THE CONCEPT OF SELF IN EDUCATION, FAMILY AND SPORTS

THE CONCEPT OF SELF IN EDUCATION, FAMILY AND SPORTS

ANNE P. PRESCOTT
EDITOR

Nova Science Publishers, Inc.
New York

For permission to use material from this book please contact us:
Telephone 631-231-7269; Fax 631-231-8175
Web Site: http://www.novapublishers.com

NOTICE TO THE READER

The Publisher has taken reasonable care in the preparation of this book, but makes no expressed or implied warranty of any kind and assumes no responsibility for any errors or omissions. No liability is assumed for incidental or consequential damages in connection with or arising out of information contained in this book. The Publisher shall not be liable for any special, consequential, or exemplary damages resulting, in whole or in part, from the readers' use of, or reliance upon, this material.

This publication is designed to provide accurate and authoritative information with regard to the subject matter covered herein. It is sold with the clear understanding that the Publisher is not engaged in rendering legal or any other professional services. If legal or any other expert assistance is required, the services of a competent person should be sought. FROM A DECLARATION OF PARTICIPANTS JOINTLY ADOPTED BY A COMMITTEE OF THE AMERICAN BAR ASSOCIATION AND A COMMITTEE OF PUBLISHERS.

Library of Congress Cataloging-in-Publication Data
The concept of self in education, family, and sports / Anne P. Prescott, editor.
    p. cm.
Includes bibliographical references and index.
ISBN 1-59454-988-5
1. Self-perception. 2. Self-perception--Social aspects. I. Prescott, Anne P.
BF697.5.S43C6545   2006
155.2--dc22   2005037788

Published by Nova Science Publishers, Inc. ✣ *New York*

CONTENTS

PREFACE

The issue of self-concept is central to the studies and practices of education and psychology. The varying degrees of self-esteem that exist between individuals can offer insight into the varying degrees of health and efficiency that exist for individuals in the worlds of education, family and sport. The research presented in this book are the latest explorations of how self-concept translates into and has an effect on these far reaching and unavoidable aspects of life.

How teachers' beliefs about assessment, teaching, learning, curriculum, and efficacy relate to each other is not well understood. The general stereotype proposes a dichotomy between a teacher transmission of surface content for accountability conception and a learner-centred, deep learning assessed for formative purposes approach. Teachers' conceptions were examined to determine the nature of their connections in chapter one. A questionnaire survey of over 230 New Zealand primary school teachers used five batteries to measure teachers' conceptions. Joint and multi-battery exploratory factor analyses of the 22 scale scores revealed four conceptions and average strength of agreement was determined. Teachers strongly agreed with the deep, humanistic and nurturing conception; moderately agreed with their ability to deliver surface learning in accountability assessments, moderately agreed with teaching and curriculum for social reform or reconstruction, and slightly agreed that assessment was bad and could be ignored because it does not improve teaching or learning, is inaccurate, and external factors prevent teachers from making improvement. This pattern revealed New Zealand teachers to be strongly child-centred with a somewhat positive orientation towards accountability. Teachers' conceptual make-up was more sophisticated than the stereotypical dichotomy.

In two longitudinal studies in chapter two, the authors examined if mathematics self-perception (self-concept and self-efficacy) predicted subsequent achievement over and above the prediction that could be made by prior achievement. They also tested if the impact of self-perception on subsequent achievement could be explained by students' goal orientation, interest, or self-esteem. The participants in study 1 were 246 middle school students whereas the participants in study 2 were 484 high school students. Achievements were indicated by final grades in mathematics in two successive school years, whereas self-concept, self-efficacy, self-esteem, interest and goal orientation were measured at the beginning of the second school year. Data were analyzed by means of structural equation modelling using the AMOS 5 program. The analyses showed that students' self-perceptions strongly predicted subsequent achievement over and above the prediction that could be made from prior achievement. Thus, both studies indicated that self-concept and self-efficacy are important mediators of academic achievement. However, there was no evidence that the effect of self-perception on subsequent achievement was mediated through students' interest in mathematics or through students' goal orientation or their self-esteem.

The purpose of chapter three is to review research on the self in disability sport and physical activity in the areas of: self-esteem, perceived competence, and body image. Based on the research findings, there is no support for the premise that individuals with disabilities have diminished self-esteem, lack physical competence, or have negative body images, compared to non-disabled people. Involvement in sport and physical activity clearly has psychological benefits. Research participants in the studies examined, ranged from children to older adults participating in activities and sports as diverse as wheelchair basketball, dance, summer camps, swimming and soccer championships, fitness activities, and road races. Athletes and physical activity participants repeatedly indicated that human movement experiences in sport and physical activity contributed to an enhanced sense of confidence to perform physical activities and sport skills, a greater sense of self-worth, and, to a lesser extent, increased body image satisfaction.

The objectives of this randomised controlled trial in chapter four were (1) to compare the changes in cardio-respiratory and muscular fitness, and the changes in physical self-concept after participation in one of two psychomotor therapy programs in a sample group of non-psychotic psychiatric patients; (2) to study the relationship between the changes in physical fitness and the changes in physical self-concept; (3) to investigate the relationship between changes in physical self-concept, global self-esteem, depression and anxiety.

The purpose in chapter five was to specify advantages and limits of dynamical perspective proposed by Nowak and Vallacher (1998) for social psychology studies. This perspective contributes massively to new knowledge in economy, biology and motor control. Theoretical models, methods, self-assessment tools, and time series analyses are complete to verify hypotheses from nomothetical approach and to determine impact of daily events on self-perception. Some example will be given with self-esteem. This new scientific path needs attention to prevent fashion effect and critic disconnection. Epistemological weaknesses, such as analogies, conceptual bounds, technological illusions, or false time series analyses, are abundant. Sport psychologists, working on behaviors, emotions and thoughts interactions (such as self-esteem, self-efficacy, motivation, and anxiety) are in phase with this perspective. Nevertheless, they must avoid weakness underlined by this paper.

The socialization of the self in the family was investigated in 315 boys and 277 girls of the fourth, fifth and sixth grade (mean age = 10.5 years) in chapter six. Self-concept was measured with Harter's Self- Perception Profile (SPPC) for children. A LISREL-model was tested in which the following variables were included: (1) *Moderator variables*: gender and age of the pre-adolescents, number of children in the family; (2) *Distal family environment variables*: structural family features such as: socioeconomic status (parental educational level and family income), and mothers' and fathers' time in employment; (3) *Proximal variables related to the parents*: parents cognition (i.e. measured perception) on conditions that alter parenting behavior such as: personal resources of the parents (financial problems), child characteristics (temperament), and contextual sources of stress (marital distress and conflict), (4) *Proximal variables related to the pre-adolescents*: pre-adolescents' cognition (i.e. measured perception) of family processes and relations, and of the family as a unit, and (5) the six SPPC-subscales, one measuring Global Self-worth and the other five assessing the child's perception of domain specific competencies or adequacies namely Scholastic Competence, Social Acceptance, Athletic Competence, Physical Appearance, Behavioral Conduct. The model tested different hypotheses with regard to the mediating influence of the proximal variables on the distal family environment variables. The fit of the model was satisfactory and 5 to 18% of the variance in each SPPC-subscales was explained. These results highlight the importance of the supportive parent-child relation, and of pre-adolescents cognition and effect in the socialization of self-concept. Pre-adolescents who feel positively reinforced in the communication with their parents have a positive metacognition. This positive metacognition enhances their global self-worth and their perceptions of competence on specific domains. These results can be seen as an empirical verification of the looking-glass self notion (Cooley).

Different frames of reference may contribute to the self-concept construal, influencing in turn the academic and working careers, the social fitness or the life satisfaction. In the present study in chapter seven, the authors focus on two particular frames of reference, defined as self-referential or internal frame of reference and comparative or external frame of reference (i.e. D'Amico and Cardaci, 2003; Marsh, Walker and Debus, 1991; Skaalvik and Skaalvik, 2002). The self referential frame leads people to evaluate their own capabilities using a personal and subjective framework (e.g. I'm quite handsome), or an internal comparison between different competency domains (e.g I'm better to play volleyball than football). The external frame of reference judgments, on the contrary, is based on comparisons with other people (e.g. I'm better than my friend in maths).

Previous studies involving adolescents, demonstrated that the different frames of reference may vary as a function of gender, and influence the self efficacy beliefs (Bong and Clark, 1999; D'Amico and Cardaci, 2003) or the scholastic and academic self concept (Pajares and Miller, 1994; Skaalvik and Skaalvik, 2002). In the present study, the authors are interested in investigating if this "dual frame of reference" is stable over time, also appearing in the self-concept construal of older people. Moreover, they aim to study if the self-referential or the comparative frames of reference influence, to a different extent, the perceptions of social well-being and life satisfaction. To this aim, about one hundred adults will be involved in the research.

The concepts of self and identity have increasingly received attention in the social psychology literature, with theory development and empirical research springing from both psychological and sociological social psychology. The cross-cultural work of anthropologists and psychologists led to the distinction between the independent self and the interdependent self. It is hypothesized that people reared in cultures with highly individualistic values tend to develop a view of self as an independent agent, while those reared in cultures with highly collectivist values develop a view of self as interdependent with others. Recent work has refined these concepts and their measurement, and has developed the theoretical ideas further. Research has found variation in these aspects of self within single cultures. There are great potential benefits of cross-fertilization between the disciplines of psychology and sociology. Chapter eight examines the conceptions of the independent and interdependent self within the framework of sociological theory, particularly Practice Theory and Identity Theory. This is approached through discussions of the development of the self and of how the self influences behavior. This effort raises new theoretical questions to be addressed in both disciplines, particularly questions related to the relationship of power to the independent and interdependent self, and self-meanings.

This study in chapter nine investigates the relationship between Social Desirability and a number of different self-concept measures. At least two of the major Social Desirability dimensions (Denial and Overconfidence) are common to some of the dimensions of self-concept. In this chapter the authors argue it is important to ensure that the self-concept tests are not influenced by a third dimension, Impression Management.

In: The Concept of Self in Education, Family and Sports
Editor: Anne P. Prescott, pp. 1-49

ISBN 1-59454-988-5
© 2006 Nova Science Publishers, Inc.

Chapter 1

INTEGRATING TEACHERS' CONCEPTIONS: ASSESSMENT, TEACHING, LEARNING, CURRICULUM AND EFFICACY

*Gavin T. L. Brown**

University of Auckland, Auckland, New Zealand

ABSTRACT

How teachers' beliefs about assessment, teaching, learning, curriculum, and efficacy relate to each other is not well understood. The general stereotype proposes a dichotomy between a teacher transmission of surface content for accountability conception and a learner-centred, deep learning assessed for formative purposes approach. Teachers' conceptions were examined to determine the nature of their connections. A questionnaire survey of over 230 New Zealand primary school teachers used five batteries to measure teachers' conceptions. Joint and multi-battery exploratory factor analyses of the 22 scale scores revealed four conceptions and average strength of agreement was determined. Teachers strongly agreed with the deep, humanistic and nurturing conception; moderately agreed with their ability to deliver surface learning in accountability assessments, moderately agreed with teaching and curriculum for social reform or reconstruction, and slightly agreed that assessment was bad and could be ignored because it does not improve teaching or learning, is inaccurate, and external factors prevent teachers from making improvement. This pattern revealed New Zealand teachers to be strongly child-centred

* Correspondence concerning this article should be addressed to Gavin T. L. Brown, Faculty of Education, University of Auckland, Private Bag 92019, Auckland, New Zealand. E-mail: gt.brown@auckland.ac.nz

Dr. Brown is a Senior Lecturer of Research Methodology in the Faculty of Education at the University of Auckland. Since leaving 13 years of secondary and tertiary teaching of English, ESOL, and reading, he has worked as an assessment researcher, at the New Zealand Council for Educational Research and the University of Auckland. He managed the Assessment Tools for Teaching and Learning (asTTle) research and development project for 5 years (see www.asttle.org.nz for details). His research interests include large-scale cognitive and attitude assessment and measurement, research design, information skills, and literacy. He can be contacted at the Faculty of Education, University of Auckland, Private Bag 92019, Auckland, New Zealand or by internet on gt.brown@auckland.ac.nz.

with a somewhat positive orientation towards accountability. Teachers' conceptual make-up was more sophisticated than the stereotypical dichotomy.

INTRODUCTION

It is generally agreed that teachers' beliefs or conceptions about teaching, learning, and curricula influence strongly how teachers teach and what students learn or achieve (Pajares, 1992; Clark and Peterson, 1986; Thompson, 1992 Calderhead, 1996). Calderhead (1996, p. 719) argued that there were five main areas in which teachers have significant beliefs (i.e., beliefs about learners and learning, teaching, subjects or curriculum, learning to teach, and about the self and the nature of teaching) and noted that "such areas, however, could well be interconnected, so that beliefs about teaching, for instance, may be closely related to beliefs about learning and the subject".

Evidence for the interconnection of these beliefs is scarce, yet there is a recurring theme that what teachers believe about one area of instruction (e.g., teaching or curriculum) impacts on practices and conceptions in other important domains (assessment or learning). For example, tertiary lecturers' conceptions of assessment impact on their understandings about student motivation, curriculum content, student ability, and student learning strategies (Dahlin, Watkins, and Ekholm, 2001). Tittle (1994, p. 151) proposed that teachers "construct schemas or integrate representations from assessments into existing views of the self, of teaching and learning, and of the curriculum, broadly construed". Delandshere and Jones (1999) argued that teachers' beliefs about assessment are shaped by how they conceptualise learning and teaching. Many teachers seem to have assessment policies based on their idiosyncratic values and their conceptions of teaching (Cizek, Fitzgerald, Shawn, and Rachor, 1995); while some use a wide variety of seemingly conflicting assessment types because they eclectically held and practiced both transmission-oriented and constructivist models of teaching and learning (Kahn, 2000). Rex and Nelson (2004) suggested that the seemingly inconsistent views of the two teachers they studied could be understood as their preference to act with honour by doing what they deem to be appropriate or feasible in the middle constrained situations of conflict and ambiguity.

Studies of teachers' understanding of the subjects they teach have shown those conceptions affect the way teachers teach and assess (Calderhead, 1996; Clark and Peterson, 1986; Thompson, 1992). For example, in mathematics, different major conceptions of the subject (i.e., relational understanding and instrumental understanding) are claimed to be "at the root of disagreements about what constitutes 'sound' approaches to the teaching of mathematics and what constitutes 'sound' student assessment practices" (Thompson, 1992, p. 133). Cheung and Wong (2002) have argued that teachers' conceptions of curriculum affect the content of assessment. Thus, it may be that teachers who believe curriculum is about transmission of traditional academic knowledge (a combination of teaching and curriculum conceptions) may well believe assessment is about student accountability and, thus, tend to use surface-oriented, factual-recall, objectively scored assessments.

From these studies, we can infer that the conceptions teachers have of teaching, learning, curriculum, and assessment are interrelated, yet, the nature of those interconnections is relatively unexplored (Dahlin, Watkins, and Ekholm, 2001). The focus of this study is to examine how teachers' conceptions of assessment relate to their conceptions of other significant educational processes (i.e., teaching, learning, curriculum, and self-efficacy). The most common models of how teachers' instructional conceptions interconnect place those connections along a continuum. One end of the continuum is a nexus of traditional, content- or material-centred curriculum, transmission-style teaching, and summative assessment conceptions. The other end is a nexus of transforming, learning- or student oriented curriculum, facilitative-style teaching, and formative assessment conceptions. For example, Delandshere and Jones (1999) proposed two major foci of teachers' conceptions to do with learning, curriculum, and assessment. The first conception is a subject-centred approach that emphasises teachers' transmission of rules and facts assessed for sanction and verification of whether or not the student has learned the content. In contrast, the second conception is a learner-centred approach that emphasises students' construction of knowledge through learning experiences assessed for the formative purpose of documenting learning and providing feedback. Carr (2001) described, in the context of early childhood education, a model that opposes an accountability-oriented folk approach that focuses on identifiable outcomes with an improvement-oriented alternative approach that focuses on the individualism of how the child develops. Torrance and Pryor (1998) contrasted an undesirable, accountability-oriented, convergent assessment approach to schooling with the more-desired, formative, divergent approach that integrates assessment with teaching through a focus on the individual child's development. In a similar vein, Philipp, Flores, Sowder, and Schappelle (1994) distinguished evaluation for reporting from assessment used to inform teaching. Figure 1 illustrates this (potentially stereotypical) portrayal of teachers' conceptions as being at either one end or the other of a single continuum. At one end lies the negatively perceived set of conceptions around teaching is telling, learning is about remembering facts and details, external obstacles hinder teacher effectiveness, curriculum is about traditional academic content, and assessment is summative for accountability. At the other, more positively regarded end, is the conceptual pattern that teaching is learner-centred, learning is about personal understanding, content is student-centred, teachers have the ability to be effective, and assessment is formative and improving. Thus, the most typical assertion is that conceptions of teaching, curriculum, learning, teacher efficacy, and assessment can be grouped into two major conceptual patterns and that these are often falsely characterised as 'teacher-surface-summative bad, student-deep-formative good'.

However, this portrayal of teachers' conceptions about the nature of curriculum, teaching, learning, assessment, and efficacy may be simplistic and inappropriate. There is evidence that more sophisticated models may better explain what teachers' conceptions really are. For example, Dwyer and Villegas (1993) described four broad, integrative domains of teacher life. The domains were teaching for student learning, creating an environment for student learning, teacher professionalism, and the organising of content knowledge for student learning. Betoret and Artiga (2004) have developed a four-way integrated categorization of teachers' instructional beliefs defined by two opposing, bipolar axes (teacher-centred versus student-centred and process-centred versus product-centred). This creates four integrated conceptions about instruction involving beliefs about teaching, learning, and assessment. One conception is the traditional paradigm (teacher-centred approach), the second is the behaviourist paradigm (product-centred approach), the third is a cognitive paradigm (student-centred approach), and the fourth is a humanist paradigm (process-centred approach). In a similar vein, Brown (2004a) found that a four factor model (i.e., assessment improves teaching and learning, assessment makes schools accountable, assessment makes students accountable, assessment is irrelevant) described teachers' conceptions of assessment better than the simple two-headed model. These examples suggest that single continua models are insufficient and unlikely to explain how teachers connect assessment, teaching, learning, curriculum, and their own sense of efficacy. Therefore, one of the ambitions of this study was to examine whether teachers' conceptions were best described by a two-factor, one continuum model or by a multi-faceted model.

	Conceptions				
Attitude	Teaching	Learning	Curriculum	Efficacy	Assessment
Agree	Child or individual centred	Personal Understanding	Learner-centred	Teacher can do	Formative (divergent) Improvement
Disagree	Teacher or group centred	Remembering Rules & Facts	Content or Subject centred	Obstacles prevent	Summative (convergent) Accountability

Figure 1. Stereotypical Pattern of Teachers' Conceptions

The study reported in this chapter was conducted within a larger study (Brown, 2002a) in which the nature of primary school teachers' conceptions of assessment were examined (reported in Brown, 2004a). The impetus for the analysis of teachers' conceptions of assessment was the finding in the earlier study that teachers had primarily deep conceptions of learning in contrast to their students' surface conceptions; yet, teachers resorted to surface approaches to teaching because of the importance of students' passing the end-of-year external examinations. The same study (Brown, 2002a) found that, in the context of interviews with 18 secondary school teachers, 27% of teachers' statements about curriculum were strongly shaped by the importance of passing examinations or maximising assessment results. When asked about their approaches to teaching, about half of the teachers' comments focused on using examination preparation approaches (e.g., teaching examination taking techniques) combined with the transmission approaches to teaching and 40% of the recent changes in teaching were classified as being examination preparation combined with teacher-controlled transmission of knowledge. The teachers clearly indicated that external factors such as socio-economic deprivation, lack of job prospects, poor student behaviour or choices, and school timetabling all conspired to prevent them from achieving their curricular or teaching goals. Note that about one-third of those goals were related to passing examinations.

Thus, the teachers interviewed in Brown (2002a) appeared to have conflicting understandings of how assessment related to conceptions of teaching, learning, curriculum, and self-efficacy. On the one hand, they emphasised humanistic and academic curriculum conceptions and had developmental and nurturing teaching perspectives. On the other hand, they expressed technological conceptions of curriculum and transmission perspectives of teaching with an explicit attention to increasing students' qualification assessment results. It appeared that teachers, despite emphasising humanistic and academic approaches to curriculum and teaching, were resorting to examination preparation processes because of the importance of the high-stakes assessment system. This early study indicated that fuller examination of how assessment related to these educational processes was warranted. Further, this descriptive, small-scale methodology could not determine how teachers connected those beliefs.

Conceptions of learning (Marton and Saljö, 1976; Biggs, 1987; Entwistle, 1997), teaching (Gow and Kember, 1993; Pratt, 1992; Samuelowicz and Bain, 1992; Trigwell and Prosser, 1997; Kember, 1997), curriculum (Eisner and Vallance, 1974; Cheung, 2000), self efficacy (Bandura, 1989; Guskey and Passaro, 1994; Tschannen-Moran, Woolfolk Hoy, and Hoy, 1998), epistemology or knowledge (Schommer, 1990; Schraw, Bendixen, and Dunkle, 2002; Wood and Kardash, 2002), and assessment (Brown, 2004a; Stamp, 1987) have been studied. These studies have focused on how teachers' conceive each domain, but what is less well understood is whether and how those beliefs interconnect with each other to create teachers' psychopedagogical (Betoret and Artiga, 2004) conceptions.

From these, and many other possible conceptions inventories that could have been used, selection had to be made to ensure that participants could complete all the survey instruments. Thus, this study focused only on teachers' conceptions of learning, teaching, curriculum, and self-efficacy, in conjunction with research into conceptions of assessment. The second major objective of the current study, using a battery of conceptions instruments and a representative sample of teachers, was to examine how teachers' conceptions about various facets of schooling and education were related.

The next section reviews the relevant models of teachers' conceptions of assessment, teaching, learning, curriculum, and efficacy. The section after that outlines the measures used, the participants involved, and the results of various factor analyses in a study of New Zealand teachers' conceptions. The chapter concludes with discussion of implications of these data and future research.

MODELS OF TEACHERS' CONCEPTIONS

Conceptions of Assessment

Assessment is any act of interpreting information about student performance, collected through any of a multitude of means or practices. Assessment, according to the Department of Education in England (as cited in Gipps, Brown, McCallum and McAlister, 1995, p. 10-11) involves "a broad appraisal including many sources of evidence and many aspects of a pupil's knowledge, understanding, skills and attitudes; or to a particular occasion or instrument….any method or procedure, formal or informal, for producing information about pupils: e.g., [sic] a written test paper, an interview schedule, a measurement task using equipment, a class quiz". Three major purposes for assessment exist: improvement of teaching and learning, making students accountable for learning partly through issuing certificates, and accountability of schools and teachers (Heaton, 1975; Torrance and Pryor, 1998; Warren and Nisbet, 1999; Webb, 1992). In addition, a fourth conception was reported by Brown (2004a); that is, assessment is fundamentally irrelevant to the life and work of teachers and students perhaps because it is bad for teachers and students, or because it can be safely ignored even if it must be used, or even because it is inaccurate.

The major premise of the improvement conception is assessment improves students' own learning and the quality of teaching (Black and Wiliam, 1998; Crooks, 1988). This improvement has two important caveats; (a) assessment must describe or diagnose the nature of student performance and (b) the information must be a valid, reliable, and accurate description of student performance. In this view, a range of techniques, including informal teacher-based intuitive judgement as well as formal assessment tools, identify the content and processes of student learning, including impediments to learning and unexpected strengths, with the explicit goal of improving the quality of instruction and student learning.

A second conception of assessment is assessment can be used to account for a teacher's, a school's, or a system's use of society's resources (Firestone, Mayrowetz, and Fairman, 1998). This conception uses assessment results to publicly demonstrate that teachers or schools are doing a good job (Butterfield, Williams, and Marr, 1999; Mehrens and Lehmann, 1984: Smith, Heinecke, and Noble, 1999) and imposes consequences for schools or teachers for reaching or not reaching required standards (Firestone, Mayrowetz, and Fairman, 1998; Guthrie, 2002). Two rationales for this conception exist; one emphasises demonstrating publicly that schools and teachers deliver quality instruction (Hershberg, 2002; Smith and Fey, 2000), and the second emphasises improving the quality of instruction (Linn, 2000; Noble and Smith, 1994).

The premise of the third conception of assessment is students are held individually accountable for their learning through assessment. This is seen in the assignment of grades or scores, checking off student performance against criteria, placing students into classes or groups based on performance, as well as various qualifications examinations in which secondary age students participate for graduation or entry selection to higher levels of educational opportunity. In New Zealand primary schools, the use of assessment for student accountability focuses much more on determining whether students have met various curriculum objectives (Hill, 2000), the criteria for a given curriculum level (Dixon, 1999), or merit placement in a certain learning group within a class. The certification of students in New Zealand is largely a secondary school activity during the final three years of schooling and there are many significant consequences for individuals dependent on their performance on such assessments, including retention in a year or grade level, graduation, and tracking or streaming (Guthrie, 2002). Together, these uses instantiate a conception wherein assessment is used as a means of making students accountable for learning.

The premise of the final conception is assessment, usually understood as a formal, organised process of evaluating student performance, has no legitimate place within teaching and learning. Teachers' knowledge of students based on long relationship and their understanding of curriculum and pedagogy preclude the need to carry out any kind of assessment beyond the intuitive in-the-head process that occurs automatically as teachers interact with students (i.e., Airasian's, 1997 'sizing up'). Assessment may be rejected also because of its pernicious effects on teacher autonomy and professionalism and its distractive power from the real purpose of teaching (i.e., student learning) (Dixon, 1999). Teachers of English in England welcomed a new National Curriculum in the early 1990s but rejected the accountability assessments because the Key Stage assessments were considered inimical to the learning and teaching values espoused in the curriculum (Cooper and Davies, 1993). It may also be that the degree of inaccuracy (e.g., standard error of measurement) published with any formal assessment contributes to teachers' conception of assessment as irrelevant.

The empirical research on teachers' conceptions of assessment, as opposed to their observed or reported assessment practices (e.g., Dixon, 1999; Gipps, et al., 1995; Hill, 2000; McMillan, Myran, and Workman, 2002; Quilter, 1998) or the literature advising teachers how to use assessment (e.g., Airasian, 1997; Linn and Gronlund, 2000; McMillan, 2001; Mehrens and Lehmann, 1984; Popham, 2000), is limited. Such literature depends largely on case studies of individual teachers or small groups and tends to place teachers' conceptions on continuum between improvement-oriented, 'formative' assessment and accountability-oriented, 'summative' assessment. For example, Garcia (1987) described a Spanish mathematics teacher who believed and practiced assessment for improvement, including seeking out information about the quality of his own teaching, and who at the same time begrudgingly implemented school-sanctioned student accountability assessment that he treated as irrelevant. Philippou and Christou (1997) found, in terms of the mathematics curriculum, that Greek and Cypriot teachers strongly agreed with using assessment for improvement (i.e., diagnosing students' difficulties, and evaluating the effectiveness of instruction), but were less supportive of assessment for accountability (i.e., assigning grades to students) and disagreed with assessment having a role in modifying the centrally determined curriculum. Warren and Nisbet (1999, p. 517), in a study of Australian teachers' uses of assessment, found that "primary teachers seemed to use assessment more often to inform the teacher with regard to teaching than to inform the learner with regard to learning and that using assessment for reporting to others was not as important as informing teaching and learning". Saltzgaver (1983) found, when describing the dominant conceptions of assessment of just one Australian teacher, ten convictions that could be mapped onto the two major assessment conceptions of improvement and irrelevance. Two teachers studied in Michigan exhibited both irrelevance and school accountability conception in their responses to the accountability pressures of high-stakes testing preparation; they prepared their students for the tests while simultaneously believing that the material on the test did not represent valuable curriculum content (Rex and Nelson, 2004). Likewise, in a study of 25 Dutch secondary school teachers' uses of assessment, it was found that 23 tempered a summative, measurement approach to assessment, at least temporarily, with formative, pedagogical goal adjustments (e.g., giving easy tests, scoring more lightly) in the hope of increasing student motivation and engagement with learning (Bulterman-Bos, Verloop, Terwel, and Wardekker, 2003).

Two larger scale studies into teachers' conceptions that identified more complex arrangements of teachers' conceptions of assessment have been conducted in Australasia. Stamp (1987) identified three major conceptions of assessment among pre-service teacher trainees in Australia -- cater for need and progress of individual pupils, assessment blocks teachers' initiative, and a more traditional-academic summative examination. The first conception used assessment in a 'formative' way to identify individual student learning needs with the purpose of catering for those individual requirements. The second conception reflected the view that teachers are required to conduct assessment but that assessment gets in the way of students' creativity and intuition. The third conception revolved around the use of tests and examinations to collect 'summative' information about students partly in order to motivate them to compete for more marks. Brown (2004a) identified four major conceptions of assessment among New Zealand practicing primary school teachers (i.e., assessment improves teaching and learning; assessment makes schools and teachers accountable, assessment makes students accountable, and assessment is irrelevant). He found that the surveyed teachers agreed with the improvement and school accountability conceptions, while rejecting the student accountability and irrelevance conceptions and, further, that the strength of teachers' conceptions was not effected by teacher characteristics (i.e., gender, role, experience) or school characteristics (i.e., size, socio-economic status, location). It is worth noting that this result is consistent with the view that teachers hold simultaneous, plural convictions.

Conceptions of Teaching

A number of independently developed models of teachers' conceptions of teaching (e.g., Gow and Kember, 1993; Pratt, 1992a; Samuelowicz and Bain, 1992; Trigwell and Prosser, 1997) have been compared (Kember, 1997) and show that three major approaches to teaching were found. The first is teacher-centred transmission of content (i.e., knowledge or information), while the second is a student-centred conceptual learning process. The third approach is a bridging one that involves student and teacher interaction or apprenticeship. The complexity of teachers' mental realities, however, means that many teachers' conceptions of teaching lay between, as much as at either end of, the more surface-like first approach and the deeper second approach. Kember (1997, p. 263) has argued that these conceptions are not hierarchical but rather "an ordered set of qualitatively differing conceptions" ranging from along the axis of teacher to student centred. Note that this position is similar to the tendency of teachers to hold simultaneously yet contradictory or pluralist convictions mentioned in reference to teachers' conceptions of curriculum.

Gow and Kember (1993) argued that conceptions of teaching affect teaching methods used by teachers, the methods students use to learn, and the learning outcomes students achieve. In other words, teachers who conceive of teaching as being teacher-centred use a transmission of knowledge method (e.g., lecture) and their students acquire a surface reproduction of knowledge. Thus, it is argued that "the methods of teaching adopted, the learning tasks set, the assessment demands made and the workload specified are strongly influenced by the orientation to teaching" (Kember, 1997, p. 270). Ho, Watkins, and Kelly (2001) showed in a study of planned change of teacher conceptions of teaching that teaching practice improved promptly and student learning eventually improved when teachers adopted a more advanced conception of teaching. Jensen, Kauchak, and Rowley (2001) showed in a study of four teacher trainees that the candidate with the most constructivist, deep learning conception of teaching actually learned much more about teaching than the candidate with the most behaviourist, transmission-oriented, surface learning conception of teaching. Samuelowicz (1994) showed that two teachers with differing conceptions of teaching had differing conceptions and practices of assessment. The first teacher, who had a deep, student-oriented conception of teaching, emphasised assessment as a means of improving teaching, providing feedback to students to improve their learning, and as a means of making students accountable. This teacher emphasised higher-order, problem solving, and decision-making processes in assessment tasks. On the other hand, the teacher who was more transmission, teacher-oriented conceived of assessment only as a means of forcing students to be accountable for their learning and emphasised recall of knowledge in assessment tasks.

Research by Pratt and associates (Hian, 1994; Pratt, 1992a; Pratt, 1992b; Pratt, 1997; Pratt and Associates, 1998; Pratt and Collins, 1998; Pratt and Collins, 2001) into teachers' conceptions about the nature of teaching has developed five perspectives of teaching that take into account the nature of teachers' intentions, actions, and beliefs. Note that Pratt and associates prefer the term perspectives to conceptions, but these terms are considered synonymous in this study. One perspective incorporates aspects of the social reform or reconstruction conception of curriculum identified by Cheung (2000). Additionally, there are four perspectives that map onto the teacher, student, and apprenticeship points of the teacher-student continuum. The most teacher-oriented conception, transmission, describes teachers who effectively communicate a well-defined and stable body of knowledge and skills to learners who must master that content. Three other perspectives are more student-oriented views of teaching. Apprenticeship assumes that the best learning happens when students work on authentic tasks in real settings of practice with learners gradually doing more of the work. The developmental perspective begins with the learners' prior knowledge and works towards restructuring how students think about that content through effective questioning and 'bridging' knowledge. The nurturing perspective respects students' self-concepts and self-efficacy in an effort to support student achievement by caring for the whole person not just the intellect. In the fifth perspective, social reform, teachers view social and structural change as more important than individual learning and so they advocate change in society as the purpose of teaching. This approach to understanding what teaching means to teachers represents a relatively complex model of teachers' conceptions of teaching.

Conceptions of Learning

Learning at all levels requires active mental processing of information, the making of meaningful connections between and among ideas and information, and repetition, practice, and memorisation (Howe, 1998). A powerful model for understanding how teachers conceive of learning is the surface-deep continuum developed in the last quarter of a century by researchers in Scandinavia (Marton and Saljö, 1976), Australia (Biggs, 1987a), and Britain (Entwistle, 1997). Marton's phenomenographic work (1981) focused attention on what students or learners claimed as their understanding of what learning meant, their intention or purpose for learning, and the processes or strategies by which the learning intention was carried out (Entwistle and Marton, 1984). A taxonomy of learning conceptions was developed that took account of the various surface and deep ways people had of understanding learning.

The surface approaches or conceptions included a) remembering things, b) getting facts or details and c) applying information. The 'surface' approach to learning is associated with the act of reproducing information that has been attended to, stored in, and retrieved from memory; for example, "in situations where the learner's aim is to gain new information or add to their store of knowledge" (Howe, 1998, p. 10). The surface intention emphasises coping with course or assessment requirements and is fulfilled by consuming or reproducing information. Further, the surface approach to learning involves learners applying teachable skills or strategies such as underlining, mind mapping, or mnemonics.

In contrast, the 'deep' approach to "learning is a qualitative change in one's way of understanding some aspect of reality" (Marton, 1983, p. 291). The deep views included understanding new material for oneself without reference to rewards, perceiving or understanding things in a different and more meaningful way, and developing or changing as a person. The deep intention is achieved by strategies that involve transforming information and integrating it into pre-existing understandings.

Learning requires deep (i.e., active processing of information to make meaningful connections) and surface (i.e., use of rehearsal and repetition) strategies, goals, practices and processes. Successful learners seem to understand that both surface and deep processes are legitimately involved in learning and are able to select and implement appropriate strategies (Purdie and Hattie, 1999). However, evidence exists that learning is portrayed and taught as largely a surface set of goals and processes. For example, MacKechnie and MacKechnie (1999) found that the strategies focused on for academically under-prepared students were largely surface skills such as note taking, time and study management, library skills, and reading skills). Anthony (1994, 1997) noted that the surface-oriented requirements of senior secondary school assessments and students' resistance to engaging in self-regulated construction of knowledge resulted in a surface approach to learning. Brown (2002b) reported that senior secondary school teachers had largely deep conceptions of learning, while their students had largely surface conceptions of learning.

Conceptions of Curriculum

Primary school teachers are generalists charged with responsibility for teaching all subjects; thus it is appropriate to examine how teachers conceive what curriculum is. Most generally, curriculum has to do with the answers to such commonplace questions as "what can and should be taught to whom, when, and how?" (Eisner and Vallance, 1974). At least five major orientations to curriculum have been found: (1) cognitive processes or skills, (2) the role of technology, (3) society and social change, (4) humanistic concern for individual development, and (5) academic knowledge or intellectual development (Eisner and Vallance, 1974; Cheung, 2000). These orientations to curriculum explain why teachers emphasise certain topics, clarify the real meaning or intent of curriculum documents, and influence both teacher professional and curriculum development. Note that Cheung and Wong (2002) prefer the term orientation to conception, but fundamentally these labels refer to the same construct.

The humanistic conception advocates that the student is the crucial source of all curriculum, the social reconstructionist perceives school as a vehicle for directing and assisting social reform or change, the technological orientation focuses on finding efficient means of reaching planned learning objectives through the use of modern technology, the cognitive processes or skill orientation focuses on the development of key competencies that can be applied to learning virtually anything, and the academic orientation aims at developing students' rational thinking and skills of inquiry. Despite the seeming antagonistic positions of these conceptions, studies have found that teachers have strong pluralist convictions in which they agree simultaneously with seemingly conflicting conceptions of curriculum (Cheung, 2000; Cheung and Ng, 2000; Cheung and Wong, 2002).

Teachers' Conceptions of Efficacy

Teacher efficacy refers to teachers' conviction or belief in their own ability to influence how well students learn or perform. Research into teacher efficacy has been shaped by two major traditions; Rotter's (1982) internal versus external locus of control and Bandura's (1989) self-efficacy (Tschannen-Moran, Woolfolk Hoy, and Hoy, 1998). Locus of control identifies whether control over outcomes resides within a person (internal) or in activities or circumstances outside the control of the individual (external). Self-efficacy, from Bandura's social cognitive theory, is belief or confidence in one's own ability to organise and take action in order to reach a goal. It is a conviction that one can successfully do what is necessary to achieve or produce a desired set of outcomes. High levels of self-efficacy impact positively on cognitive, motivational, selection, and affective processes individuals need to reach goals. For example, positive self- efficacy generates effort to achieve goals, persistence when confronting obstacles, and resilience in face of adverse situations (Pajares, 1996).

Teachers' confidence in their own ability creates initiation of and persistence in courses of action that are capable of creating learning in students (Gibson and Dembo, 1984). Teachers' sense of their own efficacy as teachers has been related not only to positive teaching behaviours (e.g., lower stress levels, willingness to remain in teaching, and willingness to implement innovations), but also to increased student achievement, student self-efficacy, and motivation (Henson, Kogan, and Vacha-Haase, 2001; Tschannen-Moran et al., 1998).

Guskey and Passaro (1994) argued that teacher efficacy consisted of two unrelated major factors: a personal internal agency ("I can") or a general occupational external agency ("teachers can"). Like Cheung (2000) and Kember (1997), they argued teacher self-efficacy represented two separate beliefs rather than two ends of the one 'teacher efficacy' belief. In other words, teachers could have high personal internal agency beliefs ("I am an efficacious teacher), but simultaneously have low external environmental agency beliefs ("Teachers are not efficacious compared to student home and family factors"). Tschannen-Moran, et al. (1998, pp. 231-232) argued that the general teacher efficacy or external belief factor is "a measure of optimism about the abilities of teachers in general to cope with adverse circumstances such as an unsupportive home environment or unmotivated students" and that it "taps teachers' tendencies to blame the home and the students for student failure". Other external factors, such as quality of curriculum resources, school leadership, school culture, and so on, may also affect external factor judgements but they are not captured in the present instruments.

For example, Delandshere and Jones (1991) argued that their three mathematics teachers took the view that students' socio-economic conditions and students' fixed level of ability in the subject absolved the teachers from responsibility for student failure to achieve expected outcomes. Brown (2002a) reported from a series of interviews with 18 secondary school teachers that external factors underpinned 96% of the attributions concerning causes for teachers' failure to achieve their own teaching goals. They especially focused on poor student motivation and negative attitude towards, or lack of interest in, learning and achievement.

Thus, there is evidence that teachers have conceptions about important educational acts, that their conceptions seem to be interrelated, and that they simultaneously have seemingly contradictory conceptions about the nature of learning, teaching, curriculum, self-efficacy and assessment. And yet we have little evidence as to how these various conceptions are interconnected. This chapter reports empirical research into the nature of teachers' conceptions of teaching, learning, curriculum, assessment, and efficacy in order to examine whether and how those conceptions interconnected. The research was conducted with New Zealand primary school teachers as part of a larger study (Brown, 2004a) into teachers' conceptions of assessment. The study examines teachers' responses to a series of questionnaires with factor analysis to determine the inter-connectedness of teachers' conceptions and speculate as to their meaning.

STUDY OF NEW ZEALAND TEACHERS' CONCEPTIONS

New Zealand Context

In the last two decades, as in other jurisdictions, large structural changes have been initiated in New Zealand schooling and education (Fiske and Ladd, 2000; Crooks, 2002; Levin, 2001). The present New Zealand Ministry of Education (MoE) is a policy only body; while other statutory bodies deal with important functions devolved from the MoE; specifically, the Education Review Office (ERO) was made responsible for quality assurance of schools, the New Zealand Qualifications Authority (NZQA) was made responsible for secondary and tertiary level qualifications. The New Zealand Curriculum Framework (NCF) consists of seven essential learning areas (i.e., Language and Languages, Mathematics, Science, Social Science, Physical Well-being and Health, Technology, and Arts) each of which has eight hierarchical levels of achievement covering Years 1–13 (primary and secondary schooling) (Ministry of Education, 1993). The goal of NCF policy developments was a seamless education system that wove together curriculum and qualifications from childhood to adulthood.

Perhaps the most radical of governance reforms was the making of all schools responsible for their own administration and management, through single-school boards (Wylie, 1997). This means that each of the approximately 2200 primary schools in New Zealand is by legislation self-governing and self-managing, including responsibility for the selection, employment, and further professional development of its own staff and for setting policies within the school to meet Ministry mandated administrative guidelines and educational goals. To balance this relatively free hand, the government has mandated accountability inspections conducted by the Educational Review Office to verify that schools were complying with this legislation. In addition, legislation (the National Educational Goals and National Administrative Guidelines) was enacted that required schools to ensure that students reached expected levels of achievement, especially in literacy and numeracy.

The Ministry's national policy in the primary school sector emphasizes voluntary, school-based assessment for the purpose of raising achievement and improving the quality of teaching programmes (Ministry of Education, 1994). There is no compulsory state mandated assessment regime and so all assessment practices are voluntary and low stakes. In the context of self-managing schools, assessment practices are school-based. At the time of the reforms, high proportions of schools reported use in at least one class of the voluntary, standardized *Progressive Achievement Tests* of language skills while half reported using the same series' mathematics tests (Croft and Reid, 1991). More recently, it was found that a large number of standardized achievement and diagnostic assessment tools were being used in New Zealand primary schools, with most teachers reporting that the use of voluntary diagnostic assessments frequently or always altered the way they taught their students (Croft *et al.*, 2000). There is no official certification consequence for these school-based assessments and it would appear that most teachers assess their students to identify their strengths and weaknesses in progress towards curriculum objectives and to evaluate the quality of teaching programmes (Hill, 2000).

A concomitant policy on assessment within primary schools is that it ought to provide clear indicators to all concerned of student performance relative to the outcomes specified in the national eight-level curriculum statements. National testing of primary-age children against the New Zealand standards-based, eight-level curriculum has been mooted, especially at key transition points within the system (Ministry of Education, 1994; New Zealand, 1998). However, unlike England or Australia, such national assessment schemes have not been adopted in New Zealand (Levin, 2001); rather voluntary-use nationally standardized assessment tools (e.g., exemplars, item resource banks, computerised teacher-managed testing tools) have been provided to teachers (Crooks, 2002). Notwithstanding the devolution of professional development responsibility, the Ministry has also funded specialized programmes that focus on improving teachers' use of assessment for improved learning (e.g., Assessment for Better Learning, Assess to Learn). Crooks (2002) provides further details of the secondary sector assessment policy and system for interested readers.

Thus, research into New Zealand primary school teachers' conceptions of assessment, teaching, learning, curriculum, and efficacy takes place in a policy and practice context of self-managed, low-stakes assessment for the purpose of improving the quality of teaching and learning. Simultaneously, schools are expected to report student performance against the objectives of various curriculum statements to parent communities, while central agencies seek to obtain evidence and surety that students and schools are meeting expected standards and outcomes. This objective has been assisted by the introduction by the Ministry of various national assessment tools and training innovations focused on assessment for learning and by a continued resistance to traditional forms of national testing. This stands in some contrast to the secondary school context where centrally administered, high-stakes qualifications assessment takes place largely to determine whether students meet various standards.

Given this mixed messages around these educational processes it might be expected that teachers would have rather more complex rather than simplistic understandings of how assessment relates to teaching, learning, curriculum, and their own efficacy.

Analysis

A general approach combing exploratory factor analysis (EFA) and confirmatory factor analysis (CFA) was used to analyse the data. In the first instance, the purported factor structure for each battery was tested using CFA. Where poor fit was found, exploratory factor analysis (EFA) using maximum likelihood extraction method with oblimin rotation (Osborne and Costello, 2005) was conducted to determine the most likely factor structure. The resulting EFA structure, where required, was subsequently tested with CFA to confirm a robust factor set of scale scores for each conception. Then, having established a robust structure of factors and scale scores for each battery, factor analyses of the scale scores was conducted (details below).

Confirmatory Factor Analysis

CFA is a sophisticated correlational technique utilizing large data sets to detect and explain relationships among meaningfully related structures (Maruyama, 1998). Because of this power, it is able to go beyond describing an individual factor to establishing the relationships (both strength and direction) between the various factors. Measurement models evaluated with CFA may contain first and second order factors representing the meaningful structures derived from the questionnaire statements to which teachers indicated their degree of agreement.

There is general agreement that the more effective measures of fit (i.e., least affected by sample size) are when the Tucker-Lewis Index (TLI), Adjusted Goodness of Fit Index (AGFI), or Comparative Fit Index (CFI) are greater than .90 and the Root Mean Square Error of Approximation (RMSEA) is below .08 (Hoyle, 1995; Hoyle and Duvall, 2004). CFA was conducted with AMOS software (Arbuckle, 2003). Sample size is also critical as the number of parameters increases (Browne and Cudeck, 1989; 1993), with numbers greater than 500 recommended for most cases (Chou and Bentler, 1995). Other than the Conceptions of Assessment instrument, all of the instruments described here have N only just over 200 cases. In order to maximise the usability of the data set, when scale scores were calculated based on the factor analyses, all missing at random data, provided that the proportion of such missing data was small, were imputed with the SPSS EM missing values procedure. The EM procedure is a two stage process of estimating the value of missing data and modelling the parameters (i.e., means, standard deviations, and correlations) assuming the missing data are as estimated. This process iterates until the change in estimated values is minimised (Hair, Anderson, Tatham, and Black, 1998). The imputed values were inspected to ensure that minimum and maximum values did not exceed the original scale and to ensure that differences in the observed means and standard deviations and the imputed values were minimal. Subsequent joint and multi-battery factor analyses were conducted using EM imputed scale scores with no missing values.

Joint and Multi-Battery Factor Analysis

Since user interpretations are made at the factor scale score level rather than at the item level it seems appropriate, provided the robustness of each scale is established, to use the scale scores to determine whether there was a meaningful pattern among the scales (Strauman and Wetzler, 1992). Further, if the ratio of cases to variables is low (e.g., less than 20 to 1) (Osborne and Costello, 2005), it becomes useful to treat the battery scale scores as if they were observed variables rather than as a latent factors. The imputation of missing at random data at the scale level would also increase the ratio of cases to variables. Interpretation of scale score based factor was used by Strauman and Wetzler (1992) in their analysis of two self-report measures of psychopathology, where they completed scale-level factor analyses of two measures separately and then combined all the scales of the two measures in one factor analysis. They found that the joint use of the two measures gave more meaningful information to clinicians than separate or individual use of either measure.

Thus, joint factor analysis of scale scores from different batteries or instruments was conducted. Joint factor analysis can be understood as similar to multitrait multimethod analysis (Campbell and Fiske, 1959) where within method and between trait correlations are used to determine whether trait or method facets explain relationships. However, in joint factor analysis, method factors may confound identification of the joint inter-battery factors. The various scale scores used here were not designed to measure the same traits (except for the social reform teaching perspective and the social reconstruction curriculum orientation), and so it would be expected that the between-battery correlations would be lower than the within-battery correlations, indicating a strong method effect. An examination of the inter-battery space more appropriately reveals the structure of the connections between instruments and leads to more appropriate understanding of teachers' instructional conceptions. Multi-battery or inter-battery factor analysis takes account of method factors (Cudek, 1982; Tucker, 1958) when constructing interpretations of scale scores from multiple sources. This procedure is appropriate when measurement models for each battery "are well-defined, but in which the traits or other aspects of performance are not so well understood" (Cudek, 1982, p. 63). The Tucker-Lewis index (TLI) can be used to evaluate the goodness-of-fit for multi-battery factor analysis (Cudeck, 1982). Cudeck (1982) has developed a software application (MBFACT) that has been successfully used in studies using both joint and inter-battery factor analysis (e.g., Finch, Panter, and Caskie, 1999).

Additionally, once interpretable joint or multi-battery scale scores are calculated it is possible to determine whether teachers have different strengths of beliefs about the underlying factors or conceptions. A simple and powerful metric for evaluating the size of differences is effect size; this turns difference in means into a proportion of pooled standard deviation (Cohen, 1977). Differences around .40 are considered average (Hattie, 1993), and values greater than .60 are large, while those smaller than .30 are small or verging on non-existent. "When implementing a new program, an effect-size of 1.0 would mean that approximately 95% of outcomes positively enhance achievement, or average students receiving that treatment would exceed 84% of students not receiving that treatment" (Hattie, 1999. p. 4). Thus, it is possible to tell whether differences in conceptions are noticeable.

Instruments

This study used two survey questionnaire inventories in order to reduce participant workload. In other words, a planned missing data design was used (Graham, Taylor, and Cumsille, 2001) such that each participant completed only one of the two survey forms but that there were common items between forms. Form A consisted of a Conceptions of Assessment questionnaire and a questionnaire on how often teachers used different assessment types (which is not reported here). Form B consisted of the Conceptions of Assessment, Conceptions of Teaching, Conceptions of Learning, Conceptions of Curriculum, and Conceptions of Teacher Efficacy questionnaires. This section overviews the instruments and reports the psychometric characteristics of each of the previously published questionnaires used to elicit data from the teachers about their conceptions of learning, curriculum, teaching, teacher efficacy, and assessment.

To ease participant workload, for each questionnaire the same response format was used regardless of the format used by the original researchers. It is likely that balanced response anchors will not provide variance when participants are inclined to respond positively to all items because they are deemed equally true or valuable. In other words, if the statement being responded to is something so socially accepted that all participants are likely to agree with it, it is difficult to elicit variance in response data with a balanced rating scale because most respondents will have generally positive affect towards the psychological object. In the case of teacher responses to conceptions of education as in this study, it is likely that they will view all or many conceptions as something they ought to or could agree with. For example, it is highly likely that teachers will simultaneously conceive that assessment makes teachers accountable, holds students accountable, and can improve the quality of teaching. Thus, a positively packed response scale (Lam and Klockars, 1982) was adopted containing four positive response points and two negative response points. The response format required teachers to identify the degree to which they agreed or disagreed with each statement using a 6-point positively-packed agreement-rating scale (Brown, 2004b). The scale responses were 'strongly disagree', 'disagree', 'slightly agree', 'moderately agree', 'mostly agree', and 'strongly agree'; each point was scored 1 to 6 respectively. This type of response format is expected to be especially effective when participants are inclined to agree with all statements; as may be the case if teachers hold a plurality of contradictory convictions.

Conceptions of Assessment. Brown's (2004a) Teachers' Conceptions of Assessment (COA-III) instrument was used. The questionnaire has 50 items in a well fitting measurement model ($\chi^2 = 3217.68$; $df = 1162$; RMSEA = .058; TLI = .967) containing nine factors (Table 1).

Table 1. Conceptions of Assessment Factors, Statements, and Psychometric Characteristics

Factors and Statements	Loading	Scale alpha
Improvement-Describe		.73
Assessment is a way to determine how much students have learned from teaching	.69	
Assessment establishes what students have learned	.61	
Assessment identifies student strengths and weaknesses	.60	
Assessment measures students' higher order thinking skills	.60	
Assessment identifies how students think	.60	
Answers to assessment show what goes on in the minds of students	.58	
Student Learning		.68
Assessment is appropriate and beneficial for children	.72	
Assessment provides feedback to students about their performance	.67	
Assessment helps students improve their learning	.65	
Assessment feedbacks to students their learning needs	.62	
Assessment is an engaging and enjoyable experience for children	.61	
Assessment is a positive force for improving social climate in a class	.45	
Assessment makes students do their best	.44	
Teaching		.78
Assessment is integrated with teaching practice	.66	
Assessment information modifies ongoing teaching of students	.63	
Assessment allows different students to get different instruction	.51	
Assessment changes the way teachers teach	.45	
Assessment influences the way teachers think	.44	
Assessment information is collected and used during teaching	.42	

Table 1. (Continued)

Factors and Statements	Loading	Scale alpha
Valid		.63
Assessment results are trustworthy	.76	
Assessment results are consistent	.69	
Assessment results can be depended on	.66	
Assessment results predict future student performance	.43	
Assessment is objective	.43	
Irrelevance		
Bad		.65
Assessment forces teachers to teach in a way against their beliefs	.64	
Assessment interferes with teaching	.62	
Assessment is unfair to students	.61	
Teachers are over-assessing	.48	
Teachers pay attention to assessment only when stakes are high	.41	
Ignore		.68
Teachers conduct assessments but make little use of the results	.81	
Assessment results are filed and ignored	.79	
Teachers ignore assessment information even if they collect it	.71	
Assessment has little impact on teaching	.55	
Assessment is value-less	.44	
Inaccurate		.78
Assessment results should be treated cautiously because of measurement error	.89	
Teachers should take into account the error and imprecision in all assessment	.62	
Assessment is an imprecise process	.38	
School Accountability		.79
Assessment provides information on how well schools are doing	.76	
Assessment is a good way to evaluate a school	.71	
Assessment is an accurate indicator of a school's quality	.71	
Assessment keeps schools honest and up-to-scratch	.61	
Assessment measures the worth or quality of schools	.59	
Student Accountability		.81
Assessment is assigning a grade or level to student work	.66	
Assessment places students into categories	.64	
Assessment determines if students meet qualifications standards	.60	
Assessment is checking off progress against achievement objectives	.59	
Assessment is comparing student work against set criteria	.51	
Assessment is completing checklists	.46	
Assessment is completing checklists	.46	
Assessment selects students for future education or employment opportunities	.44	

Factor Intercorrelations	I	II	III	IV
I. School Accountability	—			
II. Student Accountability	0.48	—		
III. Improvement	0.46	0.21	—	
IV. Irrelevance	-0.13	0.36	-0.77	—

There are four correlated major factors (i.e., conceptions of assessment is irrelevant, assessment improves teaching and learning, assessment makes schools and teachers accountable, and assessment makes students accountable) (Table 1). The assessment is irrelevant factor is a second-order factor with three first-order factors (i.e., assessment is bad, assessment is ignored, assessment is inaccurate). Likewise, the assessment improves teaching and learning factor is second-order factor with four first-order factors (i.e., assessment is valid, assessment improves teaching, assessment improves students' learning, assessment describes student thinking). Mean scale scores on this instrument were shown to be invariant across teacher roles, gender, degrees of information literacy training and degrees of teacher training. Further, mean scale scores did not differ statistically according to school size, type, or socio-economic status.

Conceptions of Teaching

Pratt and Collins' (1998) Teaching Perspectives Inventory identifies five teaching perspectives (i.e., transmission, apprenticeship, developmental, nurturing, and social reform) by enquiring into teaching intentions, actions, and beliefs within each perspective. The full instrument involves 45 statements spread equally over the five perspectives and equally over the three dimensions within each perspective. These perspectives were developed in research with adult education or tertiary level instructors.

Table 2. Teaching Perspectives Inventory Factors, Statements and Loadings

Factors and Statements	Loadings
Apprenticeship	
I link the subject matter with real settings of practice or application	.59
My intent is to demonstrate how to perform or work in real situations	.69
To be an effective teacher, one must be an effective practitioner	.53
Development	
I challenge familiar ways of understanding the subject matter	.59
My intent is to help people develop more complex ways of reasoning	.67
Teaching should focus on developing qualitative changes in thinking	.57
Nurturing	
I encourage expressions of feeling and emotion	.73
My intent is to build people's self-confidence and self-esteem as learners	.77
In my teaching, building self-confidence in learners is priority	.73
Social Reform	
I help people see the need for changes in society	.78
I expect people to be committed to changing our society	.81
Individual learning without social change is not enough	.66
Transmission	
I make it very clear to people what they are to learn	.55
My intent is to prepare people for examinations	.63
Effective teachers must first be experts in their own subject areas	.52

Note. Inter-factor correlations not available.

Teacher responses to the TPI have been collected from a number of cross-cultural studies and collected into a database of over 1,000 respondents (Pratt and Collins, 2000). The factor structure was determined using principal component analysis with equamax rotation with reliabilities for each of the five scales ranging from $\alpha = .81$ to .92. For brevity's sake, given the large number of responses required by participants completing Form B, the strongest loading statement for belief, intention, and action for each perspective was selected (J. B. Collins, personal communication, August 23, 2001). Wording of statements and factors are shown in Table 2; loadings are robust ranging between .5 and .8.

Conceptions of Learning

Six items from the Tait, Entwistle, and McCune (1998) Approaches and Study Skills Inventory for Students (ASSIST) were used to measure teacher conceptions about learning. This instrument has six statements that elicit responses along the Marton and Saljo (1976) taxonomy of learning conceptions. Three statements were designed to probe surface conceptions of learning (i.e., Learning is making sure I remember things well, Learning is building up knowledge by getting facts and information, and Learning is being able to use the information I've got); while three statements probe deep conceptions of learning (i.e., Learning is developing as a person, Learning is seeing things in a different and more meaningful way, and Learning is understanding new material for myself). Because these items were selected from a larger inventory there was no robust data to indicate the psychometric properties.

Brown (2002a) trialed these items in a survey of 81 secondary school teachers using the positively packed response scale. An exploratory maximum likelihood factor extraction with oblimin rotation found two correlated ($r = .37$) factors. The surface factor contained the 'making sure I remember things well' (1.05) and 'building up knowledge by getting facts and information' (.42) statements (Cronbach $\alpha = .61$). The deep factor contained 'developing as a person' (.55), 'seeing things in a different and more meaningful way' (.88), and 'understanding new material for myself' (.62) statements (Cronbach $\alpha = .71$). These results were consistent with the conceptions of learning identified by Marton and Saljo (1976) and sufficiently robust to warrant use of the instrument. The 'being able to use information I've got' statement loaded equally on both surface (.18) and deep (.16) factors; this poor fit with either the surface or deep factor was unexpected and suggests that use of information could be seen as either a deep or surface conception.

Conceptions of Curriculum

Cheung's (2000) conceptions of curriculum inventory consists of 20 items which are grouped into four major conceptions (i.e., academic, humanistic, technological, and social reconstruction) (Table 3). The statements all have strong loadings on their respective factors and scales had strong internal estimates of reliability (α range .73 to .79). The whole inventory had marginally acceptable fit to the model in Cheung's (2000) research with teachers (CFI =.90; RMSEA = .086). A later revision to this inventory (Cheung and Wong, 2002) had somewhat better fit (RMSEA = .073), but was unavailable at the time of this research. The inventory was adapted to New Zealand circumstances by making small wording changes. For example, the item about consummatory experience, a term introduced by Eisner and Vallance (1974), was rewritten as "Curriculum should try to provide satisfactory consumer experience for each student".

Conceptions of Teacher Efficacy

Guskey and Passaro (1994) reported a revision of Gibson and Demo's (1984) Teacher Efficacy Scale that has two relatively uncorrelated factors ($r = -.23$); personal internal agency ("I can") and a general occupational external agency ("teachers can"). Although estimates of consistency for each factor are not reported Guskey and Passaro showed that item loadings for each factor were generally greater than .40 with only three items loading less than that value. Thus, we can conclude that the items do load consistently on the factors identified.

Table 3. Conceptions of Curriculum Inventory Statements, Factors, and Loadings

Statements	Loading
Academic Subjects	
The basic goal of curriculum should be the development of cognitive skills that can be applied to learning virtually anything.	.72
School curriculum should aim at developing students' rational thinking.	.59
Curriculum should require teachers to transmit the best and the most important subject contents to students.	.54
School curriculum should aim at allowing students to acquire the most important products of humanity's intelligence.	.54
Curriculum should stress refinement of intellectual abilities.	.50
Humanistic	
Students' interests and needs should be the organising centre of the curriculum.	.64
Curriculum and instruction are actually inseparable and the major task of a teacher is to design a rich learning environment.	.62
The ultimate goal of school curriculum should help students to achieve self-actualisation.	.62
Curriculum should try to provide satisfactory consumer experience for each student.	.56
Teachers should select curriculum contents based on students' interests and needs.	.54
Technological	
Curriculum and instruction should focus on finding efficient means to a set of predetermined learning objectives.	.68
Curriculum should be concerned with the technology by which knowledge is communicated.	.65
Learning should occur in certain systematic ways.	.60
I believe that educational technology can increase the effectiveness of students' learning.	.59
Selection of curriculum content and teaching activities should be based on the learning objectives of a particular subject.	.57
The learning objectives of every lesson should be specific and unambiguous.	.50
Social Reconstruction	
Existing problems in our society should be organising centre of curriculum.	.80
Curriculum should let students understand societal problems and take action to establish a new society.	.75
Curriculum contents should focus on societal problems such as pollution, population explosion, energy shortage, racial discrimination, corruption, and crime.	.67
The most important goal of school curriculum is to foster students' ability to critically analyse societal problems.	.60

Tschannen-Moran et al. (1998) further argued that internal factor statements about self-perception of teaching competence are a poor measure of teacher efficacy because the items mix present and future or hypothetical conditions, violating the assumption that self-efficacy is context specific. Thus, the present set of instruments available to measure teacher efficacy are limited and further empirical and theoretical work is needed to improve instrumentation of this construct.

Nevertheless, use of the Guskey and Passaro (1994) instrument was justified for the time being. However, for two reasons not all items in that instrument were used. First there was a need to ensure that participants would be able to complete Form B and second, a significant number of the items in the Guskey and Passaro (1994) revision were very similar in wording. Thus, the five most strongly loading items for each scale that provided maximally unique statements about each scale were used (Table 4).

The total number of batteries of instruments used in this study was five with a total of 22 scales, and 101 items.

Table 4. Teacher Efficacy Statements, Factors, and Loadings

Factors and Statements	Loadings
Internal	
If a student masters a new concept quickly, this might be because the teacher knew the necessary steps in teaching that concept.	.62
When a student gets a better grade than he/she usually gets, it is usually because I found better ways of teaching that student.	.60
When a student does better than usually, many times it is because the teacher exerts a little extra effort	.55
When I really try, I can get through to most difficult students.	.53
If a student in my class becomes disruptive and noisy, I feel assured that I know some techniques to redirect him/her quickly.	.44
External	
I am very limited in what I can achieve because a student's home environment is a large influence on his/her achievement.	.78
Teachers are not a very powerful influence on student achievement when all factors are considered.	.66
The hours in my class have little influence on students compared to the influence of their home environment.	.56
I have not been trained to deal with many of the learning problems my students have.	.45
When a student is having difficulty with an assignment, I often have trouble adjusting it to his/her level.	.42

Participants

A random, representative sample of 800 New Zealand primary schools was surveyed. In each school, the principal was asked to give a questionnaire to a teacher and another to a leader/administrator of Year 5-7 students (i.e., ages 10 to 13). Readers in jurisdictions outside New Zealand may be concerned by this process of distributing questionnaires to participants by principals. However, given the low-stakes assessment regime and self-governing context of New Zealand schools, it was considered a valid process. An incentive to participants was that they were given confidential results for each questionnaire completed relative to the New Zealand means some 9 months after completion. A total of 525 teachers completed the Conceptions of Assessment instrument, while only between 225 and 237 completed the survey measures on Form B. This return rate was achieved without follow-up or any inducements.

The demographic characteristics of the individual teachers in this sample reasonably reflected those of the New Zealand teaching population (Table 5) as determined in the 1998 teacher census conducted for the Ministry of Education (Sturrock, 1999). The participants who completed the Form B were a sub-set of this sample and did not differ in any statistically significant way from the larger sample. Thus, the participants in this study were from a relatively homogenous sample of New Zealand primary school teachers and sufficiently representative of the New Zealand population of primary school teachers on which to base generalizations (Brown, 2004a).

Table 5. Key Demographic Characteristics Comparison

Characteristic	1998 Teacher Census	2001 CoA-III Study	2001 Instructional Conceptions Study
Sample Size	23,694	525	235
NZ European	87%	83%	83%
Female	71%	76%	77%
Long Service	49%[a]	63%	66%

Note: [a]This figure averaged for both primary and secondary sectors as separate sector information was not available.

The 235 teachers were for the most part (a) New Zealand European (83%), (b) female (77%), (c) highly experienced with 10 or more years teaching (66%), (d), reasonably well trained with two or more years training (82%), and (e) equally split between teachers (51%) and managers or senior teachers.

Table 6. Participants by School Characteristics

Characteristic	Frequency	Percent
Socio-economic status (DECILE)		
Low	81	34.5
Middle	79	33.6
High	61	26.0
Missing	14	6.0
School type		
Contributing Primary	103	43.8
Full Primary	106	45.1
Intermediate	24	10.2
Missing	2	.9

Table 6. Participants by School Characteristics (Continued)

Characteristic	Frequency	Percent
Community population type		
Urban	134	57.0
Main Urban	123	
Secondary Urban	9	
Rural	85	36.1
Minor Urban	25	
Rural	60	
Missing	16	6.8
School size		
Large (>350)	52	22.1
Medium (121-350)	101	43.0
Small (<=120)	68	28.9
Missing	14	6.0
School ethnic mix		
Majority (>26% European)	178	75.7
Minority (<=25%)	43	18.3
Missing	14	6.0
Total	235	100.0

As per design, the vast majority of the teachers were employed in contributing or full primary schools (89%) (Table 6). About one-third were employed in low socio-economic status (SES) schools, while over a quarter worked in high SES schools. This distribution represented a very acceptable sampling of the distribution of teachers by school SES. Just over half of the teachers worked in large urban area schools and just over 40% worked in medium-sized schools. Three-quarters of the teachers worked in schools whose students were predominantly of New Zealand European or Pakeha ethnicity (i.e., more than 75% of the roll—using procedure described in Hattie, 2002).

Thus, data in this study were from a relatively homogenous population of full and contributing primary school teachers, largely representative of the New Zealand population, except for an over-representation of teachers in small schools.

Results

Before examining the connections between the assessment conception and the other conceptions the psychometric characteristics of each conceptions scale was investigated. In the case of two instruments, alternative models were needed to generate close fit to the data. It should be noted that these alternative models and subsequent analyses are different to those reported in Brown (2003); in that study the model created by the various authors was accepted even though poor CFA fit statistics were reported. This study advances that research by reanalysing the Teaching Perspectives Inventory and the Conceptions of Curriculum data, identifying a different factor structure, and taking the revised scales into joint and multi-battery factor analyses of scale scores.

Conceptions of Teaching

A second-order factor structure was tested and it was found that the statements all had strong loadings on their four respective factors but the whole inventory had poor fit to the model ($\chi^2 = 296.65$; $df = 85$; TLI = .68, RMSEA = .069) and was inadmissible due to negative error variance. Instead of the hierarchical model, an inter-correlated model was found to have good fit using the same 15 statements ($\chi^2 = 277.062$; $df = 80$; TLI = .68; RMSEA =.069) (Figure 2).

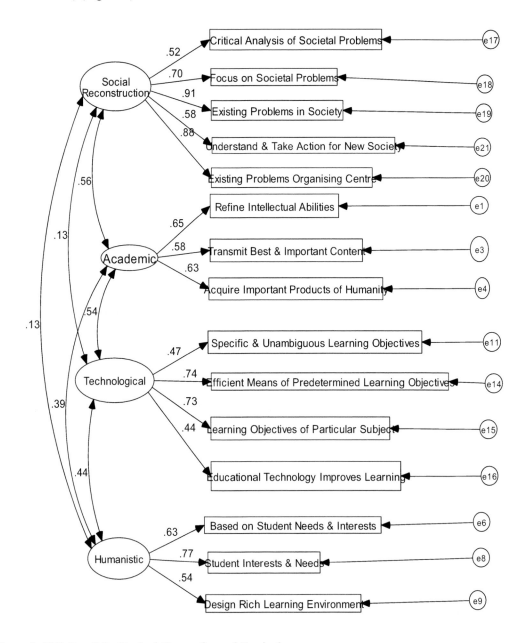

Figure 2. CFA Result for Revised Conceptions of Curriculum

Table 7. Conceptions of Teaching Results

Teaching Perspectives Scales Statements	M	SD	Loading on Scale
Apprenticeship			
Link to Real Settings	5.06	.69	.51
Show How to Perform in Real Situations	4.50	1.17	.49
Effective Practitioner	5.20	.92	.51
Average	*4.92*	*.93*	
Developmental			
Challenge Familiar Ways of Understanding	4.56	.88	.54
Develop More Complex Ways of Reasoning	4.98	.97	.61
Qualitative Changes in Thinking	4.56	1.07	.69
Average	*4.70*	*.97*	
Nurturing			
Express Feeling and Emotion	5.01	.85	.58
Build Self-Confidence and Self-Esteem	5.70	.64	.63
Build Self-Confidence	5.58	.67	.71
Average	*5.43*	*.72*	
Social Reform			
See Need for Societal Change	4.29	1.10	.64
Committed to Change Society	3.60	1.25	.84
Social Change Needed	3.72	1.34	.76
Average	*3.87*	*1.23*	
Transmission			
Prepare for Examinations	2.24	1.10	.55
Very Clear What to Learn	4.80	.94	.25
Be Experts in Own Subject Areas	3.06	1.40	.60
Average	*3.37*	*1.15*	

Scale Correlations	II	III	IV
I. Apprenticeship	.87	.71	.52
II. Developmental	1.00	.64	.76
III. Nurturing		1.00	.32
IV. Social Reform			1.00
V. Transmission			

Table 7 shows the 15 statement means, standard deviations, and CFA scale loadings for the four scales and the scale internal consistency estimates and scale inter-correlations. As might be expected with so few items loading on each scale the estimates of internal consistency were not consistently high but the items and scales were kept in order to reflect the differing conceptions of teaching. The Apprenticeship scale (3 items) had an average score of 4.92 or mostly agree, and strong correlations with the Developmental and Nurturing scales. The Developmental scale (3 items) had an average score of 4.70 or mostly agree, and strong correlations with all other scales (range .64 to .76). The Nurturing scale (3 items) had an average score of 5.43 or half-way between mostly agree and strongly agree, and weak correlations with Social Reform and Transmission scales. The Social Reform scale (3 items) had an average score of 3.87 or moderately agree, and moderate to strong correlations with Apprenticeship, Developmental, and Transmission scales. The Transmission scale (3 items) had an average score of 3.37 or close to slightly agree, and moderate to strong correlations with all scales except for Nurturing which was very weak ($r = .20$). Thus, five conceptions of teaching were found, with teachers expressing most agreement with the Nurturing conception and least agreement with the Transmission conception.

Conceptions of Learning

The data fit to the two factor model was excellent ($\chi^2 = 10.59$; $df = 8$; TLI = .955; RMSEA = .025), while intercorrelation of the two factors was moderate ($r = .39$, $p<.01$). The Surface scale (2 items) had a moderate internal estimate of consistency ($\alpha=.58$) and an average score of 3.85 or moderately agree, while the Deep scale (4 items) had a similar level of internal consistency ($\alpha=.61$) and an average score of 5.15 or mostly agree. Thus, a deep and a surface conception of learning were found with teachers agreeing noticeably more with the Deep rather than Surface conception.

Conceptions of Curriculum

A two-level factor structure was tested and it was found that the statements all had strong loadings on their four respective factors but the whole inventory had poor fit to the model ($\chi^2 = 556.88$; $df = 185$; TLI = .745, RMSEA = .092) and was inadmissible due to negative error variance. As a consequence, reanalysis of the Cheung instrument resulted in dropping several items and changing the higher order structure. The revised model had four first level factors that were correlated with each other (Figure 3) and had acceptable fit characteristics ($\chi^2 = 208.80$; $df = 84$; TLI = .859, RMSEA = .080).

Table 8 shows the 15 statement means, standard deviations, and CFA scale loadings for the four scales and the scale internal consistency estimates and scale inter-correlations. The Social Reconstruction scale (5 items) had good internal consistency ($\alpha=.85$), an average score of 3.02 or slightly agree, and very low correlations with the technological and humanistic scales. The Academic scale (3 items) had moderate internal consistency ($\alpha=.65$), an average score of 3.87 or nearly moderately agree, and moderate correlations with all three other scales. The Technological scale (4 items) had moderate internal consistency ($\alpha=.67$), an average score of 4.53 or half-way between moderate and strongly agree, and moderate correlations with the Academic and Humanistic scales. The Humanistic scale (3 items) had moderate internal consistency ($\alpha=.66$), an average score of 4.93 or moderately agree, and moderate correlations with the academic and technological scales. Thus, four conceptions of curriculum were found, with teachers expressing most agreement with the Humanistic conception and least agreement with the Social Reconstruction conception. The moderate agreement with the Academic conception of curriculum may be indicative of the lack of discipline-related degrees held by the participants (only 77 had 3 or more years of pre-service training).

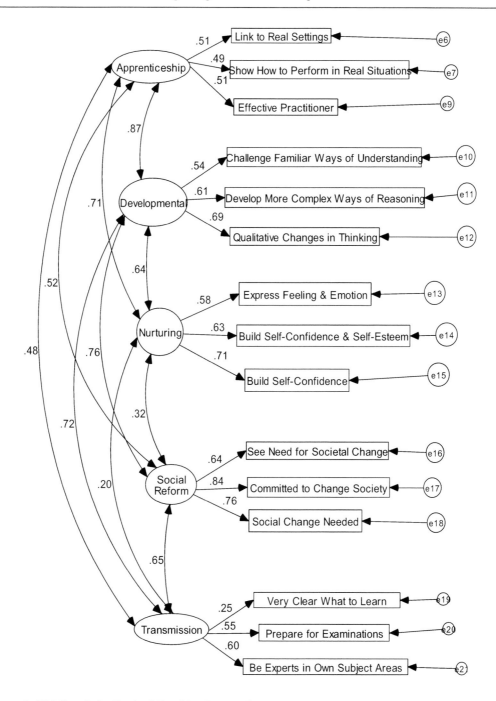

Figure 3. CFA Result for Revised Teaching Perspectives Inventory

Conceptions of Teacher Efficacy

The two first order factor model was tested and found to have good overall fit (χ^2 = 131.74; df = 31; TLI = .58; RMSEA = .074). The intercorrelation of the two scales was zero (r = .00, p=.95). The internal consistency estimates for both scales were identical at a moderate α = .65. The average score for the internal efficacy was 4.18 or moderately agree, while the average for external efficacy was 2.69 or half-way between disagree and slightly agree. Thus, two conceptions of teacher efficacy were found, with teachers expressing more agreement with the conception that they have internal efficacy to overcome learning obstacles and disagreeing with the conception that external factors prevent them from being efficacious.

Table 8. Revised Conceptions of Curriculum Results

Conceptions of Curriculum Scale and Statements	M	SD	λ	Scale α
Social Reconstruction				.85
Critical Analysis of Societal Problems	3.12	1.08	.52	
Focus on Societal Problems	3.03	1.21	.70	
Existing Problems in Society	2.79	1.02	.91	
Existing Problems as Organising Centre	2.76	1.02	.88	
Understand and Take Action for New Society	3.42	1.03	.58	
Average	*3.02*	*1.07*		
Academic				.65
Refine Intellectual Abilities	3.51	1.17	.65	
Transmit Best and Important Content	4.03	1.18	.58	
Acquire Important Products of Humanity	4.06	1.13	.63	
Average	*3.87*	*1.16*		
Technological				.67
Specific and Unambiguous Learning Objectives	5.04	1.04	.47	
Efficient Means of Predetermined Learning Objectives	4.16	1.17	.74	
Learning Objectives of Particular Subject	4.49	1.08	.73	
Educational Technology Improves Learning	4.42	.97	.44	
Average	*4.53*	*1.07*		
Humanistic				.66
Based on Student Needs and Interests	4.69	1.16	.63	
Student Interests and Needs	4.86	1.09	.77	
Design Rich Learning Environment	5.25	.93	.54	
Average	*4.93*	*1.06*		

Scale Correlations	I	II	III	IV
I. Social Reconstruction	—	.56	.13	.13
II. Academic		—	.54	.40
III. Technological			—	.44
IV. Humanistic				—

In summary, we can conclude from the individual battery analyses that this representative group of primary teachers agreed most with the following conceptions:

assessment improves the quality of teaching and learning,
teaching nurtures children,
learning means deep transformation of understanding,
curriculum is humanistic, and
teachers can effect learning changes.

Integrating Various Teachers' Conceptions

Unanswered by these separate analyses is the question of how the various conceptions related to each other. Did the teachers conceive that assessment could be used to improve deep learning while nurturing children? Were internally efficacious teachers those who believed in nurturing teaching and humanistic curriculum? Were external barriers to successful teaching associated with accountability approaches to assessment? To determine how the scales were related to each other, a multi-battery EFA on the various battery scale scores was undertaken. To determine how the teacher participants were related to each other, a hierarchical cluster analysis was conducted. Between these two approaches, patterns within items and people could be identified.

Patterns in Items—How Scale Scores Related to Each Other

Generally, the correlations between the various scale scores were higher within batteries (average Pearson $r = .28$) than between batteries (average Pearson $r = .18$), except for the two efficacy scales which had a correlation of only .04 (Table 12). The scale reliabilities were acceptable to good especially considering that only two or three items make up six of the scales. The exception is the Transmission approach to teaching which was a candidate for potential removal in future analyses.

The multi-battery factor analysis, using maximum likelihood estimation and direct quartimin oblique rotation, produced a four factor model that had good fit (TLI = .92) (Table 10). This approach showed very similar structure to the traditional joint EFA, with all but two of the scale scores loading on the same factors. The multi-battery analysis removed the two teaching perspectives scale scores of transmission and developmental approaches from the social reform or reconstruction factor; a result that clearly highlighted the trait similarity of these two scales across their different methods and which made for easier interpretation. The intercorrelations between the four conceptions factors were low, meaning the four factors were largely independent of each other.

The strength of agreement of teachers to each factor was calculated according to the original response agreement scale values ranging between 1 and 6 (Table 14). Note the two negatively loading items on factor 2 were reverse scored in subsequent analyses in order to give them the same negative meaning. Teachers agreed with factor Deep Humanistic Nurturing the most and the factor Bad Assessment Ignored That Does Not Improve Teaching and Learning had the lowest scores; factors Surface Accountability Transmitted and Social Reform had very similar values. Effect sizes between the four factors, calculated for the differences in the mean factor scores (Table 11), indicated that all differences were large except between the factors Surface Accountability Transmitted and Social Reform. These values indicated that not only were the factors independent of each other but that the teachers also responded to them quite differently. The multi-battery factor solution was evaluated with CFA but poor fit statistics were found ($N = 233$; $\chi^2 = 846.05$; $df = 205$; RMSEA = .116; TLI = .63). Clearly, further work needs to be done to improve our understanding of how these scales relate to each other. Nevertheless, this pattern of results gives us a potentially powerful insight into teachers' thinking.

Table 9. Instructional Conceptions Scale Correlations and Reliabilities

Scales	Teaching					Learning		Efficacy		Assessment									Curriculum			
	1	2	3	4	5	6	7	8	9	10	11	12	13	14	15	16	17	18	19	20	21	22
Teaching																						
1. Nurturing	(.67)																					
2. Apprenticeship	**.39**	(.50)																				
3. Transmission	**.17**	**.32**	(.37)																			
4. Social Reform	**.28**	**.36**	**.44**	(.78)																		
5. Development	**.46**	**.50**	**.49**	**.57**	(.64)																	
Learning																						
6. Deep	.54	.40	.15	.23	.41	(.61)																
7. Surface	.16	.22	.43	.21	.16	**.31**	(.58)															
Efficacy																						
8. External	-.18	-.02	.09	.03	-.09	-.08	.09	(.65)														
9. Internal	.15	.33	.37	.27	.19	.21	.27	**.04**	(.65)													
Assessment																						
10. Bad	-.07	-.08	.10	.09	-.06	-.06	.02	.31	.08	(.68)												
11. Ignore	-.05	-.10	.06	.16	-.01	-.04	-.03	.25	.07	**.61**	(.78)											
12. Inaccurate	.13	.12	-.04	.11	.16	.14	.11	.09	.07	**.28**	**.28**	(.63)										
13. Valid	.08	.14	.34	.20	.20	.11	.28	-.07	.28	**-.28**	**-.32**	**-.31**	(.73)									
14. Describe	.22	.29	.39	.26	.26	.29	.30	-.10	.31	**-.33**	**-.33**	**-.22**	**.60**	(.78)								
15. Improve Teaching	.24	.31	.13	.10	.23	.34	.19	-.17	.2	**-.39**	**-.45**	**-.11**	**.42**	**.65**	(.68)							
16. Improve Learning	.24	.35	.20	.17	.28	.25	.19	-.18	.25	**-.42**	**-.45**	**-.18**	**.57**	**.66**	**.66**	(.79)						
17. School Accountability	.13	.32	.40	.31	.28	.08	.36	.03	.38	**-.08**	**-.09**	**-.04**	**.45**	**.49**	**.34**	**.38**	(.81)					
18. Student Accountability	.08	.23	.46	.22	.25	.15	.41	.19	.29	**.18**	**.09**	**.09**	**.30**	**.31**	**.12**	**.13**	**.41**	(.75)				
Curriculum																						
19. Social Reconstruction	.14	.26	.42	.53	.32	.06	.22	.07	.32	.14	.08	.19	.22	.11	.07	.20	.35	.31	(.85)			
20. Academic	.24	.34	.41	.30	.38	.26	.37	-.00	.41	.32	.01	.23	.35	.41	.33	.29	.44	.39	**.47**	(.65)		
21. Technological	.27	.37	.27	.16	.33	.21	.27	-.02	.18	.14	-.21	.05	.34	.48	.41	.38	.33	.32	**.14**	**.40**	(.67)	
22. Humanistic	.42	.23	.06	.06	.12	.26	.15	-.04	.15	.03	-.02	.11	.13	.22	.26	.25	.17	.18	**.13**	**.28**	**.38**	(.66)

Note: Scale alpha reliabilities in brackets. Within-battery correlations in bold.

Table 10. Multi-battery EFA Results for Conceptions of Teaching, Learning, Curriculum, Teacher Efficacy, and Assessment

Scales	*Multi-battery Factor Analysis*			
	Ignore Bad Assessment, Not Improve Teaching and Learning	Surface Accountability Transmitted	Social Change	Nurturing Deep Development
11. Ignore	**.83**	.04	.08	.28
10. Bad	**.77**	.11	.00	.01
12. Inaccurate	**.49**	.04	.08	.28
16. Improve Learning	**-.43**	.14	.11	.17
15. Improve Teaching	**-.34**	.18	-.03	.17
8. External	**.23**	.17	-.00	-.17
18. Student Accountability	.19	**.50**	.01	.02
7. Surface	-.01	**.50**	.04	-.00
20. Academic	.04	**.48**	.08	.28
3. Transmission	-.01	**.46**	.20	-.15
17. School Accountability	-.13	**.43**	.20	.00
21. Technological	-.11	**.35**	-.07	.29
13. Valid	-.31	**.35**	.10	-.03
14. Describe	-.32	**.35**	-.04	.17
9. Internal	.02	**.24**	.13	.05
4. Social Reform	.06	.00	**.72**	.09
19. Social Reconstruction	.03	.12	**.59**	-.07
1. Nurturing	.00	-.07	.07	**.39**
22. Humanistic	.04	.15	-.12	**.38**
6. Deep	.00	-.02	.05	**.37**
5. Development	-.02	.04	.27	**.29**
2. Apprenticeship	-.05	.09	.16	**.27**

Table 10. Multi-battery EFA Results for Conceptions of Teaching, Learning, Curriculum, Teacher Efficacy, and Assessment (Continued)

Inter-factor Correlations				
I	1.00			
II	-.08	1.00		
III	.02	.39	1.00	
IV	-.19	.26	.23	1.00

Note. The strongest loadings are shown in bold.

Table 11. Multi-battery EFA Factor Results

	Bad Assessment Ignored	Surface Accountability Transmitted	Social Reform	Deep Humanistic Nurturing
Number of Scales	6	9	2	5
Alpha Estimate of Internal Consistency	.74	.84	.69	.75
M	2.92	3.67	3.45	5.02
SD	.53	.52	.81	.47
Effect Size Differences				
I. Bad Assessment Ignored	—	1.43	.79	4.20
II. Surface Accountability Transmitted		—	.33	2.73
III. Social Reform			—	2.45
IV. Deep Humanistic Nurturing				—

Table 12. Mean Scale Scores by Teacher Conceptual Cluster

Clus. (N)	Teaching Perspectives					Learning		Teacher Efficacy		Assessment									Curriculum			
	Nurt.	Appren.	Trans.	Soc. Ref.	Devel.	Deep	Surf.	Ext.	Int.	Bad	Ign.	Inac.	Valid	Desc.	Impr. Tchg.	Impr. Lrng.	Schl. Acc.	Stud. Acc.	Soc. Recon.	Acad.	Tech.	Hum.
1 (32)	**4.99**	4.43	2.50	2.93	3.99	4.74	2.95	3.00	3.23	2.87	2.60	3.88	2.38	3.07	3.69	3.10	1.90	2.86	2.33	2.92	3.99	4.77
2 (17)	**5.67**	**5.53**	4.10	4.29	**5.20**	**5.44**	4.85	2.99	4.04	2.41	1.54	3.80	4.19	4.72	4.91	4.74	3.88	4.23	3.76	4.82	**5.39**	**5.49**
3 (26)	**5.54**	**4.99**	3.87	4.50	**4.94**	**5.40**	4.41	3.61	4.08	3.74	3.40	4.37	3.06	3.81	4.08	3.50	3.02	4.23	3.25	4.13	4.62	**5.05**
4 (19)	**5.40**	**5.05**	2.96	3.14	4.56	**5.23**	3.66	2.25	3.44	2.04	1.68	3.75	2.96	3.76	4.58	3.98	2.41	2.94	2.43	3.67	4.46	4.53
5 (55)	**5.29**	4.58	3.27	3.82	4.44	**4.95**	3.62	3.08	3.81	3.00	2.40	3.64	3.20	3.56	3.81	3.50	2.64	3.30	2.98	3.48	4.08	4.55
6 (84)	**5.63**	**5.14**	3.52	4.16	**4.98**	**5.26**	4.04	2.60	4.01	2.34	1.96	3.69	3.73	4.31	4.71	4.26	3.30	3.63	3.23	4.27	4.82	**5.18**
Total (233)	**5.44**	4.91	3.36	3.88	4.69	**5.14**	3.86	2.88	3.82	2.71	2.26	3.78	3.31	3.90	4.29	3.85	2.89	3.50	3.02	3.87	4.52	**4.93**

Note. Bold figures represent mostly agree or greater; italic figures represent less than slightly agree; underlined figures represent disagree.

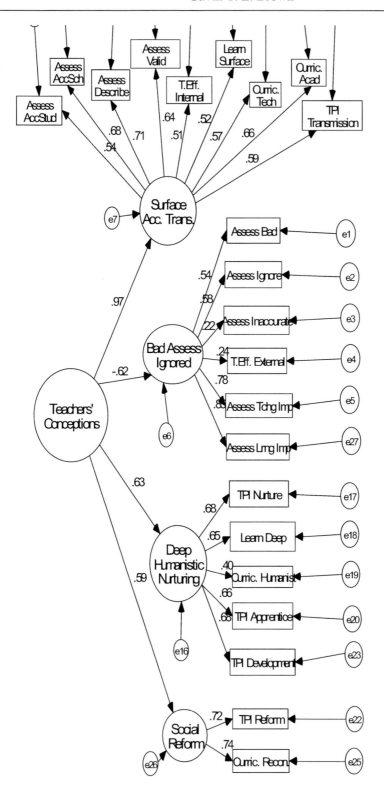

Figure 4. Multi-battery Factor Analysis of Teachers' Integrated Conceptions

The first factor (Bad Assessment Ignored that Does Not Improve Teaching and Learning) involved scales from assessment, curriculum, and efficacy and was interpreted to mean assessment is bad and can be ignored because it does not improve teaching or learning, it is inaccurate, is associated with a technological curriculum approach, and external factors prevent teachers from making improvement. Teachers only slightly agreed with this factor (Figure 4) clearly suggesting that they fundamentally did not agree with assessment systems that did not support improvements in teaching and learning. This is an interesting affirmation of the large body of literature that argues high-stakes national assessment has negative impacts on teachers, curriculum, and teaching (Cannell, 1989; Cooper and Davies, 1993; Delandshere and Jones, 1999; Firestone, Mayrowetz, and Fairman, 1998; Hamilton, 2003; Kohn, 1999; Noble and Smith, 1994; Smith and Fey, 2000; Smith and Rottenberg, 1991). These teachers appeared to recognise that such systems must be resisted and it may be legitimately inferred that if assessment assisted improvements in education then it would not be considered bad or ignored.

The second factor (Surface Accountability Transmitted) involved scales from assessment, curriculum, teaching, and efficacy and was understood to mean that a teacher would be confident that he or she could deliver surface learning through direct transmission and technological means of academic material for school and student accountability purposes and that the results would describe in a valid fashion that kind of learning. Teachers gave moderate agreement to this conception and what is of most concern here is the association of accountability assessments with surface learning. It is probably not the case that the portrayal of external high-stakes assessments as being fundamentally measures of basic fact and procedures is a function of teacher prejudice; it is probably the case that such assessments are surface (Hamilton, 2003; National Research Council, 2001). Further, as long as teachers conceive of externally mandated assessments as measuring only surface academic material (whether developers have been successful in transforming such assessments or not), it may well be that the ambitious goals of reforming education through educational assessment (e.g., Resnick and Resnick, 1989) are doomed.

The third factor (Social Reform) involved scales from teaching and curriculum only and clearly focused on the role of instruction and curriculum to reform or reconstruct society through a deliberate focus on social issues and problems. This result is consistent with the notion that these two scales measure the same trait, despite being derived from different methods. Teachers only moderately agreed with this conception; a response reminiscent of claims that schools are agents of social reproduction not transformation (Bourdieu, 1974; Harker, 1982).

The fourth factor (Deep Humanistic Nurturing) involved scales from teaching, curriculum, and learning and was interpreted to mean that teachers associated deep learning with nurturing, developmental, apprenticeship teaching and humanistic curriculum. Teachers had the highest level of agreement for this conception, mostly agreeing. This factor is very similar to Betoret and Artiga's (2004) cognitive or student-centred paradigm and Kember's (1997) student-centred conceptual learning approach. What is of concern here, in what may be seen as the most stereotypical view of what primary school instruction is about, is the absence of any of the assessment conceptions within this factor. This analysis suggests that teachers profoundly believed that such deep transformative learning can not be assessed; a matter of some serious concern for both assessment developers or publishers and policy officials.

Patterns in People—How Teachers Related to Each Other

An examination of how the conceptions related to each other was done by examining how the teachers could be classified using the scale scores. This analysis examines the pattern of distribution of the conceptions both in their scale and factor conditions—it answers the question of what patterns of conceptions can be found among teachers. Hierarchical cluster analysis of between-groups linkages across the 22 conceptions scale scores, using squared Euclidean distances, led to six clusters of teachers based on their responses across the scales (Table 12). Discriminant analysis with the 22 scale scores correctly placed 87.1% of the 233 teachers in their original clusters and 68.2% of the 233 teachers were correctly placed in their original clusters using just the four multi-battery factor scales. Thus, there was considerable accuracy in using these scales or factors to assign teachers and administrators to clustered conceptual patterns.

Table 13. Multi-Battery Factors by Teachers' Conceptual Clusters

Cluster	N	Multi-Battery Factors				Cluster Description
		Ignore Bad Assessment, Not Improve Teaching and Learning	Surface Accountability Transmitted	Social Change	Nurturing Deep Development	
1	32	M	L	L	M	Cautious, traditionalist, child-centred, anti-assessment
2	17	L	M	M	H	Progressive, child-centred, deep learning, positive users of assessment
3	26	M	M	M	H	Child-centred, developmental, deep learning, assessment tolerant
4	19	L	M	L	M	Conservative, child-centred, anti-assessment, capable
5	55	M	M	M	M	Conservative, child-centred, deep learning, no to accountability assessment
6	84	L	M	M	H	Holistic, child-centred, capable, deep learning, users of assessment

Most values fell between slightly agree (3.0) and mostly agree (5.0) and thus those below or above those values are useful in determining the meaning of each cluster. There were six scale scores that fell in the same range for all clusters and thus these scales were not useful for discriminating among the teachers (i.e., all had high values for the Nurturing perspective on teaching; all had middle values for Internal teacher efficacy, Inaccurate, Describe, Improve

Teaching, and Improve Learning conceptions of assessment). The remaining 16 scale scores were useful in describing the mental conceptions of the six clusters of teachers. The multi-battery factor analysis results were mapped onto these clusters and mean scores were classified by whether they were Low (less than 3.0), High (more than 5.0), or Medium (between 3.0 and 5.0). Six clear patterns of factor scores were evident across the clusters (Table 13).

When viewed in two dimensions (based on the first two canonical discriminant functions only—these accounted for 91.8% of variance with 22 scales and 98.5% of variance with four multi-battery factors), two major axes through the cluster centroids became apparent (Figure 5). The vertical axis was understood to reflect at the positive end a positive orientation towards assessment and the negative end reflected a negative orientation towards assessment. The bubbles used to represent each cluster are placed at the cluster centroid and are drawn relative to the number of teachers in each cluster; in other words the larger the bubble the more teachers represented by the cluster of conceptions. The first horizontal axis placed cluster 1 at the most negative point, clusters 5 and 6 in the middle region, and cluster 2 at the most positive point. The second horizontal axis cut through the middle of the first axis and had cluster 3 at the most positive point and cluster 4 at the most negative point. The horizontal axis represented at the negative end a cautious or conservative position with the positive end characterised by a progressive approach to education.

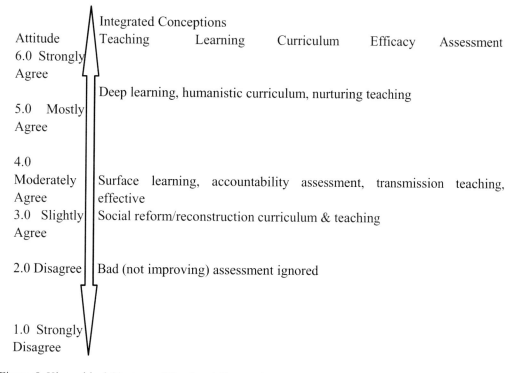

Figure 5. Hierarchical Clusters of Teachers' Conceptions

Holistic, Child-Centred, Capable, Deep Learning, Users of Assessment

Cluster 6 was the largest cluster (*N* = 84, 36%) and was at the centre point of the teachers' conceptual patterns. These teachers agreed with Apprenticeship and Developmental teaching perspectives, Deep views of learning, and Humanistic curriculum, while disagreeing with External teacher efficacy and the Bad conception of assessment. This cluster consisted of holistic, child-centred teachers who do not see assessment as bad, nor do they believe external factors prevent them from making sure students learn deep processing. In terms of the multi-battery factors, the teachers mostly agreed with the deep, humanistic, development factor and slightly agreed with the factor to do with ignoring bad assessment that is not linked to improving teaching and learning.

Conservative, Child-Centred, Deep Learning, no to Accountability Assessment

Cluster 5, the next biggest group ($N = 55$, 24%) were somewhat more negative than cluster 6, in that they explicitly rejected the Social Reconstruction approach to curriculum and the use of assessment for School Accountability, while like the first cluster, they agreed with the Deep view of learning. This cluster was characteristic of politically conservative, child-centred teachers who valued deep learning and who disagreed with the use of assessment to make schools and teachers accountable. The teachers in this cluster fell between slightly and moderately agree for all four multi-battery factors.

Cautious, Traditionalist, Child-Centred, Anti-Assessment

Cluster 1, the third largest ($N = 32$, 14%) were the most negative disagreeing with the Transmission and Social Reform perspectives of teaching, the Surface view of learning, the Academic approach to curriculum. Further, they disagreed with both the School and Student Accountability conceptions of assessment and, though agreeing that assessment was not bad, they did not agree assessment was Valid. Cluster 1 appeared to be made up of very cautious, traditionalist, child-centred teachers who were opposed to assessment in general. This cluster of teachers was noted primarily for its relatively negative position (i.e., slight agreement) towards the surface accountability transmitted and social reform multi-battery factors.

Progressive, Child-Centred, Deep Learning, Positive Users of Assessment

At the opposite end of the same spectrum was Cluster 2, the smallest ($N = 17$, 7%). These teachers agreed with Apprenticeship and Developmental perspectives of teaching, Deep views of learning, and both Humanistic and Technological approaches to curriculum. They disagreed the conception that assessment was Bad. This cluster represented progressive, child-centred teachers who used assessment for multiple purposes with the goal of achieving deep learning. This cluster of teachers agreed with the deep humanistic development multi-battery factor and disagreed with the ignoring bad assessment that is not linked to improving teaching and learning factor.

Child-Centred, Developmental, Deep Learning, Assessment Tolerant

Cluster 3, the fourth largest ($N = 26$, 11%) were closest to Cluster 5, and agreed with the Apprenticeship and Developmental perspectives on teaching, Deep learning, and Humanistic teaching. This group of teachers focused on child-centred, development of deep processing, while tolerating assessment. This cluster of teachers had strong agreement about the deep humanistic development multi-battery factor.

Conservative, Child-Centred, Anti-Assessment, Capable

Cluster 4, the second smallest (N = 19, 8%), were closest to Cluster 1. They agreed with the Apprenticeship perspective on teaching and Deep views of Learning, but their conceptions were largely negative. They disagreed with the Transmission perspective of teaching, the social Reconstruction approach to curriculum, and did not agree that External obstacles impacted on their efficacy. They also disagreed with both Accountability conceptions of assessment, and did not agree that assessment was Valid or Bad. This cluster consisted of child-centred, conservative teachers who were opposed to accountability uses of assessment, rejected the validity of assessment and telling approaches to teaching, and were confident that they could overcome external obstacles to learning. This cluster of teachers disagreed with two of the multi-battery factors: ignoring bad assessment that is not linked to improving teaching and learning and social reform.

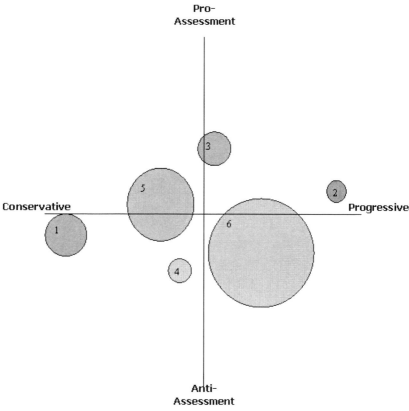

cluster	
1	*Cautious, traditionalist, child-centred, anti-assessment*
2	*Progressive, child-centred, deep learning, positive users of assessment*
3	*Child-centred, developmental, deep learning, assessment tolerant*
4	*Conservative, child-centred, anti-assessment, capable*
5	*Conservative, child-centred, deep learning, no to accountability assessment*
6	*Holistic, child-centred, capable, deep learning, users of assessment*

CONCLUSION

It is argued from these analyses that teachers' conceptions of curriculum, teaching, learning, teacher efficacy, and assessment group into four meaningful factors and that this sample of teachers exhibited six different patterns of conception. The first factor, was a strong agreement that deep learning is child-centred; the second, was a moderate agreement that accountability assessment of surface learning could be achieved through direct instruction. The third factor was a moderate agreement that education should be about social change and reform. The fourth factor was a disagreement with the conception that assessment was bad for teaching and learning and could be ignored. Cluster analysis of those four factors meaningfully identified six different mindsets which were arranged on two axes—a cautious/conservative to progressive scale and a pro to anti-assessment orientation. The six clusters were described as, in descending order of size: (6) holistic, child-centred, capable, deep learning, users of assessment; (5) conservative, child-centred, deep learning, no to accountability assessment; (1) cautious, traditionalist, child-centred, anti-assessment; (3) child-centred, developmental, deep learning, assessment tolerant; (4) conservative, child-centred, anti-assessment, capable; and (2) progressive, child-centred, deep learning, positive users of assessment.

Simple opposites did not explain how teachers melded assessment, teaching, learning, and assessment into their conceptual understanding. These factors are largely uncorrelated and independent of each other, supporting Cheung and Wong's (2002) suggestion that teachers hold apparently contradictory or pluralistic conceptions simultaneously. That the teachers had moderately positive attitude towards successfully teaching for surface accountability assessment and that they had only slight agreement toward the conception that assessment was bad and could be ignored, while they strongly agreed with deep, humanistic, and nurturing teaching clearly indicated that the simplistic dualism of the stereotype was insufficient to describe teachers' conceptions. The traditional child and learner-centred perception of primary school teachers is just inadequate to capture the rich set of conceptions these teachers held; they also believed they could deliver success on surface accountability assessments while resisting the effect of assessment on their deep learning intentions.

The model proposed by Betoret and Artiga (2004) found more support in this study in that this analysis also found two axes with four resulting quadrants. However, it is argued that this study's axes are not equivalent conceptually to that found by Betoret and Artiga. The conservative-progressive axis and the pro/anti-assessment axis in this analysis is not obviously equivalent to their student/teacher-centred axis and product/process-centred approaches. Nevertheless, an interesting future study would be to integrate the Betoret and Artiga approach with that used here. It seems highly likely that the impact and power of assessment needs to be taken into account when understanding what teachers' conceive of educational activities.

This analysis clearly indicated that New Zealand teachers do have multiple responses to the accountability and policy systems of New Zealand. Clearly, there were teachers who reflected the accountability conformity approach documented by Hill (2000) and Locke and Hill (2003), for example clusters 6 and 3, and yet similar teachers were clearly uncomfortable with such use of assessment, to wit clusters 5 and 4. What this study provides is a means of efficiently classifying teachers into orientations with reasonable accuracy and the identification of multiple patterns of conception.

These results are tentative in that much larger data sets are needed to permit analysis with all observed variables rather than the currently used 22 latent variables. Future research may well include a wider range of possible conceptions, including at least epistemology, feedback, motivation, ability, personality, and school subjects. There is also a need for greater understanding of the realities underlying the model proposed here by EFA; the fit of that model to the data could be improved. Additionally, it would be useful to identify a meaningful measure of teacher effectiveness so that a structural equation model of how teachers' conceptions relate to student learning outcomes could be developed and tested. The method of measuring the quality of student outcomes on the surface-deep axis was used in identifying effective teachers (Bond, Smith, Baker, and Hattie, 2000). This suggests that rather than focus simply on total scores or grades that the architecture of student learning could be used as a relatively objective measure of teacher effectiveness. With such a measure and sample size, a full SEM analysis of teachers' instructional conceptions could be conducted and any difference in conceptions between expert, competent, and novice teachers could be detected. It should also be noted that this study has identified factoral structure issues with Cheung's Conceptions of Curriculum and Pratt's Teaching Perspectives Inventory batteries that merit further investigation and resolution.

The relatively benign tolerance of accountability assessments (i.e., not associated with bad or ignore conceptions) as exhibited by clusters 2 and 3 may be a function of the low-stakes school-based assessment systems operating in New Zealand. A modification to that policy and practice context may well lead teachers to adjust their conception of how assessment, teaching, learning, and efficacy interrelate—in other words, their sense that assessment is bad may increase. Certainly developers of large-scale accountability assessment systems would pay to make a serious effort to ensure that deep learning is clearly measured and reported by their assessments and not assume that accountability pressures are sufficient to persuade teachers of the validity of the assessments.

It may well be that teachers who agree and comply with the surface accountability conception produce students who demonstrate surface rather than deep learning outcomes. However such compliance should not be taken to mean that teachers believe those assessments measure core values of classroom life; that is deep learning, improved quality of teaching, and student-centred development.

An important suggestion from this research is that the development of national assessment policy should be accompanied by research into teachers' conceptions. The engagement of teachers' belief systems about assessment has been a fundamentally neglected aspect in effective professional development (Hargreaves and Fullan, 1998). More generally, it is assumed that teachers' reasoning for their practices, which are their means of solving educational problems, is resistant to modification because research-based training often misses the issues relevant to teachers and because new interventions are not understood as needing to compete for belief (Robinson, 1998; Robinson and Walker, 1999). In other words, introducing a policy or innovation without taking into account the reasons and beliefs teachers have for their current practices is unlikely to be successful. This study has exposed important patterns in how teachers' conceptions of assessment, teaching, learning, curriculum, and efficacy are inter-related and these findings can be used to guide further research around the development of appropriate policies and assessments.

ACKNOWLEDGEMENTS

The author would like to acknowledge the financial assistance of the University of Auckland and thank Professor John Hattie for his supervision. An earlier version of this article was presented at the NZARE/AARE conference in Auckland 2003. Professor Robert Cudeck, Ohio State University, is thanked for supplying his MBFACT software.

REFERENCES

Airasian, P. W. (1997). *Classroom assessment* (3rd ed.). New York: McGraw-Hill.

Anthony, G. (1994). Learning strategies in the mathematics classroom: What can we learn from stimulated recall interviews? *New Zealand Journal of Educational Studies, 29*(2), 127–140.

Anthony, G. (1997). Task demands and instructional support in mathematics: Influences on strategic learning behaviours of secondary students. *set: research information for teachers,* (2), 6.

Arbuckle, J. L. (2003). AMOS (Version 5). [Computer software]. Chicago, IL: SmallWaters Corp.

Asch, R. L. (1976). Teaching beliefs and evaluation. *Art Education, 29*(6), 18-22.

Bandura, A. (1989). Human agency in social cognitive theory. *American Psychologist, 44*(9), 1175-1184.

Barnes, D. (1976). *From communication to curriculum.* London: Penguin Press.

Betoret, F. D., and Artiga, A. G. (2004). Trainee teachers' conceptions of teaching and learning, classroom layout and exam design. *Educational Studies, 30*(4), 355-372.

Biggs, J. B. (1987). Student approaches to learning and studying. Research monograph. Melbourne: ACER.

Black, P., and Wiliam, D. (1998). Assessment and classroom learning. *Educational Assessment: Principles, Policy and Practice, 5*(1), 7-74.

Bond, L., Smith, T., Baker, W. K., and Hattie, J. A. (2000). The certification system of the National Board for Professional Teaching Standards: A construct and consequential validity study. (Research Report). Greensboro, NC: University of North Carolina, Center for Educational Research and Evaluation.

Bourdieu, Pierre (1974). The school as a conservative force: scholastic and cultural inequalities. In J. Eggleston (Ed.) *Contemporary Research in the Sociology of Education,* (pp. 32-46). London: Methuen.

Brown, G. T. L. (2002a). *Teachers' Conceptions of Assessment.* Unpublished doctoral dissertation, University of Auckland, Auckland, NZ.

Brown, G. T. L. (2003, December). *Teachers' instructional conceptions: Assessment's relationship to learning, teaching, curriculum, and teacher efficacy.* Paper presented to the joint annual conference of the Australian and New Zealand Associations for Research in Education (AARE/NZARE), Auckland, NZ.

Brown, G.T.L. (2002b). Student beliefs about learning: New Zealand students in Year 11. *Academic Exchange Quarterly, 6*(1), 110-114.

Brown, G.T.L. (2004a). Teachers' conceptions of assessment: Implications for policy and professional development. *Assessment in Education: Policy, Principles and Practice, 11*(3), 305-322.

Brown, G.T.L. (2004b). Measuring attitude with positively packed self-report ratings: Comparison of agreement and frequency scales. *Psychological Reports, 94,* 1015-1024.

Browne, M. W., and Cudek, R. (1989). Single sample cross-validation indices for covariance structures. *Multivariate Behavioral Research, 24,* 445-455.

Browne, M. W., and Cudek, R. (1993). Alternative ways of assessing model fit. In K. A. Bollen and J. S. Long (Eds.), *Testing structural equation models,* (pp. 136-162). Newbury Park, CA: Sage.

Bulterman-Bos, J., Verloop, N., Terwel, J., and Wardekker, W. (2003). Reconciling the pedagogical goal and the measurement goal of evaluation: The perspectives of teachers in the context of national standards. *Teachers College Record, 105*(3), 344-374.

Butterfield, S., Williams, A. and Marr, A. (1999) Talking about assessment: mentor-student dialogues about pupil assessment in initial teacher training, *Assessment in Education,* 6(2), pp. 225-246.

Calderhead, J. (1996). Teachers: Beliefs and knowledge. In D. C. Berliner and R. C. Calfee (Eds.), *Handbook of educational psychology* (pp. 709-725). New York: Simon and Schuster Macmillan.

Campbell, D. T. and Fiske, D. W. (1959). Convergent and discriminant validation by the multitrait-multimethod matrix. *Psychological Bulletin 56,* 81-105.

Cannell, J. J. (1989). *How public educators cheat on standardized achievement tests.* Albuquerque, NM: Friends for Education.

Carr, M. (2001). *Assessment in early childhood settings: learning stories.* London: Paul Chapman.

Cheung, D. (2000). Measuring teachers' meta-orientations to curriculum: Application of hierarchical confirmatory analysis. *Journal of Experimental Education, 68*(2), 149-165.

Cheung, D., and Ng, P.-H. (2000). Science teachers' beliefs about curriculum design. *Research in Science Education, 30*(4), 357-375.

Cheung, D., and Wong, H-W. (2002). Measuring teacher beliefs about alternative curriculum designs. *The Curriculum Journal, 13*(2), 225-248.

Chou, C.-P., and Bentler, P. M. (1995). Estimates and tests in structural equation modeling. In R. H. Hoyle, (Ed.). *Stuructural equation modeling: Concepts, issues, and applications.* (pp. 37—55). Thousand Oaks, CA: Sage.

Cizek, G.J., Fitzgerald, S., Shawn, M. and Rachor, R.E. (1995) Teachers' assessment practices: Preparation, isolation and the kitchen sink, *Educational Assessment*, 3, pp. 159-179.

Clark, C., and Peterson, P. (1986). Teachers' thought processes. In M. Wittrock (Ed.), *Handbook of research on teaching.* (3rd ed., pp. 255-296). New York: Macmillan.

Cooper, P., and Davies, C. (1993). The impact of national curriculum assessment arrangements on English teachers' thinking and classroom practice in English secondary schools. *Teaching and Teacher Education, 9*(5/6), 559-570.

Croft, A. C. and Reid, N. A. (1991). How often and for what purposes are NZCER tests used in primary and secondary schools? Wellington, NZ: NZCER.

Croft, A.C., Strafford, E. and Mapa, L. (2000). Stocktake/evaluation of existing diagnostic tools in literacy and numeracy in English. Wellington, NZ: NZCER.

Crooks, T. (1988). The impact of classroom evaluation practices on students. *Review of Educational Research, 58*(4), 438-481.

Crooks, T. J. (2002). Educational assessment in New Zealand schools. *Assessment in Education: Principles Policy and Practice*, 9(2), 237–253.

Cudeck, R. (1982). Methods for estimating between-battery factors. *Multivariate Behavioral Research, 17*, 47-68.

Dahlin, B., Watkins, D. A., and Ekholm, M. (2001). The role of assessment in student learning: The views of Hong Kong and Swedish lecturers. In D. A. Watkins and J. B. Biggs (Eds.), *Teaching the Chinese learner: Psychological and pedagogical perspectives.* (pp. 47-74). Hong Kong: University of Hong Kong, Comparative Education Research Centre.

Delandshere, G., and Jones, J. H. (1999). Elementary teachers' beliefs about assessment in mathematics: A case of assessment paralysis. *Journal of Curriculum and Supervision, 14*(3), 216–240.

Dixon, H. (1999). The effect of policy on practice: an analysis of teachers' perceptions of school based assessment practice. Unpublished Masters Thesis, Massey University, Albany, NZ.

Dwyer, C. A., and Villegas, A. M. (1993). Guiding conceptions and assessment principles for The Praxis Series: Professional assessments for beginning teachers. (Research Report RR-93-17). Princeton, NJ: Educational Testing Service.

Eisner, E. W., and Vallance, E. (1974). *Conflicting conceptions of curriculum.* Berkeley, CA: McCutchan.

Entwistle, N. (1997). Contrasting perspectives on learning. In F. Marton, D. Hounsell, and N. Entwistle (Eds.). *The experience of learning: Implications for teaching and studying in higher education.* (2nd ed.). (pp. 3–22). Edinburgh: Scottish Academic Press.

Entwistle, N., and Marton, F. (1984). Changing conceptions of learning and research. In F. Marton, D. Hounsell, and N. Entwistle (Eds.). *The experience of learning.* (pp. 211–231) Edinburgh: Scottish Academic Press.

Finch, J. F., Panter, A. T., and Caskie, G. I. L., (1999). Two approaches for identifying shared personality dimensions across methods. *Journal of Personality, 67*(3), 407-438.

Firestone, W. A., Mayrowetz, D., and Fairman, J. (1998). Performance-based assessment and instructional change: The effects of testing in Maine and Maryland. *Educational Evaluation and Policy Analysis, 20*(2), 95–113.

Fiske, E. B. and Ladd, H. F. (2000). *When schools compete: a cautionary tale.* Washington, DC: Brookings Institution Press.

Garcia, E. (1987, April). *An ethnographic study of teachers' implicit theories on evaluation.* Paper presented at the Annual Meeting of the American Educational Research Association., Washington, DC.

Gibson, S., and Dembo, M. H. (1984). Teacher efficacy: A construct validation. *Journal of Educational Psychology, 76*(4), 569-582.

Gipps, C., Brown, M., McCallum, B., and McAlister, S. (1995). *Intuition or evidence? Teachers and national assessment of seven-year-olds.* Buckingham, UK: Open University Press.

Gow, L., and Kember, D. (1993). Conceptions of teaching and their relationship to student learning. *British Journal of Educational Psychology, 63*, 20–33.

Graham, J. W., Taylor, B., J., and Cumsille, P. E. (2001). Planned missing-data designs in analysis of change. In L. M. Collins and A. G. Sayer (Eds.), *New methods for the analysis of change.* (pp. 335–353). Washington, DC: APA.

Guskey, T. R., and Passaro, P. D. (1994). Teacher efficacy: A study of construct dimensions. *American Educational Research Journal, 31*, 627-643.

Guthrie, J. T. (2002). Preparing students for high-stakes test taking in reading. In A. E. Farstrup and S. J. Samuels (Eds.). *What research has to say about reading instruction* (3rd ed.), (pp. 370—391). Newark, DE: International Reading Association.

Hair, J. F., Jr., Anderson, R. E., Tatham, R. L., and Black, W. C. (1998). *Multivariate data analysis.* (5th ed.). Upper Saddle River, NJ: Prentice Hall.

Hamilton, L. (2003). Assessment as a policy tool. *Review of Research in Education, 27,* 25-68.

Hargreaves, A., and Fullan, M. (1998). *What's worth fighting for out there?* New York: Teachers College Press.

Harker, R. K. (1982). Bourdieu and education. *New Zealand Cultural Studies Working Group Newsletter.* 4, 37-49.

Hattie, J. A. (2002). *Schools like mine: Cluster analysis of New Zealand schools.* (Tech. Rep. No. 14). Auckland, NZ: University of Auckland, Project asTTle.

Heaton, J. B. (1975). *Writing English language tests.* London: Longman.

Henson, R. K., Kogan, L. R., and Vacha-Haase, T. (2001). A reliability generalization study of the Teacher Efficacy Scale and related instruments. *Educational and Psychological Measurement, 61*(3), 404-420.

Hershberg, T. (2002). Comment. In D. Ravitch (Ed.), *Brookings Papers on Education Policy: 2002.* (pp. 324-333). Washington, DC: Brookings Institution Press.

Hian, C. H. (1994). *Operationalization and prediction of conceptions of teaching in adult education.* Unpublished doctoral dissertation, University of British Columbia, Vancouver, BC.

Hill, M. F. (2000). Dot, slash, cross: How assessment can drive teachers to ticking instead of teaching. *set: Research information for teachers,* (1), 21-25.

Ho, A., Watkins, D., and Kelly, M. (2001). The conceptual change approach to improving teaching and learning: An evaluation of a Hong Kong staff development programme. *Higher Education, 42*, 143-169.

Howe, M. J. A. (1998). *Principles of abilities and human learning.* Hove, UK: Psychology Press.

Hoyle, R. H. (1995). The structural equation modeling approach: Basic concepts and fundamental issues. In R. H. Hoyle, (Ed.). *Sturctural equation modeling: Concepts, issues, and applications.* (pp. 1–15). Thousand Oaks, CA: Sage.

Hoyle, R. H., and Duvall, J. L. (2004). Determining the number of factors in exploratory and confirmatory factor analysis. In D. Kaplan (Ed.). *The Sage handbook of quantitative methodology for the social sciences* (pp. 301-315). Thousand Oaks, CA: Sage.

Jensen, J. W., Kauchak, D., and Rowley, M. L. (2001, March). *Teacher candidates' beliefs: Implications for practice.* Paper presented at the 53rd Annual Meeting of the American Association of Colleges for Teacher Education, Dallas, TX.

Kahn, E. A. (2000). A case study of assessment in a grade 10 English course. *The Journal of Educational Research, 93*, 276-286.

Kember, D. (1997). A reconceptualisation of the research into university academics' conceptions of teaching. *Learning and Instruction, 7*(3), 255-275.

Kohn, A. (1999). The schools our children deserve: Moving beyond traditional classrooms and "tougher standards". New York: Houghton Mifflin.

Lam, T.C.M., and Klockars, A.J. (1982). Anchor point effects on the equivalence of questionnaire items. *Journal of Educational Measurement, 19*(4), 317—322.

Levin, B. (2001) Reforming education: From origins to outcomes. London: RoutledgeFalmer.

Linn, R. L., and Gronlund, N. E. (2000). *Measurement and evaluation in teaching* (8 ed.). New York: Macmillan.

Linn, R.L. (2000) Assessments and accountability, *Educational Researcher*, 29(2), pp. 4-16.

Locke, T. and Hill, M. F. (2003). *The impact of changes in the nature of teachers' work on teacher professionalism*. Research Report. Hamilton, NZ, The University of Waikato.

MacKechnie, R., and MacKechnie, C. (1999). *How helpful are introductory study skills programmes? Thoughts on the experience of one programme in Hamilton, New Zealand*. Paper presented at the HERDSA Annual International Conference, Melbourne, Australia, July, 1999.

Marton, F. and Saljo, R. (1976). On qualitative differences in learning. I – outcome and process. *British Journal of Educational Psychology, 42*, 4-11.

Marton, F. (1983). Beyond individual differences. *Educational Psychology, 3*(3 and 4), 289–303.

Maruyama, G. M. (1998). *Basics of structural equation modeling*. Thousand Oaks, CA: Sage.

McMillan, J. H. (2001). Classroom assessment: Principles and practice for effective instruction (2 ed.). Boston, MA: Allyn and Bacon.

McMillan, J. H., Myran, S., and Workman, D. (2002). Elementary teachers' classroom assessment and grading practices. *The Journal of Educational Research, 95*(4), 203-213.

Mehrens, W. A., and Lehmann, I. J. (1984). *Measurement and evaluation in education and psychology* (3rd ed.). New York, NY: Holt, Rinehart and Winston.

Ministry of Education. (1993). The New Zealand curriculum framework: te anga marautanga o Aotearoa. Wellington, NZ: Learning Media.

Ministry of Education. (1994). *Assessment: policy to practice*. Wellington, NZ: Learning Media.

National Research Council. (2001). Knowing what students know: The science and design of educational assessment. Washington, DC: National Academy Press.

New Zealand. (1998). *Assessment for success in primary schools: green paper*. Wellington, NZ: Ministry of Education.

Noble, A. J., and Smith, M. L. (1994). *Old and new beliefs about measurement-driven reform: "The more things change, the more they stay the same"*. CSE Tech. Rep. 373. Los Angeles: University of California, Los Angeles, CRESST.

Osborne, J. W., and Costello, A. B. (2005). Best practices in exploratory factor analysis: Four recommendations for getting the most from your analysis. *Practical Assessment Research and Evaluation, 10*(7). Retrieved July 15, 2005, from http://pareonline.net /getvn.asp?v=1-and n=7

Pajares, M. F. (1992). Teachers' beliefs and educational research: Cleaning up a messy construct. *Review of Educational Research, 62*, 307–332.

Philipp, R. A., Flores, A., Sowder, J. T., and Schappelle, B. P. (1994). Conceptions and practices of extraordinary mathematics teachers. *Journal of Mathematical Behavior, 13*, 155-180.

Philippou, G., and Christou, C. (1997). Cypriot and Greek primary teachers' conceptions about mathematical assessment. *Educational Research and Evaluation, 3*(2), 140-159.

Popham, W. J. (2000b). Modern educational measurement: Practical guidelines for educational leaders (6th ed.). Boston: Allyn and Bacon.

Pratt, D. D. (1992a). Conceptions of teaching. *Adult Education Quarterly, 42*(4), 203-220.

Pratt, D. D. (1992b). Chinese conceptions of learning and teaching: A westerner's attempt at understanding. *International Journal of Lifelong Education, 11*(4), 301-319.

Pratt, D. D. (1997). Reconceptualizing the evaluation of teaching in higher education. *Higher Education, 34*, 23-44.

Pratt, D. D., and Associates. (1998). *Five perspectives on teaching in adult and higher education.* Malabar, FL: Krieger, Publishers.

Pratt, D. D., and Collins, J. B. (1998). *Teaching Perspectives Inventory.* [On-line]. Retrieved March 15, 2001, from http://www.edst.educ.ubc.ca/DPtpi.html

Pratt, D. D., and Collins, J. B. (2001, June). *The Teaching Perspectives Inventory (TPI).* Paper presented at the Adult Education Research Conference, Vancouver, BC.

Purdie, N., and Hattie, J. (1999). The relationship between study skills and learning outcomes: A meta-analysis. *Australian Journal of Education 43*, (1), 72–86.

Quilter, S. M. (1998). *Inservice teachers' assessment literacy and attitudes toward assessment.* Unpublished Doctoral Dissertation, University of South Carolina, Columbia, SC.

Resnick, L. B., and Resnick, D. P. (1989). *Assessing the thinking curriculum: New tools for educational reform.* Washington, DC: National Commission on Testing and Public Policy.

Rex, L.A. and Nelson, M. C. (2004). How teachers' professional identities position high-stakes test preparation in their classrooms. *Teachers College Record, 106*(6), 1288-1331.

Robinson, V. M. J. (1998). Methodology and the research-practice gap. *Educational Researcher, 27*(1), 17-26.

Robinson, V. M. J., and Walker, J. C. (1999). Theoretical privilege and researchers' contribution to educational change. In J. S. Gaffney and B. J. Askew (Eds.), *Stirring the waters: The influence of Marie Clay* (pp. 239-259). Portsmouth, NH: Heinemann.

Rotter, J. B. (1982). Social learning theory. In N. T. Feather (Ed.). *Expectations and actions: Expectancy-value models in psychology* (pp. 241–260). Hillsdale, NJ: Erlbaum.

Saltzgaver, D. (1983). One teacher's dominant conceptions of student assessment. *Curriculum Perspectives, 3*, 15-21.

Samuelowicz, K. (1994). Teaching conceptions and teaching practice: A case of assessment. In R. Ballantyne and C. Bruce (Eds.), *Phenomenography: Philosophy and practice* (pp. 343-353). Brisbane, Aus: Queensland University of Technology, Centre for Applied Environmental and Social Education Research.

Samuelowicz, K., and Bain, J. D. (1992). Conceptions of teaching held by academic teachers. *Higher Education, 24*, 93-111.

Schommer, M. (1990). The effects of beliefs about the nature of knowledge on comprehension. *Journal of Educational Psychology, 82*, 498-504.

Schraw, G., Bendixen, L. D., and Dunkle, M. E. (2002). Development and validation of the epistemic belief inventory (EBI). In B. K. Hofer and P. R. Pintrich (Eds.), *Personal Epistemology: The psychology of beliefs about knowledge and knowing* (pp. 261-276). Mahwah, NJ: Lawrence Erlbaum.

Scriven, M. (1991). Beyond formative and summative evaluation. In M. W. McLaughlin and D. C. Phillips (Eds.), *Evaluation and education: At quarter century* (Vol. Part II, pp. 19–64). Chicago: NSSE.

Smith, M. L., and Fey, P. (2000). Validity and accountability in high-stakes testing. *Journal of Teacher Education, 51*(5), 334–344.

Smith, M. L., and Rottenberg, C. (1991). Unintended consequences of external testing in elementary schools. *Educational Measurement: Issues and Practice, 10*, 7–11.

Smith, M.L., Heinecke, W. and Noble, A.J. (1999) Assessment policy and political spectacle, *Teachers College Record*, 101(2), pp. 157-191.

Stamp, D. (1987). Evaluation of the formation and stability of student teacher attitudes to measurement and evaluation practices. Unpublished doctoral dissertation, Macquarie University, Sydney, Aus.

Strauman, T. J. and Wetzler, S. (1992). The factor structure of SCL-90 and MCMI scale scores: Within-measure and interbattery analyses. *Multivariate Behavioral Research, 27*(1), 1-20.

Sturrock, F. (1999). *Teacher census: Preliminary report.* Unpublished Report. Wellington, NZ: Ministry of Education, Demographic and Statistical Analysis Unit.

Tait, H., Entwistle, N. J., and McCune, V. (1998). ASSIST: A reconceptualisation of the Approaches to Studying Inventory. In Rust, C. (Ed.), *Improving Student Learning: Improving Students as Learners* (pp. 262-271). Oxford: Oxford Centre for Staff and Learning Development.

Thompson, A. G. (1992). Teachers' beliefs and conceptions: A synthesis of the research. In D. A. Grouws (Ed.), *Handbook of research on mathematics teaching and learning.* (pp. 127–146). New York: Macmillan.

Tittle, C. K. (1994). Toward an educational psychology of assessment for teaching and learning: Theories, contexts, and validation arguments. *Educational Psychologist, 29*, 149-162.

Torrance, H., and Pryor, J. (1998). Investigating formative assessment: Teaching, learning and assessment in the classroom. Buckingham, UK: Open University Press.

Trigwell, K., and Prosser, M. (1997). Towards an understanding of individual acts of teaching and learning. *Higher Education Research and Development, 16*(2), 241–252.

Tschannen-Moran, M., Woolfolk Hoy, A., and Hoy, W. K. (1998). Teacher efficacy: Its meaning and measure. *Review of Educational Research, 68*(2), 202–248.

Tucker, L. R. (1958). An inter-battery method of factor analysis. *Psychometrika, 23*(2), 111-136.

Warren, E., and Nisbet, S. (1999, July). *The relationship between the purported use of assessment techniques and beliefs about the uses of assessment.* Paper presented at the 22nd Annual Conference of the Mathematics Education and Research Group of Australasia (MERGA), Adelaide, SA.

Webb, N. L. (1992). Assessment of students' knowledge of mathematics: Steps toward a theory. In D. A. Grouws (Ed.), *Handbook of research on mathematics teaching and learning* (pp. 661-683). New York: Macmillan.

Wood, P., and Kardash, C. (2002). Critical elements in the design and analysis of studies of epistemology. In B. K. Hofer and P. R. Pintrich (Eds.), *Personal epistemology: The psychology of beliefs about knowledge* (pp. 231-261). Mahwah, NJ: Lawrence Erlbaum.

Wylie, C. (1997). Self-managing schools seven years on: what have we learnt? Wellington, NZ: NZCER.

In: The Concept of Self in Education, Family and Sports
Editor: Anne P. Prescott, pp. 51-74

ISBN 1-59454-988-5
© 2006 Nova Science Publishers, Inc.

Chapter 2

SELF-CONCEPT AND SELF-EFFICACY IN MATHEMATICS: RELATION WITH MATHEMATICS MOTIVATION AND ACHIEVEMENT

Einar M. Skaalvik[*] and Sidsel Skaalvik
Norwegian University of Science and Technology

ABSTRACT

In two longitudinal studies we examined if mathematics self-perception (self-concept and self-efficacy) predicted subsequent achievement over and above the prediction that could be made by prior achievement. We also tested if the impact of self-perception on subsequent achievement could be explained by students' goal orientation, interest, or self-esteem. The participants in study 1 were 246 middle school students whereas the participants in study 2 were 484 high school students. Achievements were indicated by final grades in mathematics in two successive school years, whereas self-concept, self-efficacy, self-esteem, interest and goal orientation were measured at the beginning of the second school year. Data were analyzed by means of structural equation modelling using the AMOS 5 program. The analyses showed that students' self-perceptions strongly predicted subsequent achievement over and above the prediction that could be made from prior achievement. Thus, both studies indicated that self-concept and self-efficacy are important mediators of academic achievement. However, there was no evidence that the effect of self-perception on subsequent achievement was mediated through students' interest in mathematics or through students' goal orientation or their self-esteem.

---

[*] Mailing address: Einar M. Skaalvik and Sidsel Skaalvik, Norwegian University of Science and Technology, Department of Education, 7491 Trondheim, Norway. E-mail: sidsel.skaalvik@svt.ntnu.no; einar.skaalvik@svt.ntnu.no

INTRODUCTION

A widespread belief among educators is that self-perception, the various attributes and beliefs that one assigns to oneself, is a basic foundation of behaviour and achievement (Bong and Skaalvik, 2003). This belief is shared by various researchers focusing on different aspects of self-perception. Rosenberg (1979) maintains that self-concept is the individual's fundamental frame of reference and claims that it is the foundation on which all his actions are predicated. Similarly, Bong and Skaalvik (2003) maintain that individuals who are otherwise similar feel differently about themselves and choose different courses of action, depending on how they perceive themselves and what they believe they are capable of. Self-perceptions are heavily rooted in one's past experiences (Shavelson, Hubner, and Stanton, 1976), yet it is these subjective convictions about oneself, once established, which play a determining role in individuals' further growth and development (Bandura, 1997; Markus and Nurius, 1986). As Rosenberg (1979) noted in his classic book on self-concept, the individual's behavior is based not on what he or she is actually like but on what the individual *thinks* he or she is like.

The purpose of the present study was in a longitudinal perspective to examine relations between achievement and self-perception in mathematics in middle school and high school. More particularly, we examined if mathematics self-perception predicted subsequent achievement over and above the prediction that could be made by prior achievement. The underlying question was if the stability in achievement was mediated through students' self-perception. An additional purpose was to test if the impact of self-perceived abilities on subsequent achievement could be explained by goal orientation, intrinsic motivation, or self-esteem.

SELF-CONCEPT AND SELF-EFFICACY

Two research traditions can be identified in the educational and psychological research in academic self-perception: (a) the self-concept tradition and (b) the self-efficacy tradition. Researchers within the two traditions explain both the development and the effect of the constructs in different ways and use different measures (Skaalvik and Bong, 2003). Although the distinction between the constructs likely is one of degree, the difference is often emphasized (Bandura, 1986).

An important difference in how self-concept and self-efficacy are conceived includes the frame of references against which the self judgments are made. Self-concept is assumed to be influenced by reflected appraisals from significant others and both social (external) and internal comparisons (Marsh, 1986, 1987; Rosenberg, 1979; Trent, Cooney, Russel, and Warton, 1996) whereas self-efficacy researchers emphasize authentic mastery experiences as the most important source of self-efficacy (Bandura, 1981, 1986).

There are also important differences in the measurements of the two constructs. Skaalvik (1997a) points out two important differences between traditional measures of self-concept and self-efficacy. Firstly, the two constructs differ with respect to the nature of the self-judgments. Self-efficacy is concerned with judgments of how well one can execute courses of action required to deal with prospective situations (Bandura, 1977, 1981, 1982). In comparison, measures of math self-concept are concerned with feelings of doing well or poorly in mathematics (The Self Description Questionnaire; Marsh, 1990a). Whereas math self-efficacy refers to mastery expectations, answering questions like "Can I do it?" math self-concept refers to judgments of ones own abilities in mathematics, answering questions like "Am I good at it?"

Secondly, traditional measures of self-concept and self-efficacy differ with respect to the generality of the measurements. The two constructs are typically measured at different levels in the Shavelson, Hubner, and Stanton (1976) hierarchy. A typical item measuring math self-concept is: "I always do well on tests in mathematics", measuring feeling of doing well in mathematics *in general*. Self-efficacy researchers, on the other hand, emphasize that self-efficacy expectations should be measured at a *problem specific level* (Bandura, 1986, 1997; Gorrell, 1990; Pajares, 1997). For instance, mathematics self-efficacy is often measured by presenting pairs of mathematics problems to the students asking them to judge their abilities to correctly solve the problems or similar types of problems (Bandura and Schunk, 1981; Hackett and Betz, 1989).

Whereas the differences between domain-level self-concept and task-level self-efficacy are widely recognized (Marsh, Walker, and Debus, 1991; Pajares, 1996) they may not reflect inherent differences between the two constructs. Some researchers have assessed domain-level self-efficacy (Zimmerman, Bandura, and Martinez-Pons, 1992; Pajares and Miller, 1995; Bong, 2002). When measuring self-efficacy at a domain level the difference between self-concept and self-efficacy becomes less clear (Bong and Skaalvik, 2003). In this study we use the term self-perception to refer to both self-concept and self-efficacy. In the empirical studies reported here self-concept and self-efficacy are used as indicators of a self-perception latent trait.

RELATIONS BETWEEN ACHIEVEMENT AND SELF-PERCEPTION

Numerous studies have documented moderate to strong relations between both academic achievement and academic self-concept (Marsh, Byrne, and Shavelson, 1988; Marsh and Yeung, 1997; Shavelson and Bolus, 1982; Skaalvik and Hagtvet, 1990; Skaalvik and Skaalvik, 2004) and between academic achievement and academic self-efficacy (Pajares, 1996; Pajares and Kranzler, 1995; Skaalvik and Skaalvik, 2004; Zimmerman and Bandura, 1994, Zimmerman, Bandura, and Martinez-Pons, 1992). However, although the relation between academic self-perception and achievement is well established in the research literature, there is no agreement about the causal ordering of these constructs. In the self-concept literature there has been an ongoing debate about the causal relations between academic achievement and academic self-concept (see Byrne, 1996). Several authors have pointed out that causal predominance remains yet an unresolved issue (Byrne, 1996; Pottebaum, Keith and Ehly, 1986), and that it will be difficult to prove conclusively a causal direction in the relations (Wigfield, Eccles, and Pintrich, 1996). The self-efficacy literature has been less concerned with the causal ordering of self-efficacy and achievement. Still, on logical and theoretical grounds one can argue for four possible patterns of causation between academic achievement and self-perception (both self-concept and self-efficacy; see Skaalvik and Valås, 2001):

Achievement affects self-perception (skill development model). This pattern of causation is suggested by Scheirer and Kraut (1979) who argue that self-concept change is likely to be an outcome of increased achievement rather than a necessary variable for achievement to occur. Also, in the self-efficacy literature achievement (mastery experiences) is seen as the most important antecedent of self-efficacy (Bandura, 1986). In the self-concept tradition this pattern of causation is associated with the "skill development model" (Calsyn and Kenny, 1977).

Self-perception affects achievement (self-enhancement model). Based on self-consistency theory (Jones, 1973; Lecky, 1945) one may predict that students with low academic self-concept will avoid situations that may alter their self-concept, and hence make less effort to do well in school. Moreover, based on self-esteem theory and a perceived achievement-ability-worth linkage, students with low expectation of success may develop failure-avoiding tactics (Covington, 1984, 1992). Such tactics may include procrastination. As pointed out by Covington (1984) the temporary relief afforded by these failure-avoiding tactics is illusory, as they will finally destroy the will to learn. One should therefore expect low self-concept of ability to result in lower academic achievement. This view leads to a "self-enhancement model" (Calsyn and Kenny, 1977) which is consistent with self-efficacy theory, claiming that self-efficacy affects effort and persistence and therefore achievement (Bandura, 1986, 1997; Pajares, 1997; Pajares and Miller, 1995).

Achievement and self-perceptions affect each other in a reciprocal manner (reciprocal effects model). The two processes (causal orderings) described above need not contradict each other. Marsh (1984) proposed a dynamic equilibrium model suggesting that academic achievement, self-concept and self-attributions are interwoven in a network of reciprocal relations such that a change in any one would produce changes in the others in order to re-establish the equilibrium. Thus, academic achievement and self-concept may influence each other in a reciprocal manner (see also Marsh, 1990b; Wigfield, Eccles, and Pintrich, 1996; Wigfield and Karpathian, 1991). Self-efficacy researchers also assume a reciprocal relation between self-efficacy and achievement. Achievement (mastery experiences) is both regarded as the most important source of self-efficacy and as an effect of self-efficacy (Bandura, 1986, 1997).

Maruyama, Rubin and Kingsbury (1981) also contend that "third variables" (e.g., ability, support from parents, good teachers) may affect both academic achievement and self-concept (see also Pottebaum, Keith, and Ehly, 1986).

Despite the long going debate there are few empirical studies examining causal relations between academic achievement and self-concept. Most of the studies of these constructs have used cross-sectional designs showing zero-order correlations between the variables (see Byrne, 1996; Skaalvik, 1997a). The majority of the studies are therefore unsuited as a basis for suggesting causal interpretations. In a review of research Byrne (1984) notes that studies of causal predominance between self-concept and academic achievement must demonstrate a statistical relationship between the constructs, establish time precedence in longitudinal studies, and test causal models by means of statistical techniques such as confirmatory factor analyses. Marsh (1990b) also proposed optimal design features in this area of research, including longitudinal designs and multiple indicators of latent constructs. Still, few studies satisfy the prerequisites provided by Byrne (1984). Prior to 1990 Marsh (1990b) found only three such studies revealing mixed results (Byrne, 1984; Shavelson and Bolus, 1982; Marsh, 1988).

Some recent studies have addressed methodological problems by means of more sophisticated designs. Skaalvik and Hagtvet (1990) studied longitudinal relations between school achievement, self-concept of ability, and general self-esteem between grades three and four and between grades six and seven. Support for the assumptions of discriminability and factorial invariance of the concepts across time was obtained independently from estimating structural parameters. Structural equation modelling analyses revealed that in the youngest cohort, achievement at time one had a significant effect on self-concept of ability at time two, whereas prior self-concept had no significant effect on subsequent academic achievement. In the older cohort, however, there was some evidence that academic achievement and self-concept of ability had a reciprocal effect on each other. Helmke (1989) also found that self-concept of ability was affected by achievement in the fifth grade whereas the relation between these constructs was reciprocal during the sixth grade.

Marsh (1990c) examined longitudinal relations between academic achievement (grades) and self-concept of ability with data from a large representative "Youth in Transition" study. Data were collected at four points in time starting at the tenth grade. Grades at times two and three were significantly affected by prior self-concept, whereas self-concept at times two and four were not significantly affected by prior grades. The results lend support to the self-concept enhancement model of the relation between self-concept of ability and academic achievement in late adolescence.

Helmke and van Aken (1995) measured mathematics achievement and self-concept at three points of time from Grade 2 to Grade 4. Mathematics achievement was measured by both marks and math tests. Structural equation modelling analyses revealed that it made a difference whether achievement was measured with only one indicator or with two indicators (marks and tests). Analysis including two achievement indicators supported the skill development model, indicating that during elementary school years mathematics self-concept is mainly a consequence of achievement, but that it does not significantly affect later achievement.

In a longitudinal panel study Yoon, Eccles, and Wigfield (1996) studied relations between mathematics achievement (grades), mathematics self-concept of ability, and intrinsic value of mathematics in 826 sixth- and seventh-grade students. Data were collected at four points in time from sixth grade (fall semester) to seventh grade (spring semester). Structural equation modelling analyses showed that self-concept of ability at times two and four was significantly affected by prior grades whereas inconclusive results, including gender differences, were found concerning the effects of self-concept of ability on subsequent grades. The authors conclude that there are some signs of reciprocal causal relation but that the results suggest a causal priority of achievement over self-concept of ability.

Marsh and Yeung (1997) measured achievement and self-concept in high school students in three subjects (English, mathematics, and science). Self concept was measured at three points of time whereas achievement was measured at 6 points of time. Structural equation modelling analysis gave support to the reciprocal effects model. The size and consistency of the effects were strongest for mathematics.

Guay, Marsh, and Boivin (2003) conducted a longitudinal study involving of 385 French Canadian students. Data were collected at three points of time over a two year period. The participants attended 2nd, 3rd, and 4th grade at the time of the first data collection. The results indicated a reciprocal effects model and significant paths were found from self-concept at time 1 to achievement at time 2 and from self-concept at time 2 to achievement at time 3 in all three cohorts.

Some of these studies give support to a skill development model in early elementary school years, indicating that during elementary school years mathematics self-concept is mainly a consequence of achievement, but that it does not significantly affect later achievement (Helmke and van Aken, 1995; Skaalvik and Hagtvet, 1990). However, recent studies indicate that in high school achievement is affected by self-concept and that by this time there may be reciprocal causal relations between the constructs (Marsh, 1990b; Marsh and Yeung, 1997). Taken together, these results are in accordance with the developmental perspective advocated by Helmke (1989) and Skaalvik and Hagtvet (1990). In early school years the students' self-concept of academic ability has yet to be established. During this period the concept may undergo a process of shaping and reshaping dominated by the influence of academic experience. As the self-concept of ability becomes better established and more stable, it may increasingly affect performance expectancies, motivation, and study behavior, which in turn may affect academic achievement. Thus, once ability perceptions are more firmly established the relation between achievement and self-concept of ability likely becomes reciprocal (Byrne and Worth Gavin, 1996; Marsh, 1990b; Skaalvik and Hagtvet, 1995; Wigfield and Karpathian, 1991). At late adolescence self-concept of ability may even have priority over academic achievement (see for instance Marsh, 1990b). An apparent exception from the developmental model is the study by Guay, Marsh, and Boivin (2003), showing consistent effects of self-concept on subsequent teacher ratings as early as grade 2.

Like the self-concept research there are few empirical studies examining causal relations between academic achievement and self-efficacy. Most of the studies of these constructs show correlations between the variables. Although these studies show that achievement and self-efficacy are clearly related, Byrne's criteria for studying causal ordering of achievement and self-concept are equally pertinent to self-efficacy research (Pajares, 1997). We have found no studies satisfying the prerequisites provided by Byrne (1984) and Marsh (1990b), including establishing time precedence in longitudinal studies, testing causal models by means of statistical techniques such as confirmatory factor analyses, and using multiple indicators of latent constructs. The need for both longitudinal studies and experimental designs are pointed out by several researchers (e.g., Pajares, 1997).

A number of cross sectional studies analyze models letting self-efficacy predict achievement. These studies demonstrate positive relations between these constructs, but do not provide evidence of causal ordering (e.g., Pajares, 1996; Pajares and Kranzler, 1995). Although not satisfying the prerequisites provided by Byrne and Marsh some longitudinal studies suggest that self-efficacy affects achievement. In college students self-efficacy has been found to predict both subsequent academic grades and academic persistence necessary to maintain high academic performance, even when controlled for the effect of previous measures of scholastic aptitudes and high school grades (Lent, Brown, and Larkin, 1986). In high school students self-efficacy shortly after the start of the semester has been shown to predict final grades by the end of the semester when controlled for the effect of prior grades (Zimmerman et al., 1992). In all these studies self-efficacy were measured at a domain level of specificity. Whereas self-efficacy are traditionally distinguished from self-concept by its problem specific nature (e.g., Bandura, 1997; Pajares, 1997), the instruments used in these studies measure more general beliefs that one can learn well within academic areas. Such measures may not be clearly distinguished from measures of academic self-concept (Skaalvik and Rankin, 1996).

In a series of experimental studies Schunk and his colleagues have shown that achievement, persistence, and self-efficacy beliefs can be raised by specific training programs (e.g., Schunk, 1983, 1991). Posttreatment self-efficacy and achievement were clearly related, but no rigorous test of causal relations between self-efficacy and achievement were undertaken.

Despite the ongoing debate about causal predominance there is a general agreement that self-perceptions are formed through experience in the environment. More concretely, there is substantial evidence that prior academic achievement affects subsequent academic self-perceptions (Marsh, Byrne, and Yeung, 1999). The critical question is, therefore, if academic self-perception affects subsequent achievement (e.g., Guay, Marsh, and Boivin, 2003). Accordingly, one purpose of the present studies was to examine if mathematics self-perception predicted subsequent achievement over and above the prediction that could be made by prior achievement. An additional purpose was to test if the impact of self-perception on subsequent achievement could be explained by goal orientation, interest, or self-esteem.

GOAL ORIENTATION

During the last decade much research on motivation has focused on students' goal orientation. Goal orientation researchers typically differentiate between task-orientation (also termed task goals or learning goals) and performance orientation (also termed performance goals, relative ability goals or ego orientation. Task orientation means that the focus of attention is on the task (Nicholls, 1983, 1989) and that learning, understanding, and developing new skills are ends in themselves (Ames and Archer, 1988; Duda and Nicholls, 1992; Nicholls, 1989). Students with strong task orientation tend to see mastery as dependent on effort and perceptions of ability are self-referenced (Ames, 1992; Duda and Nicholls, 1992). Moreover, making mistakes are seen as a natural and inherent part of the learning process.

Performance orientation refers to the desire to be judged able. Therefore, performance orientation predicts that students are preoccupied with social comparisons and ability is normatively referenced. It follows that students who have a strong performance orientation are preoccupied by themselves in the learning situation. The goal of these students is often described as that of outperforming others or to demonstrate superior ability (Ames and Archer, 1988; Duda and Nicholls, 1992). However, students with strong performance orientation may also be concerned with not looking stupid or by avoiding being poorest. Recent research on goal orientation discriminates between two weakly correlated dimensions of performance orientation, performance-approach orientation and performance-avoidance orientation (Elliott and Church, 1997; Harackiewicz, Barron, Tauer, and Elliot, 2002; Midgley, Kaplan, and Middleton, 2001; Skaalvik, 1997b). Students with a strong performance-avoidance orientation are particularly concerned not to be poorest, not to look stupid and not to be negatively perceived by others. In comparison, students with a strong performance-approach orientation are more occupied by being best or outperforming others.

We may expect students' goal orientation to be influenced by their academic self-concept. In support of this expectation several studies have shown task orientation to be positively related to academic self-concept (Middleton and Midgley, 1997; Nicholls, 1989; Seifert, 1995; Skaalvik and Skaalvik, in press). Studies of relations between performance orientation and academic self-concept are, however, less conclusive. A possible reason for these results may be that in previous research, measures of performance orientation have failed to discriminate between performance-approach and performance-avoidance orientation. Measuring these orientations as separate constructs, Skaalvik (1997b) found academic self-concept to be negatively related to performance-avoidance orientation and positively related to performance-approach orientation (see also Skaalvik and Skaalvik, in press).

Research evidence shows that task orientation is linked to a number of adaptive learning behaviors, for instance interest, seeking challenge, help seeking behavior, and deep processing of course material (e.g., Ames and Archer, 1988; Harackiewicz, Barron, Carter, Lehto, and Elliot, 1997; Skaalvik, 1997b). We should therefore expect task orientation to be positively related to academic achievement. However, the research literature does not provide clear evidence of such a relation (see Harackiewicz et al., 1997).

Performance goals have been linked to a number of maladaptive learning behaviors, such as challenge avoidance and surface level processing (see Pintrich, 2000). Recent research supports these findings with respect to performance-avoidance orientation, whereas performance-approach orientation has been shown to be positively related to effort and achievement (e.g., Harackiewicz et al., 1997, 2000). Considered together, the research on goal orientation indicates that the impact of self-perception on achievement partly may be mediated through students' goal orientation. For instance, mastery expectations may increase students' task orientation and performance-approach orientation, which again may result in learning strategies that increases their performance. Alternatively, low mastery expectations may increase students' performance-avoidance orientation, which may lead to learning strategies that reduces their performance.

INTEREST

Interest may be conceptualized as a component of intrinsic motivation (Hidi, 2000). Intrinsic motivation differs from extrinsic motivation in that it is free of external coercion or rewards (Urdan and Turner, in press). When intrinsically motivated, individuals engage in activities for the sake of the activity itself (Sansone and Harackiewicz, 2000).

Recent research on interest distinguishes between personal (or individual) interest and situational interest (Hidi, 1990; Renninger, 2000; Schiefele, 2001). Personal interest refers to a relatively stable orientation towards specific domains or activities whereas situational interest refers to a more situation-specific attention to a topic. In this study we will be concerned with personal interest.

Interest may have different sources. Previous research has revealed a strong relation between self-concept and interest (Skaalvik, 1997b; Skaalvik and Skaalvik, 2004). For instance, Skaalvik and Skaalvik (2004) found a correlation of .80 between mathematics self-concept and a 7-item measure of interest in working with and liking to work with mathematics. Interest has also been found to predict both deep level learning strategies

(Schiefele, 1990; Schiefele and Krapp, 1996) and actual measures of learning (Kunz, Drewniak, Hatalak, and Schön, 1992). Thus, we might also expect that self-perception may affect subsequent achievement through increased interest in the topic.

SELF-ESTEEM

Historically, research on self-concept has focused on a general, overall, or global construct (see Byrne, 1984; Marsh, 1990d). A problem with this nomothetic or one-dimensional model of self-concept was that is was given a variety of definitions. The lack of a clear definition led to the construction of very different instruments for measuring a global self-concept, often labelled self-esteem. One approach was summing self-descriptions in very different areas, for instance academic, social, physical, and moral (Coopersmith, 1981; Piers and Harris, 1969). One problem with these measures is that they overlook the fact that the impact of particular self-evaluations on global self-esteem is dependent on how important each aspect is to the individual (Rosenberg, 1968, 1979). Another problem is that in such measures the meaning of general self-concept changes depending on the particular areas that researchers include in their instruments (Snow, Corno, and Jackson, 1996).

Other researchers argue that general self-esteem should be measured separate from area specific self-concepts. These researchers have therefore attempted to measure self-esteem by using items that do not refer to particular areas or contexts (Harter, 1979; Rosenberg, 1965). Implicit in these instruments is that self-esteem is defined as general self-acceptance, self-regard, or valuing of oneself (see for instance Harter, 1993; Rosenberg, 1965). It therefore refers to more generalized affective responses to oneself and is less descriptive than more particular aspects of self-concept (Campbell and Lavellee, 1993; Gecas, 1982; Rosenberg, 1979; Wigfield and Karpathian, 1991).

In the 1980s and 1990s self-concept researchers have emphasized the multidimensionality of self-concept (Byrne and Shavelson, 1986; Marsh, Byrne and Shavelson, 1988; Shavelson, Hubner, and Stanton, 1976). The focus on the multidimensionality of self-concept in contemporary research has led to a lack of attention towards general self-esteem in educational research. Some researchers explicitly state that self-esteem may not be a particularly useful construct (Bandura, 1981; Marsh, 1993). For instance, Bandura (1981) contends that global measures of self-concept detract from their power to explain behavior. Still, research strongly indicates that self-esteem is predictive of students' goal orientation (Skaalvik, Valås, and Sletta, 1994; Tice, 1993) and of mental health and depression (Battle, 1987; Harter, 1993; Kaplan, 1980; Renouf and Harter, 1990; Skaalvik, 1989; Valås and Sletta, 1996; Ystgaard, 1993). Indirectly, it may therefore also affect behaviour and achievement. Research on causes and consequences of self-esteem in educational settings is therefore a neglected, but important task for educational researchers.

THE PRESENT STUDY

As stated above, one purpose of the present studies was to examine if mathematics self-perception predicted subsequent achievement over and above the prediction that could be made by prior achievement. A second purpose was to test if the impact of self-perception on subsequent achievement could be explained by goal orientation, interest, or self-esteem.

We designed two longitudinal studies, each with data collection a three points of time. Grades in mathematics were collected at time 1 and 3. Time 1 was in June, at the end of the school year in 9th and 10th grade, respectively, whereas time 3 was one year later. Self-concept, self-efficacy, intrinsic motivation, goal orientation, and self-esteem were measured at time 2, which was in October, shortly after the beginning of the school year in 10th and 11th grade, respectively.

In Norway 10th grade is the last year in middle school. Thus one important difference between the two studies is that the participants in study 1 attended middle school at all three points of time (9th and 10th grade) whereas the participants in study 2 attended middle school at time 1 and high school at time 2 and 3. Thus, in study 2 there was a shift to a new context – new school, new classmates, new teachers. In contrast, in middle school students usually attend the same school class and have the same math teacher throughout the three middle school years. The samples in the two studies will be referred to as the *middle school sample* (study 1) and *the high school sample* (study 2)

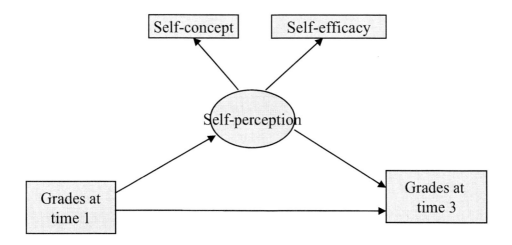

Figure 1. Simple theoretical model of relations between grades at time 1, self-perception at time 2 and grades at time 3.

We tested both simple and extended models. A simple theoretical model is presented in figure 1. The students were given one final grade in mathematics at the end of each school year. Thus, in the model grades are represented by observed variables. Self-perception is in the model a latent variable indicated by self-concept and self-efficacy. This solution was based on previous research showing that at the domain level of specificity, self-concept and self-efficacy beliefs may not be separable (e.g., Pajares, 1996; Skaalvik and Bong, 2003; Skaalvik and Rankin, 1996).

METHOD

Participants and Procedure

The participants in study 1 (the middle school sample) were 246 students (129 females and 117 males) attending 10th grade in 12 classes at four middle schools in a Norwegian city at time 2 and 3. The mean age at time 2 was 13.9. The participants in study 2 (the high school sample) were 484 students (246 females and 238 males) attending 11th grade in 33 classes at six high schools at time 2 and 3. The mean age at time 2 was 16.55. Self-concept, self-efficacy, intrinsic motivation, goal orientation and self-esteem were measured by means of a questionnaire administered to intact school classes by trained research assistants at time 2. The schools reported end of year grades in 9th, 10th, and 11th grades, respectively.

Measures

Self-concept in mathematics was in both study 1 and 2 defined as the general feeling of doing well or poorly in mathematics in school. In study 2 it was measured by an eight-item scale representing a short version of the relevant subscale of the Self-description Questionnaire II (Marsh, 1990a). In study 1 it was measured with a short (5 item) version of the scale used in study 2. An example of an item measuring math self-concept is "Mathematics is easy for me". Cronbach's alphas were .91 and .95 for the scales used in study 1 and 2, respectively.

Mathematics self-efficacy was in both studies measured by a five-item scale asking the students to indicate on a 10-point scale how certain they were that they would get a grade better than 1, better than 2 etc. in the respective school subjects (grades in Norwegian school are given on a scale from 1 to 6). The response scale ranged from 1 (not certain at all) to 10 (very certain). Cronbach's alphas were .88 and .95 in study 1 and 2, respectively.

Intrinsic motivation was only measured in study 1. It vas specified as interest in working with mathematics and was measured by a four-item interest scale representing a short version of the Skaalvik and Rankin (1995) Intrinsic Motivation Scale. An example of an item is "I like working with mathematics". Cronbach's alpha for the scale was .93.

Self-esteem was only measured in study 2. It was measured by an eight-item Norwegian version of the 10-item self-esteem subscale in the Self-description Questionnaire II. The items do not refer to any particular area. Examples of items are: "I have a lot to be proud of," "I like myself the way I am," and "I wish I were a different person." Cronbach's alpha was .88.

Two dimensions of *goal orientation* were measured in study 1 (task orientation and performance-approach orientation). In study 2 one additional dimension was added (performance-avoidance orientation). Each dimension was measured by a four-item scale (see Skaalvik, 1997b). Examples of items are: "In math classes it is important for me to learn something new" (task orientation), "I always try to do better than other students in mathematics" (performance-approach orientation), and "When I am in math classes it is important for me to avoid looking stupid" (performance-avoidance orientation). Cronbach's alphas for task orientation were .70 and .74 in study 1 and 2, respectively. Alphas for performance-approach orientation were .86 and .87 and alpha for performance-avoidance orientation in study 2 was .85.

Response categories for measures of self-concept, interest, self-esteem, and goal orientation were: false, mostly false, sometimes false/sometimes true, mostly true, and true.

Analysis

We used structural equation modelling (SEM) by means of the AMOS program (version 5) to assess the adequacy of the theoretical models and to examine direct and indirect relations between the variables. Each latent trait was defined by two indicators. Self-perception was indicated by measures of self-concept and self-efficacy. The scales measuring interest, self-esteem and each dimension of goal orientation were divided into two subscales that were used as indicators. To assess model fit, we used well-established indices such as CFI, IFI, TLI, and RMSEA. For the CFI, IFI, and TLI indices, values greater than .90 are typically considered acceptable and values greater that .95 indicate good fit to the data (Bollen, 1989; Byrne, 2001; Hu and Bentler, 1999). For well specified models, a RMSEA of .06 or less reflect a good fit (Hu and Bentler, 1999).

RESULTS

Statistical means, standard deviations, and correlations between the study variables are shown in Table 1 (middle school sample) and Table 2 (high school sample). Grades at time 1 and 3 were strongly correlated in the middle school sample (.81) whereas the correlation was somewhat lower in the high school sample (.65). A possible reason for this is that the latter correlation was between grades in middle school and grades in high school. Self-concept and self-efficacy were strongly correlated (.64 and .75) lending support to the expectation that these constructs are strongly related when measured at a domain level of specificity. In accordance with previous research we found correlations around .6 and .7 between math achievement and math self-concept and self-efficacy.

Table 1. Pearson Correlations among the Study Variables in Study 1

Variables	1.	2.	3.	4.	5.	6.	7.
1. Previous grades (time 1)	.65	.62	.54	.22	.33	.81	
2. Math self-concept	.64	.72	.43	.40	.64		
3. Math self-efficacy	.52	.31	.32	.62			
4. Interest in math	.59	.37	.57				
5. Task orientation	.27	.29					
6. Performance-approach orientation	.37						
7. Subsequent grades (time 3)							
M	3.86	16.17	29.37	12.86	11.26	7.61	3.48
SD	1.01	5.53	12.29	5.02	2.86	3.95	1.20

Table 2. Pearson Correlations among the Study Variables in Study 2

Variables	1.	2.	3.	4.	5.	6.	7.	8.
1. Previous grades (time 1)	.59	.61	.13	.24	.30 -.06	.65		
2. Math self-concept	.75	.20	.32	.41 -.16	.77			
3. Math self-efficacy	.17	.24	.35 -.11	.74				
4. Self-esteem		.25	.05 -.22	.11				
5. Task orientation	.20 -.10	.23						
6. Performance-approach orientation	.16	.34						
7. Performance-avoidance orientation	-.15							
8. Subsequent grades (time 3)								
M	3.84	23.06	28.18	31.68	14.09	7.65	6.81	3.44
SD	1.11	9.52	12.70	7.01	3.44	3.84	3.47	1.25

Note. All correlations above .09 are significant ($p < .05$)

Task orientation and performance-approach orientation were weakly, but positively correlated (.20 and .27), supporting previous findings. The two dimensions of performance orientation (approach and avoidance) were nearly uncorrelated (.16), also supporting previous results.

Simple Models

We first tested a simple model including grades at time 1 and 3 and self-perception at time 2 (see Figure 2). The models had had very good fit to the data both in the middle school sample ($\chi^2(1) = 2.34$, $\chi^2/df = 2.34$, $CFI = .99$, $IFI = .99$, $TLI = .99$, and $RMSEA < .01$) and in the high school sample ($\chi^2(1) = .236$, $\chi^2/df = .236$, $CFI = .99$, $IFI = .99$, $TLI = .98$, and $RMSEA = .05$). These results clearly demonstrated the adequacy of using measures of math self-concept and self-efficacy measured at the domain level as indicators a latent math self-perception variable.

In the middle school sample the correlation between grades at time 1 and 3 was .81. In comparison, the SEM analysis showed that the direct effect (standardized regression weight) of grades at time 1 on subsequent grades was .47, whereas the indirect effect through self-perception was .33 (Figure 2). Thus, the results strongly indicate that the stability of grades from time 1 to time 3 partly was mediated through students' math self-perception.

In the high school sample the correlation between grades at time 1 and 3 was .65 whereas the SEM analysis (Figure 2) showed no significant direct effect of grades at time 1 on subsequent grades (regression weight = .08, $p = .06$). However, a strong indirect effect (.57) was revealed. Thus, in the high school sample the results indicate that the stability of grades from time 1 to time 3 almost entirely was mediated through students' math self-perception.

Taken together the models presented in Figure 2 show that math self-perception predicts subsequent achievement over and above the prediction that can be made from prior achievement. Self-perceived abilities predicted subsequent achievement particularly strongly in the high school sample (regression weight = .82). Consequently, the indirect effect of prior achievement was much stronger in the high school sample than in the middle school sample. Following this finding, the direct effect of achievement at time 1 on subsequent achievement was close to zero in the high school sample. Thus, the results indicate not only that the stability in math achievement from one year to the next is, at least in part, mediated through students' self-perceived abilities in mathematics, but that the mediating role of students' self-perceptions increases during and shortly after transfer to a new school or a new context.

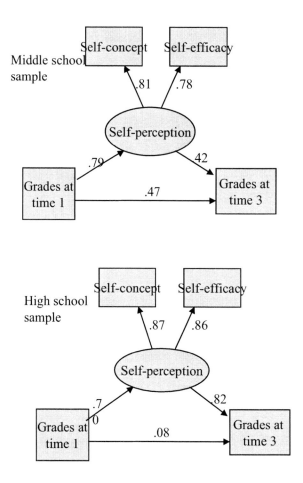

Figure 2. Simple models of relations between grades at time 1 and 3 and self-perception at time 2.

Extended Models

The next step of the analyses was to explore if the effect of self-perception on subsequent achievement was mediated through students interest in mathematics, their self-esteem, or their goal orientation. Because slightly different variables were measured in study 1 (middle school sample) and study 2 (high school sample) the extended analyses of these studies are presented separately.

The Middle School Sample

In the middle school sample we tested if the impact of math self-perception on subsequent math achievement was mediated through students' goal orientation and their interest in working with mathematics. Unfortunately, only two dimensions of goal orientation were measured in the middle school sample (task orientation and performance-approach orientation). Following previous research (e.g., Skaalvik and Skaalvik, in press) math self-perception was expected to relate positively to both dimensions of goal orientation as well as to interest in mathematics. Also task orientation in mathematics lessons was expected to relate positively to interest in mathematics (see Skaalvik and Skaalvik, in press). To test if the effect of self-perception on subsequent achievement was mediated through goal orientation and interest in mathematics the model was specified to estimate paths from these variables to achievement at time 3.

The model (Figure 3) had good fit to the data (χ^2 (26) = 44.73, χ^2/df = 1.72, CFI = .99, IFI = .99, TLI = .98, and $RMSEA$ = .05). As expected, self-perception was positively related to both dimensions of goal orientation (.45 and .47) and to interest in working with mathematics (.66). Prior achievement was indirectly and positively related to the same variables, through math self-perception.

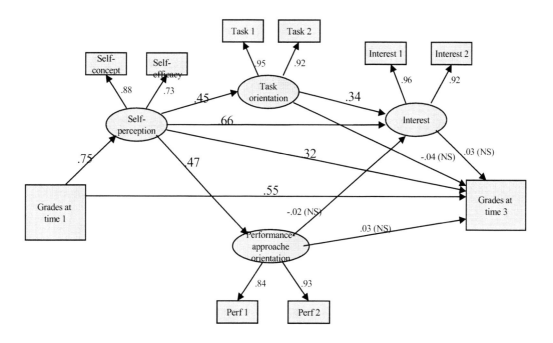

Figure 3. Extended model for the middle school sample

Neither the two dimensions of goal orientation nor interest in working with mathematics predicted subsequent grades over and above the prediction made by prior grades and self-perception (standardized regression weights = -.04, .03, and .03, respectively). Thus, the impact of self-perception on subsequent achievement was not mediated through goal orientation or interest. The model revealed a direct effect of self-perception (.32) and of prior grades (.55) even when controlled for goal orientation and interest.

The High School Sample

In the high school sample we tested if the impact of self-perception on subsequent achievement was mediated through self-esteem and goal orientation. Three dimensions of goal orientation were measured in this sample: task orientation, performance-approach orientation, and performance-avoidance orientation. Self-esteem was hypothesized to relate positively to math self-perception and task orientation and negatively to performance-avoidance orientation (see Skaalvik, Valås, and Sletta, 1994). Also, math self-perception was hypothesized to relate positively to task orientation and performance-approach orientation and negatively to performance-avoidance orientation (see Skaalvik and Skaalvik, in press). To test if the effect of self-perception on subsequent achievement was mediated through self-esteem and goal orientation the model was specified to estimate paths from these variables to achievement at time 3.

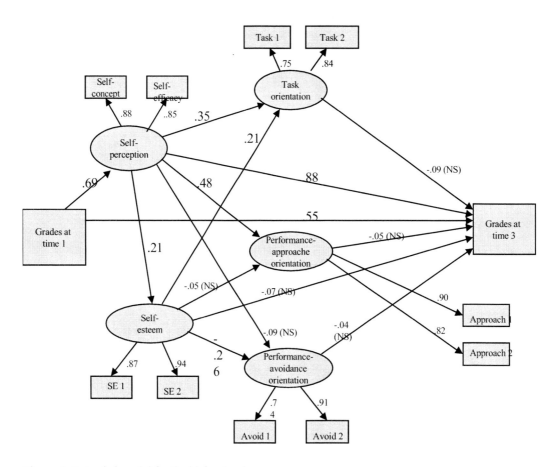

Figure 4. Extended model for the high school

The model (Figure 4) had acceptable fit to the data (χ^2 (42) = 128.14, χ^2/df = 3.05, CFI = .97, IFI = .97, TLI = .95, and RMSEA = .06). As expected, math self-perception related positively to self-esteem (.21), task orientation (.35), and performance-approach orientation (.48). However, it was not significantly related to performance-avoidance orientation (-.09). Also, as expected, self-esteem was positively related to task orientation (.21) and negatively related to performance-avoidance orientation (-.26). Self-esteem did not relate significantly to performance-approach orientation (-.05).

Neither self-esteem nor the two dimensions of performance orientation predicted subsequent achievement in mathematics over and above the prediction made by prior grades and self-perception (regression weights = -.07, -.05, and -.04, respectively). Task orientation made a small and negligible, but significantly negative prediction of subsequent achievement (-.09). Thus, the positive impact of self-perception on subsequent achievement was not mediated through self-esteem or goal orientation. The model confirmed the strong direct effect of self-perception (.88) on subsequent achievement that was evidenced in the simple model. The weak direct effect of prior grades on subsequent grades was significant in the more complex model (.08, $p < .05$).

CONCLUSION

Both studies reported here show that in early adolescence achievements in mathematics as indicated by grades were highly stable over a period of one academic year. The stability was particularly high in the middle school sample, from ninth to tenth grade (r. = .81) and somewhat weaker in the high school sample, from tenth to eleventh grade (r. = .65).

The grades used at time 3 in the middle school sample and both at time 1 and 3 in the high school sample were examination grades, which are scored anonymously by mathematics teachers at different schools than those that the students attended. Hence, neither the stability in grades nor the difference between the two samples can be explained by a tendency among teachers to perceive students abilities in a stereotypical way.

A possible interpretation of the difference in stability of grades between the samples may be that it is more difficult for students to change their relative ability as well as their self-perceptions as long as they are in the same context with the same classmates and the same teachers, resulting in relatively persistent perceived expectations from teachers and classmates. When students are transferred from middle school to high school, as was the case for the high school sample, they are placed in a new context with new classmates and new teachers. The roles and positions become less static and expectations from teachers and classmates may change more easily. For some students this may constitute new opportunities to develop and demonstrate their abilities. This may explain the lower stability in grades in the high school sample. Moreover, the lower stability in grades also increases the possibility that other variables, for example the students' self-perceived abilities, may influence their subsequent achievements.

The SEM analyses showed that students' self-perceptions strongly predicted subsequent achievement over and above the prediction that could be made from prior achievement. In the middle school sample achievement at time 1 and self-perception at time 2 predicted students' achievement at time 3 about equally strongly showing that the stability in grades in part is mediated through self-perception. In the high school sample the relation between grades at time 1 and 3 could almost entirely be explained by self-perception.

In conclusion, the results of both studies strongly indicate that self-concept and self-efficacy are important mediators of academic achievement. In other words, the studies strongly support the notion that students' self-perceptions are important prerequisites for learning and achievement. In particular, after the transmission from middle school to high school we found a very strong effect of the self-concept/self-efficacy latent trait on subsequent achievement. A possible conclusion that should be tested in future research is therefore that self-perception is particularly important in new situations or contexts.

An important question is through which processes students' self-perceptions affects subsequent achievement. In the studies reported we were not able to show that the effect of self-perception on subsequent achievement was mediated through students' interest in mathematics, which is one component of intrinsic motivation, through students' goal orientation, or their self-esteem. Still, the impact of self-perceptions must be mediated through some psychological processes or study behaviour. Gaining better understanding of these processes is very important both from a theoretical and a practical point of view. Therefore, more research needs to be done to examine through which processes students self-related beliefs affect subsequent achievement. Future studies might look at emotional variables like anxiety, but also motivational variables in terms of behaviour, for instance effort, endurance, and self-regulated learning strategies.

Self-perception was in the present studies treated as a latent variable indicated by domain-specific self-concept and self-efficacy. The difference between self-concept and self-efficacy is often emphasized in the literature. However, several researchers point out that when measuring both constructs at a domain specific level the difference between them becomes less clear at that they may be difficult to distinguish empirically (e.g., Bong, 2002). Both the parameters of the factor loadings and the fit indices of the models tested in the studies reported give support to this notion. Hence, we suggest that in future studies of academic self-perception at domain-specific levels researchers should include measures of both self-concept and self-efficacy.

Some limitations of the studies reported should be pointed out. Achievements were indicated by examination grades in both studies. Although examination grades are based on achievement tests in Norwegian school, they are not standardized tests. However, Guay, Marsh, and Boivin (2003) give four reasons to use teachers' ratings when exploring relations between achievement and self-concept and show that there is good support for the validity of teacher ratings. Also, the test-retest correlations of .81 and .65 based on evaluation from different teachers provides good support for the validity of the achievement measures.

Another limitation is that self-perception, but also interest, goal orientation, and self-esteem were measured only at one point of time. Future research should measure both achievement, self-perception, and possible variables mediating the effect of self-perception on achievement at several points of time.

REFERENCES

Ames, C. (1992). Classrooms: goals, structures, and student motivation. *Journal of Educational Psychology, 84,* 261-271.

Ames, C., and Archer, J. (1988). Achievement goals in the classroom: Students' learning strategies and motivation processes. *Journal of Educational Psychology, 80,* 260-267.

Bandura, A. (1977). *Social learning theory.* Englewood Cliffs, NJ: Prentice-Hall.

Bandura, A. (1981). Self-referent thought: A developmental analysis of self-efficacy. In J. H. Flavell and L. Ross (Eds.), *Social cognitive development: Frontiers and possible futures.* New York: Cambridge University Press.

Bandura, A. (1982). Self-efficacy mechanisms in human agency. *American Psychologist, 37,* 122-147.

Bandura, A. (1986). Social foundations of thought and action: A social cognitive theory. Englewood Cliffs, NJ: Prentice-Hall.

Bandura, A. (1997). *Self-efficacy: The exercise of control.* New York: Freeman.

Bandura, A., and Schunk, D. H. (1981). Cultivating competence, self-efficacy, and intrinsic interest through proximal self-motivation. *Journal of Personality and Social Psychology, 41,* 586-598.

Battle, J. (1987). Relationship between self-esteem and depression among children. *Psychological Reports, 60,* 1187-1190.

Bollen, K. A. (1989). A new incremental fit index for general structural models. *Sociological Methods and Research, 17,* 303-316.

Bong, M. (2002). Predictive utility of subject-, task-, and problem-specific self-efficacy judgments for immediate and delayed academic performances. *Journal of Experimental Education, 70,* 133-162.

Bong, M., and Skaalvik, E. M. (2003). Academic self-concept and self-efficacy: how different are they really? *Educational Psychology Review, 15,* 1-40.

Byrne, B. M. (1984). The general/academic self-concept nomological network: A review of construct validation research. *Review of Educational Research, 54,* 427-456.

Byrne, B. M. (1996). *Measuring self-concept across the life span. Issues and ins*trumentation. Washington DC: American Psychological Association.

Byrne, B. M. (2001). Structural equation modeling with AMOS. Basic concepts, applications, and programming. Mahwah, N.J.: Lawrence Erlbaum Ass.

Byrne, B. M., and Shavelson, R. J. (1986). On the structure of adolescent self-concept. *Journal of Educational Psychology, 78,* 474-481.

Byrne, B. M., and Worth Gavin, D. A. (1996). The Shavelson model revisited: testing for the structure of academic self-concept across pre-, early, and late adolescents. *Journal of Educational Psychology, 88,* 215-228.

Calsyn, R., and Kenny, D. (1977). Self-concept of ability and perceived evaluations by others: Cause or effect of academic achievement. *Journal of Educational Psychology, 69,* 136-145.

Coopersmith, S. (1981). *Self-Esteem Inventories.* Palo Alto, California: Consulting Psychologists Press.

Campbell, J. D., and Lavellee, L. F. (1993). Who am I? The role of self-concept confusion in understanding the behavior of people with low self-esteem. In R.F. Baumeister (Ed.), *Self-esteem. The puzzle of low self-regard* (pp. 3-20). New York: Plenum Press.

Covington, M. V. (1984). The self-esteem theory of achievement motivation: Findings and implications. *The Elementary School Journal, 85,* 5-20.

Covington, M. V. (1992). Making the grade: A self-worth perspective on motivation and school reform. Cambridge: University Press.

Duda, J. L., and Nicholls, J. G. (1992). Dimensions of achievement motivation in schoolwork and sport. *Journal of Educational Psychology, 84,* 290-299.

Elliot, A. J., and Church, M. A. (1997). A hierarchical model of approach and avoidance achievement motivation. *Journal of Personality and Social Psychology, 72,* 218-232.

Gecas, V. (1982). The self-concept. *Annual Review of Sociology, 8,* 1-33.

Gorrell, J. (1990). Some contribution of self-efficacy research to self-concept theory. *Journal of Research and Development in Education, 23,* 73-81.

Guay, F., Marsh, H. W., and Boivin, M. (2003). Academic self-concept and academic achievement: Developmental perspectives and their causal ordering. *Journal of Educational Psychology, 95*, 124-136.

Hackett, G., and Betz, N. E. (1989). An exploration of the mathematics self-efficacy/mathematics performance correspondence. *Journal of Research in Mathematics Education, 20*, 261-273.

Harackiewicz, J. M., Barron, K. E., Tauer, J. M., and Elliot, A, J, (2002). Predicting success in college: A longitudinal study of achievement goals and ability measures as predictors of interest and performance from freshman year through graduation. *Journal of Educational Psychology, 94*, 562-575.

Harackiewicz, J. M., Barron, K. E., Carter, S. M., Lehto, A. T., and Elliot, A. J. (1997). Predistors and concequences of achievement goals in the college classroom; maintaining interest and making the grade. *Journal of Personality and Social Psychology, 73,* 1284-1295.

Harter, S. (1979). *Perceived Competence Scale for Children.* Denver: University of Denver.

Harter, S. (1993). Causes and consequinces of low self-esteem in children and adolescents. In R. F. Baumeister (Ed.), *Self-esteem. The puzzle of low self-regard* (pp. 87-116). New York: Plenum Press.

Helmke, A. (1989). Mediating processes between children's self-concept of ability and mathematical achievement: A longitudinal study. In H. Mandel, E. DeCorte, N. Bennett, and H. F. Friedrich (Eds.), *Learning and instruction* (537-549). Oxford: Pergamon Press.

Helmke, A. and van Aken, M.A.G. (1995). The causal ordering of academic achievement and self-concept of ability during elementary school: A Longitudinal study. *Journal of Educational Psychology, 87*, 624-637.

Hidi, S. (2000). An interest researcher's perspective: The effects of extrinsic and intrinsic factors on motivation. In C. Sansone and J. M. Harackiewicz (Eds.), *Intrinsic and extrinsic motivation: The search for omtimal motivation and performance* (pp. 309-333). New York: Academic Press.

Hu, L.T, and Bentler, P. M. (1999). Cutoff criteria for fit indexes in covariance structure analysis: conventional criteria versus new alternatives. *Structural Equation Modeling: a Multidisciplinary Journal, 6*, 1-55.

Jones, S. (1973). Self and interpersonal evaluations: Esteem versus consistency theories. *Psychological Bulletin, 79*, 185-199.

Kaplan, H. B. (1980): *Deviant Behavior in Defence of Self.* New York: Academic Press.

Kunz, G. C., Drewniak, U., Hatalak, A., and Schön, A. (1992). Zur differentiellen bedeutung kognitiver, metakognitiver und motivationaler variabelen für das effektive lernen mit instruktionstexten und bildern. In H. Mandl and H. F. Friedrich (Eds.), *Lern- und Denkstrategien* (pp. 213-229). Göttingen: Hogrefe.

Lecky, P. (1945). *Self consistency: A theory of personality.* New York: Island Press.

Lent, R. W., Brown, S. D., and Larkin, K. C. (1986). Self-efficacy in the prediction of academic performance and perceived career options. *Journal of Counseling Psychology, 33*, 265-269.

Markus, H., and Nurius, P. (1986). Possible selves. *American Psychologist, 41*, 954-969.

Marsh, H. W. (1984). Relations among dimensions of self-attribution, dimensions of self-concept, and academic achievements. *Journal of Educational Psychology, 76*, 63-78.

Marsh, H. W. (1986). Verbal and math self-concepts: An Internal/External Frame of Reference Model. *American Educational Research Journal*, *23*, 129-149.

Marsh, H. W. (1987). The big-fish-little-pond effect on academic self-concept. *Journal of Educational Psychology*, *79*, 280-295.

Marsh, H. W. (1988). Causal effects of academic self-concept on academic achievement: A reanalysis of Newman (1984). *Journal of Experimental Education*, *56*, 100-104.

Marsh, H. W. (1990a). *SDQ II. Manual and Research Monograph.* New York: The Psychological Corporation, Harcourt Brace Jovanovich, Inc.

Marsh, H. W. (1990b). The causal ordering of academic self-concept and academic achievement: A multiwave, longitudinal path analysis. *Journal of Educational Psychology*, *82*, 646-656.

Marsh, H.W. (1990c). A multidimensional, hierarchical self-concept: Theoretical and empirical justification. *Educational Psychology Review*, *2*, 77-172.

Marsh, H. W. (1990d). The structure of academic self-concept: The Marsh/Shavelson model. *Journal of Educational Psychology*, *82*, 623-636.

Marsh, H. W. (1993). Academic self-concept: Theory, measurement, and research. In J. Suls (Ed.), Psychological perspectives on the self (Vol. 4, pp. 59-98). Hillsdale, NJ: Erlbaum.

Marsh, H. W., Byrne, B. M., and Shavelson, R. J. (1988). A multifaceted academic self-concept: Its hierarchical structure and its relation to academic achievement. *Journal of Educational Psychology*, *80*, 366-380.

Marsh, H. W., Byrne, B. M., and Yeung, A. S. (1999). Causal ordering of academic self-concept and achievement: Reanalysis of a pioneering study and revised recommendations. *Educational Psychologist*, *34*, 154-157.

Marsh, H. W., and Yeung, A. S. (1997). Causal effects of academic self-concept on academic achievement: Structural equation models of longitudinal data. *Journal of Educational Psychology*, *89*, 41-54.

Marsh, H. W., Walker, R., and Debus, R. (1991). Subject specific components of academic self-concept and self efficacy. *Contemporary Educational Psychology*, *16*, 331-345.

Marsh, H. W., and Yeung, A. S. (1997a). Causal effects of academic self-concept on academic achievement: Structural equation models of longitudinal data. *Journal of Educational Psychology*, *89*, 41-54.

Maruyama, G., Rubin, R. A., and Kingsbury, G. G. (1981). Self-esteem and educational achievement: Independent constructs with a common cause? *Journal of Personality and Social Psychology*, *40*, 962-975.

Middleton, M. J., and Midgley, C. (1997). Avoiding the demonstration of lack of ability: an under-explored aspect of goal theory. *Journal of Educational Psychology, 89*, 710-718.

Midgley, C., Kaplan, A., and Middleton, M. J. (2001). Performance-approach goals: Good for what, for whom, under what circumstances, and at what cost? *Journal of Educational Psychology*, *93*, 77-86.

Nicholls, J. G. (1983). Conceptions of ability and achievement motivation: a theory and its implications for education. In S. G. Paris, G. M. Olson, and H. W. Stevenson (Eds.), *Learning and motivation in the classroom* (pp. 211-237). Hillsdale, New Jersey: Lawrence Erlbaum Ass.

Nicholls, J. G. (1989). *The competitive ethos and democratic education.* Cambridge, MA: Harvard University Press.

Pajares, F. (1996). Self-efficacy beliefs in academic settings. *Review of Educational Research*, *66*, 543-578.

Pajares, F. (1997). Current directions in self-efficacy research. In M. L. Maehr and P. R. Pintrich (Eds.), *Advances in motivation and achievement, Vol. 10* (pp. 1-49). Greenwich, CN: JAI Press.

Pajares, F. and Kranzler, J. (1995). Self-efficacy beliefs and general mental ability in mathematical problem-solving. *Contemporary Educational Psychology*, *20*, 426-443.

Pajares, F., and Miller, M. D. (1995). Mathematics self-efficacy and mathematics performances: The need for specificity of assessment. *Journal of Counseling Psychology*, *42*, 190-198.

Piers, E. V., and Harris, D. B. (1969). *The Piers-Harris Children's Self-Concept Scale.* Nashville, Tennessee: Counselor Recordings and Tests.

Pintrich, P. R. (2000). Multiple goals, multiple pathways: The role of goal orientation in learning and achievement. *Journal of Educational Psychology*, *92*, 544-555.

Pottebaum, S. M., Keith, T. Z., and Ehly, S. W. (1986). Is there a causal relation between self-concept and academic achievement? *Journal of Educational Research*, *79*, 140-144.

Renninger, K. A. (2000). Individual interest and its implications for understanding intrinsic motivation. In C. Sansone and J. M. Harackiewicz (Eds.), *Intrinsic and extrinsic motivation: The search for optimal motivation and performance* (pp. 373-404). New York: Academic Press.

Renouf, A. G., and Harter, S. (1990). Low self-worth and anger as components of the depressive experience in young adolescents. *Development and Psychopathology*, *2*, 293-310.

Rosenberg, M. (1965). *Society and Adolescent Self-Image.* New York: Princeton University Press.

Rosenberg, M. (1968). Psychological selectivity in self-esteem formation. In C. Gordon and K. J. Gergen (Eds.), *The Self in Social Interaction.* New York: Wiley.

Rosenberg, M. (1979). *Conceiving the self.* New York: Basic Books.

Sansone, C., and Harackiewicz, J. M. (2000). Looking beyond extrinsic rewards: The problem and promise of intrinsic motivation. In C. Sansone and J. M. Harackiewicz (Eds.), *Intrinsic and extrinsic motivation: The search for optimal motivation and performance* (pp. 1-9). New York: Academic Press.

Schunk, D. H. (1983). Ability versus effort attributional feedback: Differential effects on efficacy and achievement. *Journal of Educational Psychology*, *75*, 848-856.

Schunk, D. H. (1991). Self-efficacy and academic motivation. *Educational Psychologist*, *26*, 207-231.

Shavelson, R. J., and Bolus, R. (1982). Self-concept: The interplay of theory and methods. *Journal of Educational Psychology*, *74*, 3-17.

Shavelson, R. J., Hubner, J. J., and Stanton, G. C. (1976). Self-concept: Validation of construct interpretations. *Review of Educational Research*, *46*, 407-441.

Scheirer, M. A., and Kraut, R. E. (1979). Increasing educational achievement via self-concept change. *Review of Educational Research*, *49*, 131-150.

Schiefele, U. (2001). The role of interest in motivation and learning. In J. M. Collins and S. Messick (Eds.), *Intelligence and personality: Gridging the gap in theory and measurement* (pp. 163-194). Mahwah, New Jersey: Erlbaum.

Schiefele, U., and Krapp, A. (1996). Topic interest and free recall of expository text. *Learning and Individual Differences, 8,* 141-160.

Seifert, T. L. (1995). Characteristics of ego- and task-oriented students: a comparison of two methodologies. *British Journal of Educational Psychology, 65,* 125-138.

Shavelson, R. J., Hubner, J. J., and Stanton, G. C. (1976). Validation of Construct interpretations. *Review of Educational Research, 46,* 407-441.

Skaalvik, E. M. (1989). *Verdier, selvoppfatning og mental helse. En undersøkelse blant elever i videregående skole.* Trondheim: Tapir.

Skaalvik, E. M. (1997a). Issues in research on self-concept. In M. L. Maehr and P. R. Pintrich (Eds.), *Advances in motivation and achievement, Vol. 10* (pp. 51-98). Greenwich, CN: JAI Press.

Skaalvik, E. M. (1997b). Self-enhancing and self-defeating ego orientation: relations with task and avoidance orientation, achievement, self-perceptions, and anxiety. *Journal of Educational Psychology, 89,* 71-81.

Skaalvik, E. M., and Hagtvet, K. A. (1990). Academic achievement and self-concept: An analysis of causal predominance in a developmental perspective. *Journal of Personality and Social Psychology, 58,* 292-307.

Skaalvik, E. M., and Hagtvet, K. A. (1995). Academic achievement, self-concept, and conformity to school norms: A developmental analysis. *Zeitschrift für Pädagogische Psychologie, 9,* 211-220.

Skaalvik, E. M., and Rankin, R. J. (1996, April). *Self-concept and self-efficacy : Conceptual analysis.* Paper presented at the annual meeting of the American Educational Research Association, New York.

Skaalvik, E. M., and Skaalvik, S. (2004). Self-concept and self-efficacy: A test of the Internal/External Frame of Reference model and predictions of subsequent motivation and achievement. *Psychological Reports, 95,* 1187-1202.

Skaalvik, E. M., and Valås, H. (2001). Achievement and self-concept in mathematics and verbal arts: A study of relations. In R. J. Riding and S. G. Rayner (Eds.), *Self perception. International perspectives in individual differences, Volume 2* (pp. 221-238). London: Ablex Publishing.

Skaalvik, E. M., Valås, H., and Sletta, O. (1994). Task involvement and ego involvement: relations with academic achievement, academic self-concept and self-esteem. *Scandinavian Journal of Educational Research, 38,* 231-243.

Skaalvik, S., and Skaalvik, E. M. (in press). Self-concept, motivational orientation, and help-seeking behavior in mathematics: A study of adults returning to high school. *Social Psychology of Education.*

Snow, R. E., Corno, L., and Jackson, D. (1996). Individual differences in affective and conative functions. In D. C. Berliner and R. C. Calfee (Eds.), *Handbook of Educational Psychology* (pp. 243-330). New York: Prentice Hall International.

Tice, D. (1993). The social motivations of people with low self-esteem. In R. F. Baumeister (Ed.), *Self-esteem. The puzzle of low self-regard* (pp. 37-53). New York: Plenum Press.

Trent, L. M. Y., Cooney, G., Russel, G., and Warton, P. M. (1996). Significant others' contribution to early adolescents' perceptions of their competence. *British Journal of Educational Psychology, 66,* 95-107.

Urdan, T., and Turner, J. C. (in press). Competence motivation in the classroom. In A. Elliot and C. Dweck (Eds.), *Handbook of competence and motivation*. Guildord Press.

Valås, H., and Sletta, O. (1996, August). *Social behavior, peer relations, loneliness, and self-perceptions in middle school children: A mediational model*. Paper presented at the XIVth Biennial Meetings of the international Society for the study of Behavioural Development, Quebec City.

Wigfield, A., and Karpathian, M. (1991). Who am in and what can in do? Children's self-concepts and motivation in academic situations. *Educational Psychologist, 26*, 233-262.

Wigfield, A., Eccles, J. S., and Pintrich, P. R. (1996). Development between the ages of 11 and 25. In D. C. Berliner and R. C. Calfee (Eds.), *Handbook of Educational Psychology* (pp. 148-185). New York: Prentice Hall International.

Yoon, K. S., Eccles, J. S., and Wigfield, A. (1996, April). *Self-concept of ability, value, and academic achievement: A test of causal relations*. Paper presented at the Annual Meeting of the American Educational Research Association in New York.

Ystgaard, M. (1993). *Sårbar ungdom og sosial støtte* [Vulnerable yongsters and social support]. Report number 1/93, Oslo, Center for social nettwork and health.

Zimmerman, B. J., and Bandura, A. (1994). Impact of self-regulatory influences on writing course attainment. *American Educational Research Journal, 31*, 845-862.

Zimmerman, B. J., Bandura, A., and Martinez-Pons, M. (1992). Self-motivation for academic attainment: The role of self-efficacy beliefs and personal goal setting. *American Educational Research Journal, 29*, 663-676.

In: The Concept of Self in Education, Family and Sports
Editor: Anne P. Prescott, pp. 75-89

ISBN 1-59454-988-5
© 2006 Nova Science Publishers, Inc.

Chapter 3

THE SELF IN DISABILITY SPORT
AND PHYSICAL ACTIVITY

*Jeffrey Martin**
Wayne State University

ABSTRACT

The purpose of this chapter is to review research on the self in disability sport and physical activity in the areas of: Self-esteem, perceived competence, and body image. Based on the research findings, there is no support for the premise that individuals with disabilities have diminished self-esteem, lack physical competence, or have negative body images, compared to non-disabled people. Involvement in sport and physical activity clearly has psychological benefits. Research participants in the studies examined, ranged from children to older adults participating in activities and sports as diverse as wheelchair basketball, dance, summer camps, swimming and soccer championships, fitness activities, and road races. Athletes and physical activity participants repeatedly indicated that human movement experiences in sport and physical activity contributed to an enhanced sense of confidence to perform physical activities and sport skills, a greater sense of self-worth, and, to a lesser extent, increased body image satisfaction.

INTRODUCTION

The purpose of this chapter is to review research on the self in disability sport and physical activity. Findings are reported in three broad areas: self-esteem, perceived competence, and body image. Although I discuss each of these areas separately it should be noted that they are not independent and represent reciprocal influences on each other

---

* Send correspondence to: Jeffrey J. Martin; Division of Kinesiology, Health and Sport Studies, 265 Matthaei Building, Wayne State University, Detroit MI 48202; Phone (313) 577-1381 Fax (313) 577-5999; aa3975@wayne.edu

(Bandura, 1997; Martin, 1999a). The rationale for a literature review in this area is three-fold. First, individuals with disabilities constitute a large number of people. People with disabilities are considered a "silent" minority (Shapiro, 1993) and are the largest minority group in the world. In the USA alone, there are 54 million people with a disability (McNeil, 1997). For these reasons, and others, research examining individuals with disabilities involvement in physical activity is considered a national priority in the USA (Rimmer, Braddock, and Pitetti, 1996). Second, researchers have noted that individuals with disabilities might lack self-regard and have low perceived competence (Kunnen, 1990), and poor body image (Martin, 1999b). Thus, it is important to examine if there is research support for such claims. Third, authors (e.g., Baake, 1978) have often argued that sport has character building (i.e., self-esteem) qualities but few researchers (Hutzler, and Bar-Eli, 1993) have examined if this is true for disability sport and physical activity.

Individuals with disabilities face reduced opportunities for sport participation, health complications due to aging with a disability, low employment rates, reduced social contact, and discrimination (Fine and Asch, 1988; Yuker, 1987) and stigmatization (Goffman, 1963). People with disabilities, for example, are at risk for physical and sexual abuse (Sobsey, 1994).

According to Martin and McCaughtry (2004) and Martin (in press-a) the above injustices and challenges make opportunities for sport and physical activity involvement critical to the psychological, physiological and social well being of individuals with disabilities. For example, Goodwin and Staples (2005) found that a sport camp for children with disabilities was vital in helping them connect with similar others and reduced their sense of isolation. Determining if sport and physical activity participation promotes favorable self-worth, increased competence and enhanced body image cognitions would provide empirical support for the anecdotal claims of the benefits of disability sport and physical activity participation. I conclude my review by noting the limitations in the research cited and by summarizing the most important findings. It should be noted that I confine my review of the literature to individuals with physical disabilities (e.g., amputee, spinal cord injury, vision loss, cerebral palsy, etc) and I do not review research on people with intellectual disabilities.

SELF-ESTEEM

Self-esteem refers to how well people like who they are. Two major antecedents of favorable self-esteem are: Success experiences which promote feelings of mastery (James, 1890) and favorable judgments of worth from significant others (i.e., reflected appraisals). One perspective, grounded in the above processes, for why individuals with disabilities may experience low self-esteem is that their disability directly and indirectly limits their ability to experience success. For instance, Smyth and

Anderson (2000) reported that children with movement difficulties, compared to children without movement difficulties, fail more in sport and physical activity. Poorly coordinated children may also withdraw, watch, and be less active at play thereby limiting their opportunities for success (Bouffard, Watkinson, Thompson, Causgrove-Dunn, and Romanow, 1996).

A second major source of self-esteem, thought to be lacking, are the favorable appraisals from significant others and, conversely, increased negative feedback. Adults with developmental coordination disorder (DCD), for instance, sometimes experience humiliation and anxiety as a result of other's reactions to their condition (Fitzpatrick and Watkinson, 2003). On the other hand, Cacciapaglia, Beauchamp and Howells (2004) found non-disabled people more willing to talk to a person with a visible disability (i.e., amputee) than the same person who "hid" their disability. As Cacciapaglia et al (2004) notes, the research findings on interactions among disabled and non-disabled individuals are complex and likely to be disability and context specific.

In sport and physical activity contexts, positive and negative appraisals may be contingent on ability perceptions. Parents of children with disabilities, for instance, believe that peers are more accepting of their children with physical disabilities in physical activity and sport settings if they were viewed as being physically capable (Martin, in review). This finding is similar to previous research examining able bodied children (Weiss, Smith, and Theeboom, 1996). Some individuals with disabilities note that their participation in sport and physical activity is trivialized and their physical abilities often doubted (Taub, Blinde, and Greer, 1999).

Even well intended offers of aid can go awry. Goodwin (2001), for instance, interviewed 12 early to later elementary aged children in order to understand their perceptions of help from peers in physical education classes. She reported that children's self-esteem was threatened when they perceived that help was offered based on a negative assessment of their ability (e.g., "he thinks that I don't have muscles" p. 297). In contrast, Rees, Smith and Sparkes, (2003) reported on the experiences of six men with spinal cord injuries who became disabled as a result of a rugby accident. One of the themes emerging from a discussion of social support was how others (e.g., father, therapist) bolstered their self-esteem and perceptions of ability.

Martin (1999b) examined varied self-referent cognitions of adolescents swimmers with varied physical disabilities (e.g., Cerebral Palsy) and found self-esteem scores comparable to elite adolescent soccer players, gymnasts and figure skaters (Martin, Engels, Wirth, and Smith, 1997b). Campbell and Jones (1994) found no self-esteem differences between wheelchair athletes and non-athletes and further suggested that sport participation has self-esteem boosting qualities. Additional analyses indicated that the international level athletes reported higher self-esteem compared to national, regional, and recreational level athletes supporting the notion that a high level of sport involvement (and presumably success) may be necessary to generalize to increases in global self-esteem. Using Harter's (1988) multi-dimensional self-concept scale, Sherrill, Hinson, Gench, Kennedy, and Low (1990) surveyed 158 youth athletes (M age = 14) with disabilities to determine if their self-esteem scores paralleled those of non-disabled youth based on established norms. The pattern of scores across the global self-worth scale and 8 subscales indicated no differences. However, the close friends and job competence subscale scores were .10 below the range of normative scores. Sherrill et al (1990) suggested these results were emblematic of youth's unmet needs in these areas as people with disabilities are often socially isolated and underemployed (Shapiro, 1993).

In one of the few sport intervention studies assessing self-esteem, Hedrick (1985) examined if a 4 week wheelchair tennis program increased children's (N=36) general perceived competence (i.e., self-worth) and, as he anticipated, found no support. As Hedrick (1985) notes, increases in self-esteem likely require increases in mastery behavior over a significant range of behaviors (i.e. not just sport) over a period of time longer than 4 weeks.

Goodwin, Krohn, and Kuhnle (2004b) reported both children ($N = 5$, ages 6-14) and their parents saw wheelchair dance as instrumental in promoting a stronger sense of self. Finally, Valliant, Bezzubyk, Daley, and Asu (1985) compared athletes with disabilities to non-athletes with disabilities. They found athletes with disabilities had higher global self-esteem compared to non-athletes with disabilities. It should be noted, however, that the disability group was quite heterogeneous (i.e., wheelchair, amputee, blind, cerebral palsy) and was significantly ($N = 139$) larger than the comparison group ($N = 22$).

In conclusion, the limited research examining the self-esteem scores of individuals with disabilities does not support the notion that they have lower self-esteem compared to non-disabled individuals. Furthermore, it is not likely that intervention programs of short duration focused only on sport skill mastery are likely to have a significant impact on global self-esteem unless program participants have low self-esteem and their athletic identity constitutes a significant aspect of their self-worth (Martin, Eklund, and Mushett, 1997a). Sport and physical activity based interventions have potential to enhance multidimensional self-esteem if the specific component of self-esteem targeted (i.e., such as social self-esteem, friendships) is an area where participants have had limited opportunities to interact with peers and particularly peers with similar disabilities and life experiences (Goodwin and Staples, 2005; Martin and Smith, 2002).

BODY IMAGE

Rose and Larkin and colleagues have conducted a line of research examining children with motor control difficulties (i.e., clumsy children). Rose, Larkin and Berger (1997), for instance, compared children with high and low motor coordination (LMC) and found that the LMC children had lower physical appearance perceptions compared to the high motor coordinated children (HMC). In contrast, with an older sample of adolescents, they reported stronger physical appearance cognitions for LMC adolescents compared to a control group matched for age and gender (Larkin and Parker, 1997). Similar to able bodied research (Martin et al., 1997b), Rose and Larkin (2002) reported that physical appearance perceptions contributed significantly to feelings of global self-worth.

Martin-Ginis et al (2003) reported that after a 3 month exercise intervention program adult participants ($N = 21$) with spinal cord injury (SCI), compared to controls with SCI, increased their satisfaction with their physical appearance. In a related study Martin-Ginis and colleagues (Hicks et al., 2003) determined that at 9 months exercise participants exhibited an upward linear trend of increasing satisfaction with their appearance, compared to the controls. Yuen and Hanson (2002) investigated multi-dimensional body image among adults with ($N=30$) and without ($N=30$) acquired mobility disability such as a lower body amputation. Individuals in both groups varied in their physical activity levels and analyses were conducted to determine if individuals with or without a disability who were active or inactive varied in their body image perceptions. Participants with disabilities who were active, rated their appearance better, were more satisfied with various body parts, were more concerned about their fitness levels and, finally, rated their health higher than non-active individuals with disabilities. Furthermore, on most of the scales, participants with disabilities scored similarly to individuals without disabilities. However, participants with disabilities were more focused on their appearance compared to the able bodied controls. This finding in particular may reflect participant's awareness of their physical "differentness". Finally, as might be expected, the non-disabled individuals rated their health more favorable.

In a relatively recent line of research in exercise psychology, scientists have examined a body image related construct: social physique anxiety. Social physique anxiety is anxiety experienced or anticipated as a result of the perception that others are devaluing ones body. Researchers (e.g., Taleporos and McCabe, 2002) have suggested that it is difficult for individuals with disabilities to have a positive body image because they often receive cues from the environment (e.g., stares) that they are unattractive. In two review articles, Rumsey and colleague (Rumsey, 2002; Rumsey and Harcourt, 2004) also affirm how "visible differences" in appearance, as a result of social anxiety, can have a negative impact on body image. Although Rumsey and colleague focus on disfigurement (e.g., cleft lip) her conclusions can be cautiously extended to individuals with a visibly "different" appearance due to a physical disability (e.g., amputee). Of importance to the current review are Rumsey and Harcourt's (2004) assertion that, despite the above assertion, many people still effectively adapt to their condition and often appear relatively unaffected by it from a body image perspective.

In regard to social anxiety about the body (i.e., social physique anxiety), Kleck and De Jong (1983) found that able bodied children viewed children with disabilities as less attractive compared to non-disabled children. Children with disabilities participating in Goodwin, Thurmeier, and Gustafson's (2004c) study reported that the "poor you" (p. 288) look they received from others was quite common. Thus, individuals with disabilities my sense more negative evaluative judgments about their appearance from others.

Martin (1999b) found that adolescent athletes with disabilities had low levels of SPA that were comparable to SPA anxiety reported by college males (Martin, Kliber, Kulinna, and Fahlmann, in review) and females (Crawford and Eklund, 1994; Eklund and Crawford, 1994). Martin (1999b) suggested that athlete's successful sport mastery experiences combined with self-assessments made in comparison to similar self-referent groups (i.e., others with disability) contributed to the healthy levels of SPA.

Finally, it is important to note that researchers have also reported that women with disabilities and disfigurements were less concerned about weight related issues compared to matched controls and reported virtually no strong negative appraisals of their bodies from others (Ben-Tovim and Walker, 1995). The authors suggested that women with serious health (i.e., disability condition) issues view weight concerns as relatively unimportant in the bigger picture (Ben-Tovim and Walker, 1995). This last research finding illuminates the importance of considering the sample specificity of various research efforts when considering the findings. In conclusion, although individuals with disabilities may experience heightened awareness of their physical self-presentation and others perceptions of them, the research in this area doesn't support the conclusion that individuals with disabilities will "automatically" have greater body image dissatisfaction compared to people without disabilities. Similar to individuals without disabilities, though, it is likely that body image perceptions play a role in self-esteem perceptions.

PERCEIVED COMPETENCE

Researchers have examined self-efficacy, a situation specific form of confidence or competence. Greenwood, Dzewaltowski, and French (1990) found that wheelchair tennis players exhibited stronger mobility efficacy than non-tennis playing wheelchair users. Greenwood et al. (1997) concluded that sport involvement increases participant's efficacy in their physical capabilities. Lowther, Lane and Lane (2005) asked 15 elite male amputee soccer players, participating in the World Cup, to rate their self-efficacy for their competition goals. Mean scores ($M = 13$-15 on an 18 pt scale) reflected a relatively strong and stable sense of efficacy over the 6 game competition. Martin (2002) found that elite level wheelchair road racers had strong self-efficacy (on a 10 point scale) for overcoming racing ($M = 7.88$) barriers (e.g., wet roads), racing a time relative to their personal race time goal ($M = 7.05$) and for overcoming ($M = 6.23$) training barriers (e.g., poor weather). Furthermore, the pattern of scores exhibited above would suggest athletes are most confident in a specific one time competitive situation such as a race, compared to maintaining their efficacy over prolonged training periods.

Cairney, Hay, Faught, Mandigo, and Flouris, (2005) examined self-reported physical activity levels and physical activity self-efficacy of children with and without developmental coordination disorder (DCD). They found that children with DCD had lower free play and organized physical activity levels, and lower physical activity self-efficacy compared to children without DCD. However, it should be noted that the self-efficacy scale employed was flawed as it included items assessing preference for, and enjoyment of, physical activity which are clearly inconsistent with Bandura's (1997) theoretical formulation of self-efficacy. In addition, the scale is a comparative scale forcing children to make self-assessments in reference to "other children" (Cairney et al., 2005).

Campbell and Jones (1997) assessed national level wheelchair athlete's self-confidence leading up to competition. In support of Lowther et al's (2005) findings they found that athletes had fairly stable self-confidence over a one week period to 30 minutes prior to competition. Mean scores ($M = 23.33$-26.85 on a 36 pt scale) were indicative of favorable and robust self-confidence. Botvin Madorsky and Kiley (1984) reported on a case study of a paraplegic wheelchair mountaineer who ascended an 8,751 foot mountain. Similar to Greenwood et al. (1997) the authors concluded that his successful mountain climbing experience was responsible for increased efficacy.

Ashton-Shaeffer, Gibson, Autry and Hanson (2001) provided qualitative data on the experiences of 15 adults with disabilities attending a 2 day sport camp. One of the themes that emerged was the value of the camp as a site for empowerment. Campers indicated feelings that the researchers interpreted as self-confidence for physical activity as well as increased confidence to "engage in the world again" (p. 109).

Taub et al. (1999) interviewed 24 male college students engaged in sport and physical activity as to their motives for participation. Sport and physical activity involvement was perceived as an excellent vehicle to demonstrate competence and refute stereotypes of incompetence resulting from their disability. Furthermore, the demonstration of competence achieved by exhibiting skill, was distinguished from portraying competence via a fit body. A common theme throughout the interviews was the ability to use sport and physical activity as a forum to challenge stereotypes of people with disabilities as lacking physical competence and physical fitness (Taub et al., 1999).

Blinde and McCallister (1999) also interviewed sport and physical activity participants, but focused on women's (N=16) experiences. The majority of the women preferred fitness versus sport types of activities. A reoccurring and dominant theme captured by the researchers was the women's motivation to use fitness activities to maintain (versus gain) functionality. Similar to the college aged men, most of the women cited a greater sense of physical competence which generalized to other aspects of their lives such as work and relationships. Related to a enhanced vision of their competence was an increased feeling of control. Also, like the men, about half of the women noted how they came to see their bodies as a source of strength.

The emphasis on maintaining functionality may reflect an "adult" perspective as children in a wheelchair dance troupe saw their experience as a form of self-expression whereas their parents and instructors discussed the rehabilitative value of the program (Goodwin et al., 2004b). Participating in sport to maintain physical condition post spinal cord injury (SCI) was also the number one reason provided by 678 individuals with SCI (Tasiemski, Kennedy, Gardner, and Blaikley, 2004). Finally, women aging with a disability, have also noted that they viewed physical activity as a mechanism to maintain functionality and offset secondary disabilities associated with aging (Goodwin and Compton, 2004a).

Blinde and McClung (1997) reported on men and women's perceptions of their recreational and physical activity involvement. An important theme running throughout their results was the combination of increased confidence in their physical abilities and an awareness of an even greater physical activity potential than previously thought. Additionally, participants indicated a greater willingness to try novel physical activities including risk taking behaviors.

In another study by Blinde (Blinde and Taub, 1999) she and colleagues interviewed 28 male college students with physical and sensory disabilities with a focus on how sport and physical activity empowered participants. Participants overwhelmingly indicated that they gained confidence in their capabilities. Blinde and Taub (1999), however, reported a multidimensional portrayal of the manner in which students expressed this new found competence. First, participants gained confidence in their physical abilities that extended beyond sport and physical activity into daily activities of living. Second, they perceived a greater sense of their potential and increased their aspirations. Third, students reported a reduced sense of dependence and increased independence and inner locus of control. Finally, subjects indicated that they experienced a feeling of mastery from their accomplishments which in some cases, led to feelings of self-actualization. Interestingly, Blinde and Taub (1999) indicated that participants with acquired disabilities cited the above benefits of sport and physical activity participation more frequently than students with congenital disabilities.

The sport and physical activity link to self-actualization has also been reported Patrick and Bignall's (1984) six month in depth study of 11 of the top wheelchair racers in the USA. A wheeler, Clint, exclaimed "It's a great feeling. I go out early in the morning and there's nothing else on the road.... I get this physical exertion and freedom feeling-it's really an excellent feeling" (Patrick and Bignall, 1984, p. 217). Pensgaard and Sorensen (2002) and Hutzler (1989) view confidence (i.e., efficacy), control, and self-esteem as critical mediators of empowerment and provide an empowerment model to guide sport and physical disability research in this area. They both urged practitioners to provide programs that help individuals with disabilities gain a sense of control and efficacy.

Another theme running throughout the work of Blinde and colleagues is the notion that confidence gained in sport and physical activity generalizes to other life activities. Adnan, McKenzie and Miyahara (2001) specifically examined if wheelchair or quad rugby (QR) players would report stronger self-efficacy for QR and for activities of daily living (ADL) compared to a control group of non-QR players with quadriplegia. As expected, players, compared to the control group, reporter stronger self-efficacy on all 11 items constituting the QR self-efficacy scale. For efficacy regarding ADL, QR players scored higher than the control group on 4 of the 28 items indicating minimal generalizability. However, all 4 items represented transferring ability (e.g., transferring from seat to wheelchair) suggesting that the transferring involved in games and practices contributed to enhanced efficacy for transferring in non sport and physical activity environments (Adnan et al., 2001).

Some of the few exercise intervention studies conducted with individuals with disabilities also supports the value of physical activity in promoting competence in physical functioning (Hicks, et al., 2003; Martin-Ginis, et al., 2003). Martin-Ginis and colleagues had SCI participants exercise 2 times a week for nine months. They found that SCI adults who exercised reported an increase in their physical self-concept function after both 3 and 9 months, compared to the control group.

Kunnen (1990) compared 9 year old children with ($n = 62$) and without physical disabilities ($n = 62$) for multi-dimensional competence. She found no differences in perceived physical competence between the two groups although some findings suggested the children with physical disabilities were less realistic in their appraisals. Hedrick (1985) examined the impact of an instructional wheelchair tennis program on children's ($N=36$) tennis self-efficacy and physical competence. He found that not only did the children increase in their tennis specific competence (i.e., tennis efficacy) but that they also enhanced their more general physical competence. Furthermore, he found that the tennis experience did not further generalize to increases in social, cognitive or general competence.

Causgrove Dunn (2000) found moderate to strong levels of perceived competence ($M =$ approximately 5 on a 7 point scale) among 11 year old ($N = 65$) children with movement difficulties. Perhaps an even more significant set of findings revolved around her test of a competence and motivation model. Using structural equation modeling techniques, Causgrove Dunn (2000) found that children who perceived a strong mastery motivational climate in physical education (PE) class reported higher levels of competence compared to children who perceived a weaker mastery motivational climate. A mastery motivational climate in PE reflects an atmosphere where teachers and students emphasize personal goals, trying hard and self-improvement. Additionally, a mastery climate mediated the relationship between a task orientation (i.e., a personal disposition to focus on effort and self-improvement) and perceived competence. Causgrove Dunn's (2000) results support the perspective that adults should strive to create mastery climates for children where the standard of comparison for perceptions of competence is self-referenced and therefore controllable, versus other referenced and thus uncontrollable.

In a similar theoretical research effort, Valentini and Rudisill (2004) examined the impact of a 12 week mastery climate intervention on motor skill development. Students with and without disabilities were randomized into intervention and control groups. Both intervention groups showed increases in object control and locomotor skills compared to the comparison group. Finally, Goodwin et al. (2004c) noted that adolescents and young adults perceived that their sport participation increased how able others viewed them. Meg, for instance, stated "people have a higher perception of you when you are more active (Goodwin et al., 2004c, p. 393).

In conclusion, it is quite clear that most individuals participating in physical activity and sport believe it enhances their physical capabilities and, subsequently, their perceptions of competence. Furthermore, there is evidence to suggest that increased feelings of competence can, in some cases, transfer to a greater sense of efficacy in other related areas in addition to promoting more favorable global perceptions about the self (e.g., empowerment, control, self-esteem). Finally, athlete self-efficacy is positively related to sport social support suggesting the value of group based (i.e., teams) interventions that enhance social cohesion (Martin and Mushett-Adams, 1996).

RESEARCH LIMITATIONS

Much of the research cited in this chapter is qualitative or cross-sectional and correlational in nature. Even the few intervention studies reported on often either lacked a control group and/or participants were not randomized into groups, when control groups were employed. Thus a major causal mechanism alluded to in many studies, such as the ability of sport and physical activity to enhance efficacy and self-esteem, is speculative despite their intuitive appeal and the theoretical grounding (e.g., self-efficacy theory) of much of the research. It is quite plausible and theoretically consistent (i.e., reciprocal determinism) that the pathways are bi-directional. Such a perspective would acknowledge that while sport has efficacy, body image, and self-worth building possibilities, it is equally reasonable to assume that individuals with a resilient sense of efficacy, who are content with their bodies, and a healthy sense of self-regard are most likely to engage in sport and physical activity. In contrast, individuals who lack efficacy, suffer from SPA, and doubt their worthiness, are more likely to shy away from participating in sport and physical activity.

It should be noted that not all participants in the various research efforts reviewed had unanimously positive perceptions of their sport and physical activity experiences. For instance, the qualitative research studies that Blinde was involved in (Blinde and McCallister, 1998; 1999; Blinde and McClung; 1997; Blinde and Taub, 1999; Taub et al., 1999) participants would sometimes report feelings of frustration and inadequacy when attempting to accomplish activities that they were inexperienced in or lacked the skills to be successful in. Ashton-Shaeffer et al. (2001) reported that a few participants in her study compared how severe their disability was to others in the camp and subsequently experienced some guilt about being less disabled. This finding shares some similarity with the results of Mastro, Burton, Rosendahl and Sherrill (1996) who documented that even athletes with disabilities may have some negative attitudes towards athletes with more severe disabilities.

Finally, the above research efforts represent a diversity of disability type and conditions (e.g., cerebral palsy, spinal cord injury, low motor coordination, vision loss, etc). Additionally, in many research efforts the samples are quite heterogeneous in terms of disability type, severity and onset (i.e., congenital versus acquired). For instance, athletes who are hearing impaired have a different mode of communication, not a disability that affects their motor skills (Dummer, Haubenstricker, and Stewart, 1996), although they are often considered physically disabled in the disability sport world.

CONCLUSION

A number of themes and patterns emerged throughout this literature review and warrant summarizing and repeating. First, many individuals with disabilities, particularly adults, likely see sport and physical activity participation to have very pragmatic purposes such as maintaining and preventing loss of function. Second, the majority of participants in the qualitative research lines conducted by Goodwin and colleagues, and by Blinde and colleagues, indicated that participating in sport and physical activity enhanced their feelings of physical competence. Third, while feelings of competence may generalize to other life areas they are most likely to do so for life skills that are similar in function (e.g., transferring) to sport skills. Additionally, sport and physical activity may simply serve as "vehicles" that allow increased social interaction and promote social support among individuals who share similar life experiences (i.e., shared social reality).

Fourth, disabilities, particularly visible (i.e., severe) disabilities, may serve to heighten individual's awareness of their body image. However, there is no compelling evidence to suggest people with disabilities suffer from adverse body image dissatisfaction any more or less than individuals without disabilities. Finally, the frame of reference and the context in which individuals make competence judgments is critical to the process. For example, older women with serious disability and health related issues are far less likely to be concerned with weight gain and body image compared to adolescent girls who are undergoing puberty related body changes during a time of heightened awareness of their bodies (Martin, 1999b; Tiggemann, 2004).

From a sport competence perspective, if adults promote a master climate in which children make competence judgments in reference to effort, learning, and self-improvement than they are not likely to suffer from low perceived competence. In contrast, if children (able bodied or disabled) develop competence judgments based on other's capabilities than the potential to feel inefficacious is heightened. Martin (in press-b) for example, speculated that athletes in his study made physical competence inferences based on other competitors with similar disabilities. The process by which individuals use a frame of reference established by significant others (e.g., peers on their team, other competitors) to make self-concept and competence assessments has been referred to as the Big Fish Little Pond Effect (BFLPE) by Marsh (1998). Research support for this phenomenon is strong in academic studies (Marsh, 1987) and supportive in investigations with athletes examining physical self-concept (Marsh, 1987, 1993, 1998). As Block, Griebenauw, and Brodeur (2004) note, the dynamics of social comparison processes in determining perceived competence also has a developmental component with younger children (i.e., under 10 years of age) looking more towards adults whereas children 10-14 years of age rely more on peers for information about their competence.

To finish, it is clear that physical activity and sport can provide wonderful psychological benefits to individuals with various disabilities. My conclusions are consistent with both Block et al (2004) and Hutzler and Bar-Eli (1993) who reached similar conclusions based on their reviews of some of the literature on the psychosocial dynamics of disability sport and physical activity.

Researchers are urged to continue theory based research into the many self-referenced emotional and cognitive benefits of human movement opportunities for individuals with disabilities. Given the short careers of many disability sport participants, it is critical to investigate how to maintain sport and physical involvement for athletes with disabilities across the lifespan, and avoid the deleterious effects of sport and physical activity cessation (Martin, 1996; 1999c).

REFERENCES

Adnan, Y., McKenzie, A., and Miyahara, M. (2001). Self-efficacy for quad rugby skills and activities of daily living. *Adapted Physical Activity Quarterly*, 18, 90-101.

Ashton-Shaeffer, C., Gibson, H.J., Autry, C.E., and Hanson, C.S. (2001). Meaning of sport to adults with physical disabilities: A disability sport camp experience. *Sociology of Sport Journal*, 18(1), 95-114.

Baake, T. (1978). Judo for the blind: A path to self-confidence. *The Physician and Sports Medicine*, 3, 141-142.

Bandura, A. (1997). *Self-efficacy: The exercise of control.* New York: Freeman and Co.

Ben-Tovim, D. I., and Walker, M. K. (1995). Body image, disfigurement and disability. *Journal of Psychosomatic Research*, 39, 283-292.

Blinde, E.M. and McCallister, S.G. (1998). Listening to the voices of students with physical disabilities: Experiences in the physical education classroom. *Journal of Physical Education, Recreation, and Dance*, 69(6), 64-68.

Blinde, E.M. and McCallister, S.G. (1999). Women, disability, and sport and physical fitness activity: The intersection of gender and disability dynamics. *Research Quarterly for Exercise and Sport*, 70(4), 303-312.

Blinde, E.M., and McClung, L.R. (1997). Enhancing the physical and social self through recreational activity: Accounts of individual with physical disabilities. *Adapted Physical Activity Quarterly*, 14, 327-344.

Blinde, E.M. and Taub, D. E. (1999). Personal empowerment through sport and physical fitness activity: Perspectives from male college students with physical and sensory disabilities. *Journal of Sport Behavior*, 22, 181-202.

Block, M. E., Griebenauw, L-M., Brodeur, S. (2004). Psychosocial factors and disability: Effects of physical activity and sport. In M. R., Weiss (Ed.) *Developmental Sport and Exercise Psychology: A Lifespan Perspective* (pp.425-452) Morgantown, WV: Fitness Information Technology, Inc.

Botvin Madorsky, J.G., and Kiley, D.P. (1984). Wheelchair mountaineering. *Archives of Physical Medicine and Rehabilitation*, 65, 490-492.

Bouffard, M., Watkinson, E. J., Thompson, L. P., Causgrove Dunn, J. L., and Romanow, S. K. E. (1996). A test of the activity deficit hypothesis with children with movement difficulties. *Adapted Physical Activity Quarterly*, 13, 61-73.

Cacciapaglia, H. M., Beauchamp, K. L., and Howells, G. N. (2004). Visibility of disability: Effect on willingness to interact. *Rehabilitation Psychology*, 49, 180-182.

Cairney, J., Hay, J., Faught, B., Mandigo, J., and Flouris, A. (2005). Developmental coordination disorder, self-efficacy toward physical activity and play: Does gender matter. *Adapted Physical Activity Quarterly*, 22, 67-82.

Campbell, E. and Jones, G. (1994). Psychological well-being in wheelchair sport participants and nonparticipants. *Adapted Physical Activity Quarterly*, 11, 404- 415.

Campbell, E. and Jones, G. (1997). Precompetition anxiety and self-confidence in wheelchair participants. *Adapted Physical Activity Quarterly*, 14, 95-107.

Causgrove Dunn, J. (2000). Goal orientations, perceptions of the motivational climate, and perceived competence of children with movement difficulties. *Adapted Physical Activity Quarterly*, 17, 1-19.

Chubon, R.A. (1994). *Social and Psychological Foundations of Rehabilitation*. Springfield, IL: Charles C. Thomas.

Crawford, S., and Eklund, R. C. (1994). Social physique anxiety, reasons for exercise and, attitudes toward exercise settings *Journal of Sport and Exercise Psychology*, 16, 70-82.

Dummer, G. M., Haubenstricker, J. L., and Stewart, D. A. (1996). Motor skill performances of children who are deaf. *Adapted Physical Activity Quarterly*, 13, 400-414.

Eklund, R. C. and Crawford, S. (1994). Active women, social physique anxiety, and exercise. *Journal of Sport and Exercise Psychology*, 16, 431-448.

Fine, M. and Asch, A. (1988). Disability beyond stigma: Social interaction, discrimination, and activism. *Journal of Social Issues*, 44(1), 3-21.

Fitzpatrick, D.A. and Watkinson E.J. (2003). The lived experience of physical awkwardness: Adults' retrospective views. *Adapted Physical Activity Quarterly*, 20, 279-297.

Goffman, E. (1963). Stigma: Notes on the management of spoiled identity. New York: Simon and Shuster.

Goodwin, D.L. (2001). The meaning of help in PE: Perceptions of students with physical disabilities. *Adapted Physical Activity Quarterly*, 18, 289-303.

Goodwin, D.L. and Compton, S.G. (2004a). Physical activity experiences of women Aging with disabilities. *Adapted Physical Activity Quarterly*, 21, 122-138.

Goodwin, D.L., Krohn, J., and Kuhnle, A. (2004b). Beyond the wheelchair: The experience of dance. *Adapted Physical Activity Quarterly*, 21, 229-247.

Goodwin, D. L., and Staples, K. (2005). The meaning of summer camp experiences to youths with disabilities. *Adapted Physical Activity Quarterly*, 22, 160-178.

Goodwin, D.L., Thurmeier, R., Gustafson, P. (2004c). Reactions to the metaphors of disability: The mediating effects of physical activity. *Adapted Physical Activity Quarterly*, 21, 379-398.

Greenwood, M.C., Dzewaltowski, D.A., and French, R. (1990). Self-efficacy and psychological well-being of wheelchair tennis participants and wheelchair nontennis participants. *Adapted Physical Activity Quarterly*, 7, 12-21.

Harter, S. (1988). Manual for the self-perception profile for adolescents. Denver. University of Denver.

Hedrick, B.N. (1985). The effect of wheelchair tennis participation and mainstreaming upon the perceptions of competence of physically disabled adolescents. *Therapeutic Recreation Journal*, 19(2), 34-46.

Hicks, A. L., Martin-Ginis, K. A., Ditor, D. S., Latimer, A. E., Craven, C., Bugaresti, J., and McCartney, N. (2003). Long term exercise training in persons with spinal cord injury:

effects on strength, arm ergometry performance and psychological well- being. *Spinal Cord*, 41, 34-43.

Hutzler, Y. (1989). The concept of empowerment in rehabilitative sports. In G.Doll-Temper, C. Dahms, B. Doll, and H. von Selzam (Eds.) *Adapted Physical Activity: An Interdisciplinary Approach, Proceedings of the 7th International Symposium*(pp. 43-51) Berlin: Springer-Verlag.

Hutzler, Y., and Bar-Eli, M. (1993). Psychological benefits of sports for disabled people: A review. *Scandinavian Journal of Medical Science and Sports*, 3, 217-228.

James, W. (1890). *The principles of psychology.* (Vol 1). New York: Holt.

Kleck, R., and De Jong, W. (1983). Physical disability, physical attractiveness, and social outcomes in children's small groups. *Rehabilitation Psychology*, 28(2), 79-91.

Kunnen, S. (1990). Development of perceived competence in physically handicapped and non-handicapped children. In L. Oppenheimer (Ed.) *The Self Concept: European Perspectives on its Development, Aspects, and Applications* (pp.143-158) Berlin: Springer-Verlag.

Larkin, D., and Parker, H. (1997, May). *Physical self-perceptions of adolescents with a history of developmental coordination disorder.* Poster presented at the NASPSPA Conference, Denver, USA.

Lowther, J. Lane, A. and Lane, H. (2004). Self-efficacy and psychological skills during the amputee soccer world cup. *The Online Journal of Sports Psychology*, **4** (2), 1-8. Retrieved 7/24/04 from http://www.athleticinsight.com/Vol4Iss2/SoccerSelfEfficacy. htm

Marsh, H. W. (1987). The Big-Fish-Little-Pond-Effect on academic self-concept. *Journal of Educational Psychology, 79,* 280-295.

Marsh, H. W. (1993). The multidimensional structure of physical fitness: Invariance over gender and age. *Research Quarterly for Exercise and Sport, 64,* 256-273.

Marsh, H. W. (1998). Age and gender effects in physical self-concepts of adolescent elite athletes and nonathletes: A multicohort-multioccasion design. *Journal of Sport and Exercise Psychology, 20,* 237-259.

Martin, J.J. (1996). Transitions out of competitive sport for athletes with disabilities. *Therapeutic Recreation Journal*, 30(2), 128-136.

Martin, J.J. (1999a). A personal development model of sport psychology for athletes with disabilities. *Journal of Applied Sport Psychology*, 11, 181-193.

Martin, J.J. (1999b). Predictors of social physique anxiety in adolescent swimmers with physical disabilities. *Adapted Physical Activity Quarterly*, 16, 75-85.

Martin, J. J. (1999c). Loss experiences in disability sport. *Journal of Loss and Interpersonal Loss, 4,* 225-230.

Martin, J.J. (2002). Training and performance self-efficacy, affect, and performance in wheelchair road racers. *The Sport Psychologist*, 16, 384-395.

Martin, J. J. (in press-a). Sport psychology consulting with athletes with disabilities. *Exercise and Sport Psychology Review*.

Martin, J. J. (in press-b). Psychosocial aspects of youth disability sport. *Adapted Physical Activity Quarterly*.

Martin, J. J. (in review). Parent's perceptions of their children with disabilities involvement in physical activity and sport. *Disability and Rehabilitation Journal*.

Martin, J.J., Eklund, R.C. and Adams Mushett, C. (1997a). Factor structure of the athletic identity measurement scale with athletes with disabilities. *Adapted Physical Activity Quarterly*, 14, 74-82.

Martin, J. J., Engels, H.J., Wirth, J.C., and Smith, K. (1997b). Predictors of social physique anxiety in elite female youth athletes. *Women in Sport and Physical Activity Journal, 6,* 29-48.

Martin, J. J., Kliber, A., Kulinna, P. H., and Fahlman, M. (in review). Social physique anxiety and body image cognitions in active college males. *Sex Roles*.

Martin, J. J., and McCaughtry, N. (2004). Coping and emotion in disability sport. In D. Lavallee, J. Thatcher, and M. V. Jones (Eds.) *Coping and emotion in sport* (pp.225- 238) New York: Nova Science Publishers, Inc.

Martin, J. J., and Smith, K. (2002). Friendship quality in youth disability sport: Perceptions of a best friend. *Adapted Physical Activity Quarterly, 19*, 472-482.

Martin-Ginis, K. A., Latimer, A. E., McKechnie, K., Ditor, D. S., McCartney, N., and Hicks, A. L. (2003). Using exercise to enhance subjective well-being among people with spinal cord injury: The mediating influences of stress and pain. *Rehabilitation Psychology*, 48, 157-164.

Mastro, J.V., Burton, A.W., Rosendahl, M., and Sherrill, C. (1996). Attitudes of elite athletes with impairments toward one another: A hierarchy of preference. *Adapted Physical Activity Quarterly*, 13, 197-210.

McNeil, J. M. (1997). Americans with Disabilities: 1994-95, U. S. Bureau of the Census. Current population reports. Washington, D. C: U. S. Government Printing Office.

Patrick, D.R. and Bignall, J.E. (1984). Creating the competent self: The case of a wheelchair runner. In J. Kotarba and A. Fontana (Eds.) *The Existential Self in Society* (pp. 207-221) Chicago: The University of Chicago Press.

Pensgaard, A.M. and Sorneson, M. (2002). Empowerment through the sport context: A model to guide research for individuals with disability. *Adapted Physical Activity Quarterly*, 19, 48-67.

Rees, T., Smith, B., Sparkes, A.C. (2003). The influence of social support on the lived experiences of spinal cord injured sportsmen. *The Sport Psychologist*, 17, 135-156.

Rimmer, J.H., Braddock, D. and Pitetti, K.H. (1996). Research on physical activity and disability: An emerging national priority. *Medicine and Science in Sports and Exercise*, 28(8), 1366-1372.

Rose, E. and Larkin, D. (2002). Perceived competence, discrepancy scores, and global self-worth. *Adapted Physical Activity Quarterly*, 19, 127-140.

Rose, B., Larkin, D. and Berger, B.G. (1997). Coordination and gender influences on the perceived competence of children. *Adapted Physical Activity Quarterly*, 14, 210-221.

Rumsey, N. (2002). Body image and congenital conditions with visible differences. In T. F. Cash and T. Pruzinsky (Eds.) *Body image: A handbook of theory, research and clinical practice* (pp.226-233). New York: The Guildford Press.

Rumsey, N., and Harcourt, D. (2004). Body image and disfigurement: issues and interventions. *Body Image*, 1, 83-97.

Shapiro, J. (1993). No pity: People with disabilities forging a new civil rights movement. New York, NY: Random House, Inc.

Sherrill, C., Hinson, M., Gench, B., Kennedy, S.O., and Low, L. (1990). Self-concepts of disabled youth athletes. *Perceptual and Motor Skills*, 70, 1093-1098.

Smyth, M. M., and Anderson, H. I. (2000). Coping with clumsiness in the school playground: Social and physical play in children with coordination impairments. *British Journal of Developmental Psychology*, 18, 389-413.

Sobsey, D. (1994) *Violence and Abuse in the Lives of People with Disabilities: The End of Silent Acceptance*. Baltimore, MD: Paul H. Brooks Publishing Co.

Taleporos, G., and McCabe, M. P. (2002). Body image and physical disability-personal perspectives. *Social Science and Medicine*, 54, 971-980.

Tasiemski, T., Kennedy, P., Gardner, B. P., and Blaikley, R. A. (2004). Athletic identity and sports participation in people with spinal cord injury. *Adapted Physical Activity Quarterly*, 21, 364-378.

Taub, D.E., Blinde, E.M., and Greer, K.R. (1999). Stigma management through participation in sport and physical activity: Experiences of male college students with physical disabilities. *Human Relations,* 52(11), 1469-1483.

Tiggemann, M. (2004). Body image across the adult life span: Stability and change. *Body Image*, 1, 29-41.

Valentini, N.C. and Rudisill, M.E. (2004). An inclusive mastery climate intervention and the motor skill development of children with and without disabilities. *Adapted Physical Activity Quarterly*, 21, 330-347.

Valliant, P. M., Bezzubyk, I., Daley, L., and Asu, M. E. (1985). Psychological impact of sport on disabled athletes. *Psychological Reports*, 56, 923-929.

Weiss, M. R., Smith, A. L., and Theeboom, M. (1996). "That's what friends are for:" Children and teenagers' perceptions of peer relationships in the sport domain. *Journal of Sport and Exercise Psychology*, 18, 347-379.

Yuen, H. K., and Hanson, C. (2002). Body image and exercise in people with and without acquired mobility disability. *Disability and Rehabilitation*, 24, 289-296.

Yuker, H.E. (1987). *Attitudes towards persons with disabilities*. New York, Springer Publishing.

In: The Concept of Self in Education, Family and Sports
Editor: Anne P. Prescott, pp. 91-114

ISBN 1-59454-988-5

Chapter 4

COMPARISON OF CHANGES IN PHYSICAL FITNESS, PHYSICAL SELF-CONCEPT, GLOBAL SELF-ESTEEM, DEPRESSION AND ANXIETY FOLLOWING TWO DIFFERENT PSYCHOMOTOR THERAPY PROGRAMS IN NON-PSYCHOTIC PSYCHIATRIC INPATIENTS

*Jan Knapen[a,b], Herman Van Coppenolle[a,b],
Joseph Peuskens[b,c], Guido Pieters[b] and Koen Knapen[d]*

[a] Department of Rehabilitation Sciences, Faculty of Kinesiology and Rehabilitation
Sciences, Katholieke Universiteit Leuven, Tervuursevest, Leuven, Belgium
[b] University Center Sint-Jozef, Leuvensesteenweg, Kortenberg, Belgium
[c] Faculty of Medicine, Katholieke Universiteit Leuven, Belgium
[d] SAS Institute NV, Tervuren, Belgium

ABSTRACT

Introduction

Generally, depressed and anxious psychiatric patients have a weak physical fitness and low physical self-concept and global self-esteem.

Objectives

The objectives of this randomised controlled trial were (1) to compare the changes in cardio-respiratory and muscular fitness, and the changes in physical self-concept after participation in one of two psychomotor therapy programs in a sample group of non-psychotic psychiatric patients; (2) to study the relationship between the changes in physical fitness and the changes in physical self-concept; (3) to investigate the relationship between changes in physical self-concept, global self-esteem, depression and anxiety.

Setting

Three treatment units of a university psychiatric hospital in Belgium.

Subjects

One hundred ninety-nine patients with severe symptoms of depression and/or anxiety, and/or personality disorders.

Interventions

A general program of psychomotor therapy, consisting of different forms of physical exercises and relaxation training, and a personalized psychomotor fitness program, consisting of aerobic and resistance training. These programs were followed three times a week for a period of 16 weeks.

Outcome Measures

Cardio-respiratory fitness and muscular strength were measured by means of an incrementally graded exercise test and the 1-repetition maximum method. Physical self-concept, global self-esteem, depression and anxiety, were evaluated using the Physical Self-Perception Profile, the Rosenberg Self-Esteem Inventory, the Beck Depression Inventory and the Trait Anxiety Inventory, respectively.

Conclusion

At the end the 16-week programs, both groups exhibited an improvement in muscular fitness, but only the psychomotor fitness group had improved in cardio-respiratory fitness. Both groups showed a more positive physical self-concept. The two programs seem to be equally effective in enhancing physical self-concept. The improvements in physical self-concept were not related to the progress in physical fitness. The gains in fitness did not play an essential role in the enhancement in physical self-concept. In both groups, the improvement in physical self-concept was correlated with increased global self-esteem and decreased depression and anxiety levels. This relationship supports the potential role of the physical self-concept in the recovery process of depressed and anxious psychiatric inpatients.

INTRODUCTION

Psychiatric disorders are associated with a high incidence of co-morbid somatic illness [1]. This is especially true concerning patients with depression. They run a higher relative risk of cardiovascular disease and osteoporosis than the general population [2]. In general, depressed and anxious psychiatric patients exhibit a less active life-style and have a reduced cardio-respiratory fitness in comparison with the general population [3,4]. Several symptoms of the depressive syndrome such as loss of energy, interest and motivation, and general fatigue are directly related to a more sedentary life-style, a decreased cardio-respiratory capacity and poor physical health. Patients with anxiety disorders tend to avoid aerobic exercise because they fear that physical effort may provoke physiological reactions such as tachycardia, hyperventilation, sweating and dyspnoea, which they associate with symptoms of panic attacks [5]. In these patients a vicious circle between avoidance of exercise, deterioration of cardio-respiratory capacity and a loss of control over functioning of the body may develop.

Low self-esteem is closely related to mental illness and diminished psychological well-being. It frequently accompanies psychiatric disorders such as clinical depression, anxiety disorders and personality disorders [6-8]. Most recently, Beck et al. [9], and Van de Vliet et al. [10] have indicated an inverse relationship between level of self-esteem and severity of depression and anxiety in sample groups of psychiatric outpatients and inpatients, respectively. The latter also detected that Flemish depressed psychiatric inpatients had significantly lower self-esteem and physical self-concept scores when compared with non-patients. A prospective study suggested that low self-esteem may play a causal role in major depressive disorder [11]. Improvement of self-esteem has therefore regularly been described as one of the main treatment aims for psychiatric patients. Self-esteem is defined as the 'way in which an individual is able to express a positive idea about him/herself'. This includes a personal evaluation, based on cognitive comparison, and is considered to be the evaluative component of the self-concept [12]. 'Self-concept' is described as a multidimensional system of constructs, which contains more specific perceptions in different areas. These constructs are therefore regarded as components or domains of the global self-concept. Roles in several life domains may contribute to the global self-concept and include perceptions of the self at work or in school (academic self-concept), in social relationships (social self-concept), in emotional relationships (emotional self-concept), and also perceptions about the body and physical abilities (physical self-concept). Physical self-concept is dictated by qualities related to physical acceptance and physical competence [13]. During the last 20 years, much value has been attached to body attractiveness, health-related physical fitness, motor skills and sporting performances as these features of the physical domain are consistently tied to the global self-concept. As a result, the physical self-concept may be important for the development and the enhancement of global self-concept especially for individuals with low self-concept such as psychiatric patients. Leith [14] indicated that clinical populations in particular (e.g. depressed adults, persons with mental retardation, rehabilitation patients) have problems with self-concept. He also reported that exercise programs lead to a significant improvement in self-concept in 10 out of 13 conducted investigations with these groups. The 'Exercise and Self-Esteem Model' [EXSEM], developed by Sonstroem and Morgan [15] and further by Fox [16] represents the theoretical framework of the hierarchical model of self-concept. This model proposes that physical self-perceptions can be improved through physical activity participation. Improvements in specific physical self-perceptions (e.g. stamina, muscular strength, attractiveness of body) may generalize to physical self-worth in general. In turn, physical self-worth is related to global self-esteem. Finally, increased global self-esteem can lead to a reduction of depression and anxiety.

There have been over 25 years of systematic investigation examining the relationship between exercise, especially aerobic forms and weight training, and negative affect. Recently, two meta-analyses were conducted in the area of exercise and depression. Craft and Landers [17] reported that regular exercise is as beneficial as individual or group psychotherapy and other behavioural interventions. Lawlor and Hopker [18] inferred from their meta-analysis of 14 randomized controlled trials, that physical activity is more effective than no treatment and as effective as traditional forms of treatment including cognitive therapy and antidepressant medication. Landers and Petruzzello [19] examined in a meta-analysis the results of 27 narrative reviews on the relationship among exercise and anxiety. These authors found that in 81% of the conducted studies, the researchers had concluded that physical activity has a moderate anxiety reducing effect.

Notwithstanding the strong inverse relationship between level of global self-esteem and severity of depression and anxiety, and the potential mediating roles of exercise participation, the physical self and the global self-esteem in the recovery process of clinically depressed and anxious individuals, there are only four studies containing randomized controlled clinical trials in the field of the EXSEM and negative affect [20-23]. Ossip-Klein et al. [20] investigated the effects of two exercise programs on self-esteem in a group of 40 clinically depressed women. The subjects, volunteers recruited by the media, were randomly assigned to three research conditions: running, weight lifting and a waiting list. After eight weeks, both exercise groups significantly improved on self-esteem and perceptions of energy and fitness in comparison with the no-exercise control group. There were no significant differences between the two exercise groups. However, in this study no analysis of the possible effects on depression was conducted. Bosscher [21] compared the effects of an eight-week running therapy program and a movement treatment-as-usual, consisting of a great variety of physical exercises and relaxation training, on depression, self-esteem and body-satisfaction in a group of 24 depressed psychiatric inpatients. The running therapy group showed a significant improvement in all variables, whereas the subjects in the movement treatment-as-usual did not improve significantly on any measure. No correlations between increase of scores on body-satisfaction, self-esteem and decrease on depression were calculated. Donaghy and Mutrie [22] explored the effects of exercise on the physical self-concept of 117 alcoholics in a randomised controlled trial. The experimental condition consisted of a three-week supervised exercise program in a hospital, followed by a twelve-week home-based program; the placebo control group received a stretching program for three weeks and was advised to continue exercising for the next twelve weeks. Measurements taken one and two months after entering the supervised program indicated that the exercise group demonstrated significant improvements in physical self-worth and perception of strength and physical condition. After 5 months there was no significant difference in physical self-perceptions between the groups, possibly attributable to a diminished adherence to the exercise regime. A randomised controlled trial by Blumenthal et al. [23] compared the effectiveness of a 16-week aerobic exercise program, a treatment with antidepressants, and the combination of the treatment with antidepressants and the same exercise program. The sample group consisted of 156 older people with major depression. The subjects, volunteers recruited by means of media advertisements, were healthy enough and sufficiently motivated to participate in vigorous aerobic exercises. The outcome measures, i.e. level of depression and global self-esteem improved significantly in all three groups, but the improvements were not significantly different across the groups. It is difficult to compare these randomized trials, because there are big differences between types of dependent variables, subject groups, age ranges, control groups, sample sizes, duration of exercise programs, etc. All the researchers concluded that exercise programs are associated with significant enhancements of physical self-concept and/or global self-esteem and/or reductions of depression. However, none of them investigated whether improvements in physical self-concept are accompanied with an increase in global self-esteem and a decrease in negative affect.

In psychiatric patients, a low physical self-concept and poor physical health and fitness, in interaction with other barriers to participation in exercise, such as psychosomatic complaints and hypochondria, lack of energy, and general fatigue may lead to a vicious cycle of loss of self-confidence, an increased avoidance of physical activity and decreased levels of physical health and fitness [4,24,25]. For that reason, the integration of exercise therapy into the comprehensive treatment programs for psychiatric patients is highly recommended. During the last three decades, both clinical experience of psychomotor therapists and research findings in the area of physical activity and mental and physical health have, in most psychiatric hospitals, led to an 'evidence-based' implementation of exercise and body awareness techniques as psychomotor therapy (PMT). The general objectives of PMT are the improvement of both psychological and physical well-being and the maintenance or enhancement of physical fitness in patients suffering from various mental illnesses such as psychotic, eating, personality, mood and anxiety disorders. In psychiatric hospitals in the Netherlands and Belgium, the most commonly PMT program consists of a great variety of sports and games, physical activities and relaxation training [21]. In this article the usual therapy program is called general program of psychomotor therapy (GPMT). Since 1992, psychomotor fitness training (PF) has been developed as a specialized form of PMT at the University Centre Sint-Jozef in Kortenberg (Belgium) [26,27]. The development of this type of PMT was based on (a) the scientific findings regarding therapeutic effects of aerobic exercise and weight training on the symptoms of depression and anxiety in sample groups of mainly non-clinical subjects [24] (b) on the evidence that well-balanced exercise programs improve physical health and fitness [28] (c) on patient's reports about psychological and physical benefits from personalized and gradual exercise programs [29].

The aim of the present randomised controlled parallel-group trial is threefold. First, to compare the effectiveness of two types of psychomotor therapy: the general program of psychomotor therapy (consisting of different forms of physical activities and relaxation training) and the psychomotor fitness training (consisting of resistance and aerobic exercise) on physical fitness and physical self-concept in a sample group of non-psychotic psychiatric patients. Second, to study the relationship between the changes in physical fitness and the changes in physical self-concept. The third objective was to investigate the relationship between changes in physical self-concept and changes in global self-esteem and negative affect.

METHODS

Subjects

Subjects were patients hospitalised in three cognitive-behavioural treatment units in a university psychiatric hospital in Belgium. Patients already had a long psychiatric history (M=7.78 years, SD=9.21). Most of them formerly did not respond successfully to the usual pharmacological and psychological interventions in primary and/or secondary care. Eight to 10 weeks before the beginning of the specialized treatment in one of the three wards, patients were placed in an observation unit and treated with psychotropic drugs and short-term supportive psychotherapeutic interventions. During this period of time, 98% patients received one or more psychotropic medications at adequate dosage (81% antidepressants, 37% hypnotics, sedatives or anxiolytics, 24% antipsychotics). Patients continued pharmacological treatment without changes throughout the trial. All patients who were admitted with severe depressive and/or anxious symptoms, and/or personality disorders over a period of 20 months, were asked to take part in the study. Patients suffering from psychosis were excluded. The somatic exclusion criteria were severe orthopaedic, neurological or cardiopulmonary diseases that absolutely would not allow regular training. The patients were diagnosed by psychiatrists according to the Diagnostic and Statistical Manual for Mental Disorders, Fourth Edition [6] for syndrome diagnosis (axis I) and diagnosis of personality disorders (axis II). Multiple diagnoses were possible on both axes and mostly psychiatrists made three or more diagnoses. The principal diagnoses, subdivided in clusters according to the recommendations in the DSM-IV, are represented in Table 1.

Table 1. Principal diagnoses (n = 199)

Mood disorders	63
Anxiety disorders	32
Adjustment disorders 13	13
Personality disorders	70
A. paranoid/schizoid/schizotypal	6
B. antisocial/histrionic/narcissistic/borderline	39
C. avoidant/dependent/obsessive-compulsive/personality disorder not other specified	25
Substance-related disorders	10
Other diagnoses	11

Measures

Cardio-respiratory fitness was evaluated by means of a submaximal incrementally Graded Exercise Test (GXT) on an electronically braked bicycle ergometer (Ergo 2000) according to the Franz test [30]. In this test protocol the work load is increased by 10 Watts every minute, starting with a work load that corresponds to the body weight. Since such a work load was not feasible for many of the patients, the first stage work load was reduced by 30 Watts for males participants and 50 Watts for the females. The end point heart rate was

80% of the estimated maximal heart rate reserve. The physical work capacity at 60% and 80% of the estimated maximal heart rate reserve (PWC 60% MHRR and PWC 80% MHRR) were retained as measures of cardio-respiratory fitness. Previous research showed that the Franz test has a good reliability in a sample group of psychiatric inpatients (r ranged from 0.74 to 0.90) [31].

Maximum dynamic muscular strength was measured by the one-repetition maximum method (1-RM) [32]. Dynamic muscular endurance was assessed using a weight that was 70% of the 1-RM value. The outcome was the number of repetitions that the subject completed at a set cadence of 30 repetitions per minute. The subjects went to four subsequent measurements of 1-RM, as well as muscular endurance tests on a variable-resistance machine (bench press, leg press, arm curl and latissimus pull down).

Abdominal muscle endurance was measured using the three-stage test of the Eurofit test battery for adults [33] and the conventional maximal sit-up test, endorsed by the Eurofit Coordinating Group [34]. The first test is carried out in three sequential levels, the aim being to perform five sit-ups on each level. If the subject managed 15 sit-ups, he/she carried out the conventional maximal sit-up test during 30 sec. The result of this examination was the sum of the correctly performed sit-ups in both tests.

Habitual physical activity was assessed using the Baecke questionnaire [35]. Philippaerts and Lefevre [36] showed the Baecke questionnaire to be a reliable and valid instrument in the assessment of habitual physical activity in a Belgian sample group

Physical self-concept was assessed using the Dutch version of the Physical Self-Perception Profile [10]. This questionnaire consists of the domain scale of physical self-worth (six items), and three subdomain scales, namely perception of sports competence and physical condition (12 items), perceived physical strength (six items), and perceived attractive body (six items). Each item is scored on a scale from 1 to 4, with higher scores indicating more positive self-perceptions. The range of possible total scores is 0-24, for the scale sports competence and physical condition: 0-48. Van de Vliet et al. demonstrated an adequate reliability and validity of The Dutch version of the Physical Self-Perception Profile in a sample group of Flemish psychiatric inpatients [10].

The Rosenberg Self-Esteem Scale RSES [37] was used to evaluate *global self-esteem*. This self-rating scale is composed of 10 items. Higher total scores indicate higher self-esteem (range: 10-40). The Dutch version of the RSES is regarded as one of the better measures of global self-esteem [37].

The severity of depression was measured using the Dutch translation of the Beck Depression Inventory (BDI) [38]. The range of possible total scores is 0 to 63; with higher scores indicating greater depression. The Dutch translation of the BDI has shown to be a valid and reliable instrument for the measurement the seriousness of depression [38].

Anxiety disposition was assessed by means of the Dutch version of the Trait Anxiety subscale [TAI] of the State-Trait Anxiety Inventory [STAI] [39]. The range of possible total scores is 20-80, higher score indicate higher levels of anxiety. The TAI represents one of the most reliable and valid instruments for assessing trait anxiety in psychiatric settings, and has been validated for use in Dutch by Hermans [39].

Procedure

A randomised controlled trial with repeated measures was developed where patients received either the psychomotor fitness training or the general program of psychomotor therapy. Except for the allocation to one of them all patients followed identical cognitive behavioural therapy programs. During the first week of admission in three treatment units, the head nurses allocated patients to the psychomotor fitness training or the general program of psychomotor therapy, using a stratified randomisation with respect to treatment unit, gender and motivation towards exercises and physical activities. Each treatment unit had 6 randomisation lists, 3 for males and three females. These 3 randomisation schemes per gender, corresponded with three categories of the initial motivation. Initial motivation was assessed by means of a visual analogue scale, ranging from 0 (not at all motivated) to 10 (highly motivated). The 18 randomisation schemes, corresponding to all possible strata of treatment unit, gender and motivation level (3, 2 and 3 levels respectively, $3*2*3 = 18$), were computer-generated by means of the SAS Ranuni random number generator [40].

Eleven physical fitness outcomes and physical self-concept were measured three times at fixed time intervals: at week zero (Time 1), at week eight (Time 2) and at week sixteen (Time 3). Patients performed all physical examinations at the three points in time at the same hour of day in standardized conditions. A couple of days before completing the physical tests, patients filled out the questionnaires. The level of habitual physical activity prior to admission was measured at baseline only [35].

The study procedures were approved by the Ethical Committee of the Faculty of Medicine of the Katholieke Universiteit Leuven in accordance with the principles of the Declaration of Helsinki of 1975, and all participants gave the research coordinators their informed consent.

Interventions

The general program of psychomotor therapy was the usual exercise program in psychiatric hospitals in Belgium and the Netherlands that includes a great variety of sports and games, physical activities and relaxation training [21]. This 16-week program consisted of different forms of physical exercises, two times a week during 45 minutes, and progressive relaxation training according to Jacobson, one time a week during 45 minutes. In this exercise program, the therapists offered a great variety of physical activities, such as floor gymnastics, badminton, body awareness techniques and specially adapted versions of sports and games (e.g. netball, soccer, indoor hockey, soft-tennis, ect.). Following the recommendations for enhancing physical self-concept [14-16], the psychomotor therapists adapted sports and games in such a way that the competitive aspects were minimized and that the co-operative elements of these activities were emphasized. Most often, the activity was chosen in agreement with the participants. The exercise intensity varied from low to moderate depending on the type of activity. For the relaxation training, Jacobson's progressive relaxation was selected, because this technique is regarded as a gold standard in relaxation methods [41]. The objectives of the relaxation training were improving body awareness and teaching an effective method for coping with tension.

Since 1992, psychomotor fitness training has been developed as a specialized form of psychomotor therapy at the University Centre Sint-Jozef in Kortenberg (Belgium) [26]. The development of this type of psychomotor therapy was based upon: the scientific findings regarding therapeutic effects of aerobic and resistance training on the symptoms of depression and anxiety [17,18]; and the evidence that balanced exercise programs, including aerobic exercise, resistance exercise, and flexibility exercise enhance physical health and fitness [28]. The length of the program (16 weeks), the workout frequency (three times a week) and the duration of each session (45 minutes) were the same as in the general program of psychomotor therapy. In this program patients participated in endurance, muscular strength and flexibility. Depending on the outcome of the initial fitness assessments and patient's earlier experiences with physical exercises, the psychomotor therapists developed a gradual exercise program by applying the general recommendations of the American College of Sports Medicine [28]. The moderate intensity, measured by heart rate monitors, ranged from 40% to 60% of the estimated maximal heart rate reserve. Perceived exertion, rated by the Borg Category Ratio 10 Scale, was used as an adjunct for the intensity prescription at each exercise apparatus. The rate of perceived exertion, especially in clinical groups, is a valuable aid in teaching participants to monitor exercise tolerance taking account of their own level of fatigue, shortness of breath and muscular sensations [4]. The resistance training constituted an all-rounded program exercising major muscle groups. Muscular strength and endurance were developed by the progressive overload principle according to which repetitions and weight load are gradually increased. The program was monitored using exercise cards and the patients were informed regularly about their progress by the psychomotor therapists. At all times, the therapists avoided between-patient comparisons.

In both programs, participants and therapist discussed their experiences with the exercises and the relaxation training during the last 5 minutes of each session. All discussions were focused on personal experiences with the activities (e.g. social interactions, fair-play, emotions, tension reduction, sense of mastery, enjoyment and satisfaction) and on body awareness (e.g. breathing, muscle tone and relaxation, degree of effort, body-acceptance). The two therapeutic interventions were based on personal responsibility, social reinforcement, self-evaluation, constructive feedback by therapist, hedonic properties of exercise and process internalization [13,42]. The main differences between the treatment conditions were the following: in the structured psychomotor fitness training, the moderate exercise intensity was adapted exactly to the individual physical abilities and exercise tolerance. This exercise program focused more on perceived fitness gains, success achievement, mastery experiences and sense of control over the body and it's functioning. In the less structured general psychomotor therapy, on the other hand, the greater variety of activities was based on the personal preference of each participant (self-determination). This program concentrated more on the sense of belonging and significance through social interaction with peers, and had a low to moderate exercise intensity.

Both programs were presented as equally acceptable and attractive. The subjects were not informed about the investigator's hypotheses. Therefore, the interventions were offered as 'physical health-related programs' and not as 'programs for improving psychological well-being'. In both programs, patients exercised in groups with an equal number of participants (8-10), under supervision of 4 qualified psychomotor therapists, assisted by eight students of the postgraduate specialization course in psychomotor therapy. During each session, one psychomotor therapist and, for the most part, one student were present. The psychomotor therapists and the students met the two groups of each treatment unit on the same days and at the same time, in order to control for the influence of daily mood fluctuations. The therapists and students were rotated across the groups to minimize the possible effects of personal supportive contact with a particular therapist or student.

Statistical Analysis

The sample size estimation was based on an 80% desired power to discern a 10% difference in physical fitness outcome between the two groups at alpha-significance level 0.05 [43]. Based on our previous research on fitness training in a group of psychiatric patients, the sample size calculation resulted in two groups, each with 48 participants [27].

The nine measurements of muscular fitness were aggregated into one overall muscular fitness factor by summing the nine respective z-scores (standardized scores).

Outcomes variables were assessed in both groups using repeated measures ANOVAs corrected for multiple testing with Bonferroni-Holm p-value adjustments [44].

The effect sizes (ES) were calculated as the difference between the mean score after and before the exercise programs, divided by the standard deviation of the intra-individual difference scores. An ES of 0.20 to 0.50 is considered to be a small effect, 0.50 to 0.80 medium, and a value of more than 0.80 large [45].

In order to investigate the responsiveness of each subject who completed the 16-week study, the reliable change index (RC) of all these patients was calculated by means of the formula of Christensen and Mendoza [46].

The relationship between changes in the variables was examined using Pearson product-moment correlation coefficients.

The significance level in all of the tests was set at 0.05 level (two-tailed).

RESULTS

Recruitment and Drop-Out

In the course of the research project, 237 patients (84 males and 153 females) were admitted into the three treatment units. Twenty-nine patients did not meet the inclusion criteria or were excluded according to the exclusion criteria. Three individuals refused to take part in the study; six (2.93%) dropped out the after randomisation but before intervention was initiated due to dissatisfaction with their program assignments. Substantial numbers of patients were discharged prior to Time 2 (T2) at week eight or Time 3 (T3) at week sixteen (see flow diagram). The reasons for discharge of these drop-outs were unrelated to the psychomotor therapy programs. The drop-out rates did not vary across the two programs (drop-out before T2: $\chi^2=1.23$, p=0.27; drop-out before T3: $\chi^2=0.001$, p=0.97).

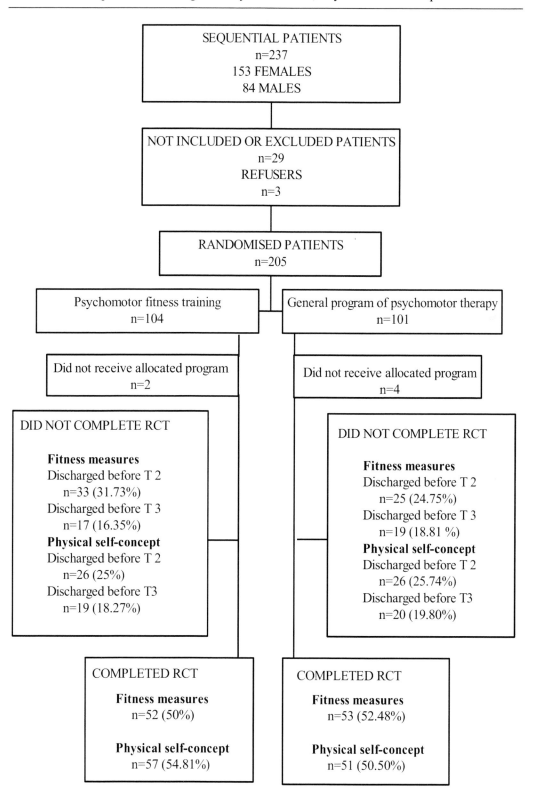

Figure 1. Flow diagram of the trial

Sample Characteristics

The mean age of the PF subjects (M=35.54 years, SD=10.76) was significantly higher than that of the GPMT subjects (M=32.44 years, SD=10.75) (p=0.04). Males showed a significantly higher initial motivation (M=6.88, SD=2.44) in comparison with females (M=6.16, SD=2.44) (p=0.045). However, because gender stratification was performed, there was no difference between the groups of both conditions. Study drop-outs did not significantly differ from patients who remained in the study until Time 2 or Time 3 on baseline measures of motivation, physical self-perceptions, depression, global self-esteem and age; drop-outs did only demonstrate lower TAI scores at baseline (p=0.02).

Adherence to Treatment

All patients, except the six who dropped out immediately after randomisation, remained in the study until their discharge. The attendance of both groups was similar, with patients in the psychomotor fitness training attending 85.42% of the scheduled sessions and patients in the general psychomotor therapy attending 84.33%. In those cases where a participant's program had been interrupted, the patient remained a few weeks longer in the study until all 48 sessions had been completed.

Changes in Cardio-Respiratory Fitness

The within-group comparison for the PF group revealed that the PWC 60% MHRR and the PWC 80% MHRR had significantly increased at Time 2 and Time 3 (F- and p-values ranged from $F1,117=10.79$, $p<0.01$ to $F1,117=23.62$, $p<0.0001$). On the other hand, the GPMT group demonstrated no significant improvements in the PWC outcomes (F- and p-values ranged from $F1,117=0.01$, $p=0.91$ to $F1,117=2.87$, $p=0.01$). The between-group comparison of training effects after 16 weeks revealed a significant difference in the PWC 60% MHRR ($F1,117=8.84$, $p=0.01$), but no significant difference in the PWC 80% MHRR ($F1.51=3.06$, $p=0.09$). The changes in PWC 60% MHRR and PWC 80% MHRR after 16 weeks in the PF represented effect sizes of 0.87 and 1.43, representing large improvements; those in the GPMT effect sizes of 0.01 and 0.20, representing no and small effects. Patients in the PF group achieved an average gain of 13.59% in the PWC 60% MHRR and 14.53% in the PWC 80% MHRR; patients of the GPMT group showed no or only minimal enhancements in both PWC measures (0.31% and 2.28%). In the PF condition 77.78% and 84% of patients had a positive reliable change index, and 6.67% and 4% a negative reliable change index; in the GPMT condition 45.45% and 50% of patients had a positive reliable, and 34.09% and 30% a negative reliable change index. There were no significant differences in response during the initial eight-week period between those patients who were discharged after the second evaluation and those who completed the whole 16-week study.

Changes in Muscular Fitness

The changes in muscular fitness were calculated as the difference between the sums of the nine z-scores of the nine muscular fitness measurements at the three points in time. The within-group differences revealed that both groups demonstrated significant improvement in the overall muscular fitness factor during the first eight-week period (PF: $F_{1.120}=147.41$, $p<0.0001$; GPMT: $F_{1.120}=25.20$, $p<0.0001$). During the second eight-week period both groups made further progress (PF: $F_{1.120}=124.76$, $p<0.0001$; GPMT: $F_{1.120}=35.07$, $p<0.0001$). The between-group comparison of training effects after eight and 16 weeks showed that the PF group had made significantly more progress than the GPMT (at T2: $F_{1.120}=27.62$, $p<0.0001$; at T3: $F_{1.120}=13.83$, $p=0.0003$).

Changes in Physical Self-Perceptions

After 8 weeks, both groups showed significantly higher scores on the PSPP-scales (F- and p-values ranged from $F_{1.195}=11.32$, $p=0.0037$ to $F_{1.195}=34.73$, $p<0.0001$), except the PF group on the scale attractive body and the GPMT group on the scales strength and physical self-worth. After 16 weeks, the within-group comparison revealed that both groups displayed significant increases on all PSPP-scales (F- and p-values ranged from $F_{1.195}=9.13$, $p=0.0114$ to $F_{1.195}=32.67$, $p<0.0001$). The between-group comparison of differences between means after 8 and after 16 weeks was not significant. The changes after 16 weeks in the PF condition demonstrated effect sizes varying from 0.50 to 0.73, representing moderate enhancements; in the GPMT condition effect sizes varied from 0.34 to 0.64, considered as small to moderate improvements. The percentages of patients in both groups who showed a positive reliable change index after 16 weeks were comparable: in the PF condition the percentages varied from 60% to 74%, while in the GPMT the range was 61% to 69%. There were no significant differences in response over the period of the first 8 weeks between the patients who were discharged after the second evaluation and those who completed the 16-week programs. We found no significant therapy-by-time interaction effects.

Relationship between Changes in Physical Fitness and Changes in Physical Self-Concept

For the second purpose, only the patients who completed the 16-week programs were included. Cardio-respiratory and muscular fitness were related to their respective subdomains of physical self-concept i.e., perception of sports competence and physical condition, and perceived physical strength, respectively. The changes in cardio-respiratory fitness were expressed as percentages of changes in the physical work capacity at 60% the estimated maximal heart rate reserve. The changes in muscular fitness were the differences between the sums of the nine z-scores (overall muscular fitness factor). There were no statistically significant correlations found in the PF group nor in the GPMT (cardio-respiratory fitness, in PF: r=-0.17, p= 0.28; in GPMT: r=0.31, p=0.06; muscular fitness, in PF: r =0.15, p=0.37; in GPMT: r=-0.12, p=0.50).

Changes in Additional Variables: Global Self-Esteem, Depression and Anxiety

The within-group differences revealed that both groups demonstrated significant improvement on RSES, BDI and TAI scores during the period of the first 8 weeks (F- and p-values ranged from $F_{1,192}=6.91$, p=0.0278 to $F_{1,195}=31.39$, p<0.0001). During the second 8 weeks both groups made further progress on these instruments (F- and p-values ranged form $F_{1,145}=13.82$, p=0.0009 to $F_{1,195}=31.66$, p<0.0001). The between-group comparison of differences between means was not significant either at 8 weeks or 16 weeks follow-up. The effect sizes of progress after 16 weeks in the PF condition were considered to be moderate (0.60 to 0.72), and in the GPMT condition as small to moderate effects (0.46 to 0.61). Substantial and comparable percentages of patients of both groups showed a positive reliable change on RSES (PF 54%, GPMT 63%), BDI (PF 65%, GPMT 71%) and TAI (PF 63%, GMPT 60%). There were no significant differences in response over the period of the first 8 weeks between the patients who dropped out after the second evaluation due to discharge and those who completed the 16-week study. We found no significant therapy-by-time interaction effects.

Relationship between Changes in Physical Self-Worth, Global Self-Esteem, Depression and Anxiety

For the third objective, the patients who completed the 16-week programs were used (n=108). For the relationship between the changes in physical self-worth and the changes in depression, the patients with at least a mild to moderate depression level (BDI>15) were included (n=94). In both groups, all correlation coefficients were significant in the expected direction (r ranged from 0.45 to 0.81, p<0.01).

DISCUSSION

Main Findings

The changes in physical fitness, physical self-concept, global self-esteem, depression and anxiety after two psychomotor therapy programs were compared in non-psychotic psychiatric inpatients. A representative sample group of 199 subjects was recruited. All patients were hospitalised within one of three specialized treatment units at the University Centre Sint-Jozef at Kortenberg. It should be stressed that subjects were recruited in tertiary care. In contrast with many other investigations in the field of exercise and psychological well-being using non-clinical volunteers [18], patients were not 'selected' and all of them were sequentially referred to the study. Patients were not volunteers for exercise, considering that they initially sought treatment to discuss psychological ailments and to ask for assistance with their social problems, usually expecting a psychopharmacological and psychotherapeutic treatment. At onset of treatment, most psychiatric patients tended to be passive receivers. Psychomotor therapy, which appeals to the patient's own active participation and responsibility, does initially not meet their immediate needs [25]. It is therefore reasonable to assume that the compliance with exercise in psychiatric patients would be worse than in the general population. Many psychiatric patients demonstrate multiple risk factors for non-compliance in exercise programs, such as learned helplessness, hypochondria, a loss of energy and interest, smoking, general fatigue, a negative physical self-concept, a low intrinsic motivation and a poor physical health and fitness [4,18,24,25]. Despite these psychological and physical barriers to participate in exercise, there was a good adherence to both interventions. This may be attributable to the motivational strategies and the supportive and task-oriented climate put into place by the psychomotor therapists [47]. Except for the 6 individuals who dropped out after randomization due to dissatisfaction with their program assignment, no drop-out of patients with a low initial motivation occurred.

The PF group showed significant improvements in cardio-respiratory fitness, whereas the GPMT group did not. The exercise stimuli in the GPMT were not sufficient to increase aerobic fitness. In this exercise intervention, in which the participants trained less specific, at a lower frequency of two times a week (and one session relaxation training), the intensity was not individualized and was, in general, lower when compared with the PF program. Thus, the GPMT group did not show any increase in physical work capacity outcomes. In this condition, which was more centred on group activities, it was extremely difficult for the psychomotor therapists to adapt the exercise stimuli to the heterogeneous fitness levels of the participants (eight to ten) in each group. On the other hand, in the PF the moderate exercise intensity could be adapted exactly to the individual physical abilities, side effects of psychotropic medication, exercise tolerance and perceived exertion of the particular participant. The average increase in physical work capacity outcomes (13,59% and 14.53%) in the PF group was remarkable higher than those reported in the meta-analysis of Craft and Landers [17]. The latter indicated that only five of the 30 studies, claiming to use aerobic programs, resulted in cardio-respiratory fitness gains over of 5%. The higher response in the present study could be attributed to certain characteristics of the sample group (e.g. very low fitness levels) and to the specific characteristics of the exercise program (i.e., length, quantity and quality of exercise stimuli, well-monitored exercise schedules, social support and motivational strategies). Training effects are also dependent on the individual's genetic constitution as well as current training status [48]. Therefore, improvements should be interpreted with respect to the characteristics of the exercise programs (i.e., the quantity, quality and specificity of exercise stimuli), the genetic variation and the current training status. Since, in our study there was no significant baseline difference in current training status between both groups (Baecke $F_{3,130}$=1.67, p=0.20), the increase in cardio-respiratory fitness in the PF condition is attributed to a program-specific effect and/or random differences in genetic constitution.

After 8 and 16 weeks, both groups made progress in muscular fitness. The improvements were greater in the specific fitness training compared with the less specific general psychomotor therapy. Thus, in general, the exercise stimuli of the activities in the GPMT condition were sufficient for increasing muscular fitness. On the other hand, the GPMT participants did not, on average, exhibit any increase in cardio-respiratory fitness. Patients suffering from anxiety, in particular, avoid taking part in any aerobic activities and, to a lesser extent, strength-oriented activities. The reason for this is that aerobic effort provokes more anxious aversive stimuli (e.g. increase in heart rate and in respiratory frequency, sweating and other indices of sympathetic arousal) than resistance exercises. A number of GPMT patients with somatic-related anxiety avoided intensive aerobic efforts (e.g. running) during more stamina-oriented sports and games. In the individualized graded PF program, aerobic training represents on a cognitive-behavioural approach a form of exposure technique, in which the anxious patient on a well-considered gradual way is confronted with these feared internal stimuli [5].

Both programs were associated with significant improvements in the different domains of physical self-concept (ES varying from 0.34 to 0.73). This finding suggests that PMT programs help patients to develop a more positive attitude towards their physical self. However, without a no-exercise control group we cannot be certain that either of these programs caused these changes (see limitations of the study described below). The enhancements in the two groups were of similar magnitude, and the differences between the groups were not significant. This finding suggests that PMT programs help patients to develop a more positive attitude towards their physical self. The magnitude of the improvement in the two groups was similar, and the differences between the groups were not significant. These findings are in accordance with the hypothesis of Fox [8,13], who posits that several psychosocial mechanisms (see below) all have an influence upon the improvement in physical self-concept and that due to a complex interaction among these mechanisms identification of the specific role of different mechanisms is difficult. The majority of patients in both groups exhibited statistically reliable improvements on the four scales of the Dutch version of the Physical Self-Perception Profile (percentages varied from 60% to 74%). It is plausible that not all patients experienced positive effects on physical self-concept. One possible explanation for this is that a large number of patients suffered from recurrent depressive and/or anxious episodes, often associated with an underlying complex personality disorder. In most cases, these patients had failed to recover in treatment in primary and/or secondary care. They were characterized by persistent feelings of incompetence and failure, overestimation, overgeneralization and internal attributions with regard to negative events. Many of them exhibited low self-acceptance or high self-criticism and were therefore unable to reach their unrealistic expectations. A second explanation for not experiencing progress in physical self-concept is related to the barriers to exercise participation that psychiatric patients experience [4,24,25].

No statistically significant correlations were found between changes in physical fitness and changes in subdomains of physical self-concept. This indicates that the gain in fitness itself did not play an essential role in the improvement in physical self-concept. Our finding is similar to that of the meta-analytic review of Landers and Arent [49]. They suggested that it is the participant's own perception of improvement in physical fitness rather than the objective change itself is responsible for the improvement in the individual's physical self-worth. The lack of specific effect associated with increase in physical fitness indicates that psychological mechanisms are more important. Fox [13] as well as Sonstroem [42] pointed out that several mechanisms operate in the enhancement in physical self-concept. The mainly are: perceived improvement in fitness, enhanced body image, a sense of control over the body, feelings somatic well-being, social experiences and reinforcement, goal achievement, success experiences, self-evaluation, process internalisation and self-determination.

Both groups significantly increased in global self-esteem and decreased in severity of depression and anxiety (ES varying from 0.46 to 0.72). Substantial percentages (varying from 54% to 71%) of patients showed positive reliable changes on these variables. The improvements in physical self-worth went along with an increase in global self-esteem and a decline in depression and anxiety levels. This finding corroborates the Exercise and Self-Esteem Model [15,16], which is based on the self-efficacy theory of Bandura [50]. This hierarchical model proposes that improvements in physical self-concept lead to enhancements in global self-esteem. In turn, increased global self-esteem can lead to a reduction of depression and anxiety. This means that the relationship between changes in primary and secondary outcomes provide some interesting information regarding the potential role of the physical self in the recovery process of depressed and/or anxious psychiatric inpatients. However, it remains possible that changes in secondary outcomes improve subject's physical self-concept.

Strengths of the Study

In his chapter regarding methodological considerations in the research area of physical activity and mental health, Morgan indicated:

"It is imperative that future inquiry in this area be approached with rigorous research designs, appropriate and powerful statistical models, and state-of-the-art psychometric methods" (Morgan, 1997, p. 3) [51].

However, Craft and Landers [17] found, in a meta-analysis on the effects of exercise on clinical depression, smaller effect sizes for randomised controlled studies in comparison with non-random pre-experimental and quasi-experimental investigations. Randomised controlled trials, which are considered to be the gold standard and the most rigorous research design, could be problematic if there are patients who are not allocated to their preferred form of physical exercise [24,25]. This is due to the fact that improvement in psychological well-being occurs mainly as a response to participation in specific exercise, in which the participant is highly interested and in which he or she experiences a certain degree of autonomy [13,42]. It is possible that the responses of particular patients in our randomised controlled trial were low or negative due to the fact that those subjects had not been allocated to their preferred exercise programs. Therefore, it is quite possible that our outcomes in physical self-concept and physical fitness underestimate the likely effectiveness of PMT in daily practice.

It is well established in PMT for psychiatric patients that psychological and physical outcomes following PMT programs are governed to a large degree by individual differences [52]. It. Individuals differ widely on psychological variables such as physical self-concept, anxiety, depression, extroversion, intrinsic motivation, coping strategies and internal locus of control. In addition, individuals differ on a wide variety of physical variables such as exercise experience, current training status, muscle fibre types, lactate threshold, exercise tolerance, percent body fat etc. All these variables are related to response in psychological well-being and physical fitness, respectively. In the present work, we have made quite some effort to take into account the influence of these 'confounding variables'. A randomisation procedure with stratification has been employed with the intention of balancing both groups for the variables motivation towards PMT, gender and treatment unit. Clinical experience indicates that the individual differences in response to PMT are great. For some patients, PMT seems to be highly beneficial, while in others the psychological and/or physical benefits are minimal. We have identified the responders and non-responders by calculating the reliable change index for each patient who completed the 16-week study [46].

In order to check whether both programs were perceived by patients as equally interesting (cf. presentation of the two programs before randomisation), the changes in motivation after 16 weeks were compared. The repeated measures ANOVA revealed that the initial motivation significantly increased across the groups ($F_{2,136}$=4.52, p=0.01). However, the therapy-by-time interaction effect was not significant.

Limitations of the Study

The subjects in this study were inpatients who were treated within multi-disciplinary treatment programs. Other therapy forms and their interactive effects with the psychomotor therapy programs could have influenced the response in all outcome variables. All patients were on a stable medication regimen at an adequate dosage for at least 8 to 10 weeks prior to inclusion, and the medication scheme was not altered during the study. 81% of patients were treated with antidepressants. These drugs have been shown to have an onset of action of 4 to 6 weeks [53,54]. Onset of action of hypnotics, sedatives, anxiolytics and anti-psychotics that were prescribed is even shorter [53]. This makes it unlikely that medication accounts for important effects on outcome variables. A second limitation was the absence of a no-exercise control group to control for placebo effects and potential spontaneous recovery. After much consideration of this issue during the initial planning of the study, by the ethical committee, we decided to assign patients only to two active exercise groups. It was deemed unethical to create a no-exercise control group, for the reason that psychomotor therapy in multi-disciplinary treatment programs is the only therapy that focuses on physical fitness and physical self-concept. Moreover, several studies have already addressed this topic, showing that exercise programs to be associated with reductions of depression and anxiety and enhancements of physical self-concept [8,13,17-19].

Another limitation is that increased scores in physical self-concept may be influenced by behavioural artefacts, such as demand characteristics and positive expectancies that people associate with exercise [49,55]. Regarding demand characteristics, Morgan [51] pointed out that non-volunteers may be less sensitive to this behavioural artefact than volunteers. Positive expectancies with respect to exercise are probably highly related to a high motivation to take part in PMT. In order to control for the influence of motivation before program onset, the level of motivation was included as a covariate in analysing the response profile of physical self-worth. The analysis of co-variance did not demonstrate that initial motivation had played a significant role in the response profile of physical self-worth (therapy*motivation $F_{1,190}$=2.14, p=0.15). In other words, the co-variance analysis revealed that patients improved in physical self-worth even with initial motivation statistically controlled.

Evidence-Based Guidelines for Psychomotor Therapy and Advice for Long-Term Prophylactic Effects

It is conceivable to suppose that the results could be generalized to similar psychomotor therapy settings in Belgium. The following features of the study might guarantee a certain value of generalization:

- An unselected sample group of 199 patients of both sexes was recruited in three specialized treatment units of a large psychiatric hospital over a period of 20 months.
- The complexity of psychiatric problematic of most patients seems to be representative of those of non-psychotic patients who are treated in other psychiatric hospitals.
- The low drop-out rate directly related to the study.
- The rotation of psychomotor therapists across both groups.

Physical Fitness
- In order to improve general muscular fitness, both programs are suitable when followed for a period of at least eight weeks at a frequency of three times a week.
- In order to increase cardio-respiratory fitness a gradual aerobic training program is necessary over a period of at least 8 weeks.
- Thus, to improve both muscular and cardio-respiratory fitness a balanced personalized training program, which includes aerobic and resistance training, is required during a period of at least eight weeks. In designing well-considered training schedules based on fitness assessments, psychomotor therapists should take into account emotional, cognitive and physiological components of mental illness [4]. The moderate exercise stimulus should be adapted to the individual physical abilities, training status, patient's own expectation and goals, side effects of psychotropic medication, exercise tolerance and perceived exertion of the particular participant. Obviously, the minimal intensity threshold to improve cardio-respiratory fitness in very active individuals is significantly higher than that in low active people [28]. Furthermore the preferred intensity of non-experienced exercisers may be lower than that of experienced exercisers [25]. Therefore, rigid prescriptions for all individuals to exercise at the same relative intensity (e.g., 50% of maximal heart rate reserve) might be insufficient and perceived as aversive.
- Clinical experience of psychomotor therapists suggests that for patients with somatic-related anxiety, who tend to avoid aerobic efforts, the PF program is to be preferred rather than the GPMT. The graded PF program appears to be more suitable for the implementation of cognitive behavioural techniques, in which the patient is gradually confronted with feared physical stimuli.

Physical Self-Concept
- In order to enhance physical self-concept both programs are recommended over a period of at least 16 weeks.
- The study on the association between changes in physical fitness and changes in physical self-concept shows that increases in physical fitness are not necessary for an improvement in physical self-concept. Thus, patients and therapists are at liberty to

choose those types of physical activity in which the individual is interested, and do not need to focus on training effects. On the other hand, strategies for improving physical self-concept seem to be essential.

For specific information on strategies for enhancing physical self-concept and exercise adherence, the reader is referred to Dishman [56], Fox [8,13,16], Sonstroem [42] and Leith [14]. The latter pointed out that various behaviour-change strategies, such as contracting, behavioural contingencies, self-recording, cost-benefits analysis, stimulus cuing, goal setting, relapse-prevention training and social reinforcement have been found to be effective for helping people adhere to physical exercise. These strategies could be incorporated in PMT to enhance both the patients' motivation and their long-term adherence to exercise, taking into account emotional, cognitive and physiological components of mental illness.

In addition, some criteria for long-term success in mental health treatment should be implemented in psychomotor therapy [25]. On the whole, these would consist of:

- The rationale providing structure that patients believe they can control their own behaviour, well-being, fitness and health (internal locus of control).
- Teaching of problem-solving skills to the patient.
- Self-management: an emphasis on independent use of these skills; a central concept in self-management is the self-efficacy-confidence to carry out a behaviour necessary to reach a desired goal.
- The attribution of improved psychological and physical well-being to the patient's personal mastery skills (positive internal attributions).

These components have been applied in the present PMT programs by the psychomotor therapists in an optimal way.

Finally, there is much evidence that relapse prevention in mental care should include the follow-up and stimulation of exercise. For this purpose, information is required on the benefits of exercise in the treatment of people with mental illness for general practitioners and psychiatrists. Interesting information on the psychiatrist's role and the therapist-patient collaborative process in improving exercise compliance can be found in Pollock [57].

Future Research

The relationship between the improvement in physical self-worth and the increase in global self-esteem and the decline in negative affect suggests that changes in the physical self-concept might lead to enhancement in mental health. Psychiatric illnesses, especially mood disorders, have a high risk of relapse. The value of exercise training in relapse prevention is highly dependent on the degree to which the patients maintain physical activity after termination of supervised PMT programs. We plan a follow-up study to determine and to compare the exercise adherence and the long-term protective effects in both groups after discharge.

REFERENCES

[1] Osborn DP. The poor physical health of people with mental illness. *West J Med* 2001;175:329-32.

[2] Dinan TG. The physical consequences of depressive illness. Include coronary artery disease and reduced bone mineral density. *BMJ* 1999;318:826.

[3] Martinsen EW, Strand J, Paulsson G. Physical fitness level in patients with anxiety and depressive disorders. *Int J Sport Med* 1989;10:58-61.

[4] Meyer T, Broocks A. Therapeutic impact of exercise on psychiatric diseases: Guidelines for exercise testing and prescription. *Sports Med* 2000;30:269-79.

[5] Broocks A, Meyer TF, Bandelow B. Exercise avoidance and impaired endurance capacity in patients with panic disorders. *Neuropsychobiology* 1997;36:182-187.

[6] American Psychiatric Association: *Diagnostic and Statistical Manual of Mental Disorders,* ed 4. Washington, American Psychiatric Association, 1994.

[7] Butler AC, Hokanson JE, Flynn HA: A comparison of self-esteem liability and low trait self-esteem as vulnerability factors for depression. *J Pers Soc Psychol* 1994;66:166-177.

[8] Fox KR: Self-esteem, self-perceptions and exercise. *Int J Sport Psychol* 2000;31:228-240.

[9] Beck AT, Brown GK, Steer RA, Kuyken W, Grisham J: Psychometric properties of the Beck Self-Esteem Scales. *Behav Res Ther* 2001;39:115-124.

[10] Van de Vliet P, Knapen J, Onghena P, Fox K, Van Coppenolle H, David A, Pieters G, Peuskens J: Assessment of physical self-perceptions in normal Flemish adults versus depressed psychiatric patients. *Pers Individ Dif* 2002;32:855-863.

[11] Maciejewski PK: Self-efficacy as a mediator between stressful life events and depressive symptoms: differences based on history of prior depression. *Br J Psychiatry* 2000;176:373-378.

[12] Campbell RN: *The New Science: Self-Esteem Psychology.* Lanham, University Press of America, 1984.

[13] Fox KR: The effects of exercise on self-perceptions and self-esteem; in Biddle SJH, Fox KR, Boutcher SH (eds): *Physical Activity and Psychological Well-Being.* London, Routledge, 2000, pp 88-117.

[14] Leith LM: *Foundations of Exercise and Mental Health.* Morgantown, Fitness Information Technology, 1994.

[15] Sonstroem RJ, Morgan WP: Exercise and self-esteem: Rationale and model. *Med Sci Sports Exerc* 1989;21:329-337.

[16] Fox KR: The physical self and processes in self-esteem development; in Fox KR (ed): *The Physical Self: From Motivation to Well-Being.* Champaign, Human Kinetics, 1997, pp 111-140.

[17] Craft LL, Landers DM: The effect of exercise on clinical depression and depression resulting from mental illness: A meta-analysis. *J Sport Exerc Psychol* 1998;20:339-357.

[18] Lawlor DA, Hopker SW: The effectiveness of exercise as an intervention in the management of depression: Systematic review and meta-regression analysis of randomised controlled trials. *BMJ* 2001;322:763-767.

[19] Landers DM, Petruzzello SJ: Physical activity, fitness and anxiety; in Bouchard C, Shephard RJ, Stephens T (eds): *Physical Activity, Fitness and Health*. Champaign, Human Kinetics, 1994, pp 868-882.

[20] Ossip-Klein DJ, Doyne EJ, Bowman ED, Osborn KM, McDougall-Wilson IB, Neimeyer RA: Effects of running and weight lifting on self-concept in clinically depressed women. *J Consult Clin Psychol* 1989;57:158-161.

[21] Bosscher RJ: Running and mixed physical exercises with depressed psychiatric patients. *Int J Sport Psychol* 1993;24:170-184.

[22] Donaghy ME, Mutrie N: A randomized controlled study to investigate the effect of exercise on the physical self-perceptions of problem drinkers. *Physiotherapy* 1998;84:169.

[23] Blumenthal JA, Babyak MA, Moore KA, Craighead WE, Herman S, Khatri P, Waugh R, Napolitano MA, Forman LM, Appelbaum M, Doraiswamy M, Krishnan KR: Effects of exercise training on older patients with major depression. *Arch Intern Med* 1999;159:2349-2356.

[24] Biddle SJ, Mutrie N. *Psychology of Physical Activity. Determinants, Well-being and Interventions*. London, Routledge, 2001.

[25] Salmon P. Effects of physical exercise on anxiety, depression, and sensitivity to stress: A unifying theory. *Clin Psychol Rev* 2001;21:33-61.

[26] Van Coppenolle H, Pieters G, Knapen J, Peuskens J: Pychomotor therapy in depressive patients. *Issues Spec Educ Rehabil* 1993;2:29-34.

[27] Van de Vliet P, Van Coppenolle H, Knapen J, Pieters G, Peuskens J: Physical fitness as a driving force to enhance psychological well-being in the treatment of depressive disorders; in Morisbak I, Jorgensen PE (eds): *Quality of Life through Adapted Physical Activity and Sport: a Lifespan Concept*. Trykk, Ham Trykk, 1997, pp 414-429.

[28] Pollock M, Gaesser G, Butcher J, Després JP, Dishman R, Franklin B, Garber C: The recommended quantity and quality of exercise for developing and maintaining cardiorespiratory and muscular fitness, flexibility in healthy adults. *Med Sci Sports Exerc* 1998;30:975-991.

[29] Knapen J, Van de Vliet P, Van Coppenolle H, Pieters G: Physical fitnesstraining als psychomotorische therapie bij depressieve stoornissen: follow-up onderzoek [Physical fitness training as psychomotor therapy for depressive disorders: follow-up study]. *Bewegen & Hulpverlening* 1996;13:284-291.

[30] Franz I: Vergleichende Untersuchungen zur Messung der PWC 170; in Hansen G, Mellerowicz H (eds): *Internationales Seminar für Ergometrie*. Berlin, Institut für Leistungsmedizin, 1972, pp 136-142.

[31] Knapen J, Van de Vliet P, Van Coppenolle H, Peuskens J, Pieters G: Evaluation of cardio-respiratory fitness and perceived exertion for patients with depressive and anxiety disorders: A study on reliability. *Disabil and Rehabil* 2003;27:1312-1315.

[32] American College of Sports Medicine (US). *A.C.S.M.'s Guidelines for Exercise Testing and Prescription*, ed 6. Baltimore, Williams & Wilkins, 2000.

[33] Oja P, Tuxworth B: *Eurofit for Adults: a Test Battery for the Assessment of Health-related Fitness of Adults*. Strasbourg, Council of Europe, Committee for Development of Sport, 1995.

[34] Council of Europe: *European test of Physical Fitness*. Rome, Council of Europe, Committee for the Development of Sport, 1988.

[35] Baecke JAH, Burema J, Frijters JER. A short questionnaire for the measurement of habitual physical activity in epidemiological studies. *Am J Clin Nutr* 1982;36: 936-941.

[36] Phillipaerts R, Lefevre J. Reliability and validity of three physical activity questionnaires in Flemish males. *Am J Epidemiol* 1998;147:982-90.

[37] Helbing JC: Zelfwaardering: Meting en validiteit [Self-esteem: Measurement and validity]. *Nederlands Tijdschrift voor de Psychologie* 1982;37:257-277.

[38] Bosscher RJ, Koning H, van Meurs R: Reliability and validity of the Beck Depression Inventory in a Dutch college population. *Psychol Rep* 1986;8:696-698.

[39] Hermans D: De 'Zelf-Beoordelings-Vragenlijst' [The State-Trait Anxiety Inventory]. *Gedragstherapie* 1994;27:145-148.

[40] SAS Institute: *SAS Language and Procedures: Usage 2*, Version 6 (computer program). Cary, SAS Institute Inc, 1991.

[41] Kerr K: Relaxation techniques: A critical review. *Crit Rev Phys Rehabil Med* 2000;12:51-89.

[42] Sonstroem RJ: Improving compliance with exercise programs; in Torg JS, Shephard RJ (eds): *Current Therapy in Sports Medicine.* St Louis, CV Mosby, 1995, pp 608-619.

[43] Kraemer H, Thiemann S. *How Many Subjects? Statistical Power Analysis in Research.* London, Sage Publications, 1991.

[44] Littell RC, Milliken GA, Stroup WW, Wolfinger RD: *SAS System for Mixed Models.* Cary, SAS Institute Inc, 1996.

[45] Cohen J: *Statistical Analysis for the Behavioural Sciences*, ed 2. Hillsdale, Lawrence Erlbaum, 1988.

[46] Maassen GH: The unreliable change of reliable change indices. *Behav Res Ther* 2001;39:495-498.

[47] Weinberg R, Gould D: *Foundations of Sport and Exercise Psychology*, ed 3. Champaign, Human Kinetics, 2003.

[48] Bouchard C: Gene-environment interaction in human adaptability; in Malina RB, Echert HM (eds): *The academy papers.* Champaign, Human Kinetics Publishers, 1988, pp 55-66.

[49] Landers DM, Arent SM: Physical activity and mental health; in Singer RN, Hausenblas HA, Janelle CM (eds): *Handbook of Sport Psychology.* New York, John Wiley & Sons, 2001, pp 740-765.

[50] Bandura A: Self-efficacy: Towards a unifying theory of behavior change. *Psychol Rev* 1977;84:191-215.

[51] Morgan WP: Methodological considerations; in Morgan WP (ed): *Physical Activity and Mental Health.* Washington, Taylor & Francis, 1997, pp 3-32.

[52] Van de Vliet P, Vanden Auweele Y, Knapen J, Rzewnicki R, Onghena P, Van Coppenolle H: The effect of physical exercise on depressed patients: An intra-individual approach. *Psychol Sport Exerc* 2004;5:153-167.

[53] Taylor D, Paton C, Kerwin R. *The South London and Maudsley NHS Trust 2003 Prescribing Guidelines,* ed 7. London Martin Dunitz, 2003.

[54] Montgomery SA: New developments in the treatment of depression. *J Clin Psychiatry* 1999;60(suppl 14):10-15.

[55] Sonstroem RJ: The physical self-system: A mediator of exercise and self-esteem; in Fox KR (ed): *The Physical Self: From Motivation to Well-Being.* Champaign, Human Kinetics, 1997, pp 3-26.

[56] Dishman RK, Buckworth J: Adherence to physical activity; in Morgan WP (ed): *Physical Activity and Mental Health*. Washington, Taylor & Francis, 1997, pp 63-80.

[57] Pollock KM: Exercise in treating depression: broadening the psychotherapist's role. *J Clin Psychol* 2001;57:1289-1300.

In: The Concept of Self in Education, Family and Sports   ISBN 1-59454-988-5
Editor: Anne P. Prescott, pp. 115-151   © 2006 Nova Science Publishers, Inc.

Chapter 5

THE DYNAMICS OF SELF-ESTEEM

Grégory Ninot, * *Didier Delignières*
Faculty of Sport Sciences, University Montpellier I, Montpellier, France
and Marina Fortes
University of Nantes, France

ABSTRACT

The purpose was to specify advantages and limits of dynamical perspective proposed by Nowak and Vallacher (1998) for social psychology studies. This perspective contributes massively to new knowledge in economy, biology and motor control. Theoretical models, methods, self-assessment tools, and time series analyses are complete to verify hypotheses from nomothetical approach and to determine impact of daily events on self-perception. Some example will be given with self-esteem. This new scientific path needs attention to prevent fashion effect and critic disconnection. Epistemological weaknesses, such as analogies, conceptual bounds, technological illusions, or false time series analyses, are abundant. Sport psychologists, working on behaviors, emotions and thoughts interactions (such as self-esteem, self-efficacy, motivation, and anxiety) are in phase with this perspective. Nevertheless, they must avoid weakness underlined by this paper.

INTRODUCTION

The operational basis of social psychology aims to demonstrate linear relations between cause and consequence to explain reality. The postulate is that knowledge of simple structure and function can explain seeming complexity of thought, feeling and behavior in manifest or imaginary social situation (Allport, 1985). This analytic and reductionism approach was the

---

* *Author for correspondence:* Grégory Ninot. JE 2416 Faculty of Sport Sciences, University Montpellier I, 700 avenue du Pic saint Loup, 34090 Montpellier – France; Phone: +33 467 41 57 54 - fax: +33 467 41 57 08; Email: gregory.ninot@univ-montp1.fr

only path to explore construct during the first century of social psychology. If this paradigm underlines relations between variables, some psychologist produced critics for the poor practical interest and heuristic limits (Kimiecik and Blissmer, 1998). Moreover, this reductionism allows researchers to neglect or underestimate time and ecological context influence to characterize studied variable. Thus, causal relationships derived from analytic methods stay limited to generalization of thought, feeling and behavior, to explain individual behavior in ecological context and to produce some prevision of behaviors.

According to the philosopher Thomas Kuhn, science does not evolve with simple accumulation of knowledge, but rather with change of manner to conceive and treat scientific problems. Recently, Nowak and Vallacher (1998) consider that complexity in psychology has its own reality and can not be reduced to several elements, even if they are cumulated. They proposed to develop a new approach named dynamical social psychology. This orientation includes recent works from physics and biology about complexity illustrated with the formula the whole is not the sum of parts, new properties emerge from the overview of system.

Self-esteem represents one's general or typical feelings of self-worth and self-liking (Greenier, Kernis, McNamara, Waschull, Berry, Herlocker and Abend, 1999). The term physical self, on the other hand, has a more specific meaning. It reflects the domain of perceptions of one's body, and the corresponding feelings of physical self-worth, with these perceptions particularly focused on sub-domains such as physical condition, sport competence, physical strength, and attractive body (Fox and Corbin, 1989; Sonstroem, Speliotis, and Fava, 1992; Sonstroem, Harlow, and Josephs, 1994).

Classic works in social psychology using questionnaires with Likert-type response scales and a few reports presenting longitudinal data have shown that the mean group level of self-esteem does not significantly differ over time in adults, suggesting good stability across situations (Burke, Kraut, and Dworkin, 1984; Demo, 1992; McCrae and Costa, 1994). This stability may reflect self-consistency with the development of feelings of unity, independence, predictability, and control (Epstein, 1979). The notions of self-schemata (Markus, 1977) and the primary basis of security (Rogers, 1959) were advanced as explanations of this stability such that, if an individual were to experience no critical life events, and if measurement error could be eliminated by directly assessing the content of the person's mind, self-esteem would be characterized as a single point on an appropriately labeled scale.

Nevertheless, dynamical psychology considered declarative perception of the self as a highly complex process (Nowak, Vallacher, Tesser and Borkowski, 2000; Vallacher, Nowak, Froehlich and Rockloff, 2002). Self-esteem can be considered as phenomena emerging from the interplay of the many elements included in a system. The mind cannot be reduced to separate mechanisms, but instead mutual influences and coordination must be taken into account. Specific brain structures carry out cognitive and emotional functions in parallel but also interact to produce higher order structures with emergent properties. Thus, the functioning of self-esteem could be more complex than proposed by classical studies. The purpose of this chapter was to examine how self-esteem functions overtime at an intra-individual level using a brief questionnaire, daily assessment and time series analyses. The first part focuses on theoretical and methodological exigencies. The second part shows some recent works about instability and dynamics of self-esteem.

THE DYNAMICAL STUDY OF SELF-ESTEEM

Theoretical Aspects

Limits of Classic Approaches in Social Psychology

The study of psychological constructs used predominantly static nomothetic method, in other words based on few repeated measures spaced at least one month. The results showed inter-individual differences and correlates without never determine causal functioning or predict change of studied dimensions for a subject (Kimiecik and Blissmer, 1998; Nowak and Vallacher, 1998). This lack to answer to both main aims of social psychology needs a new approach in which intra-individual variability will play a crucial role. The priority attributed to personality according to the structuralist and dispositional perspective (Coopersmith, 1967; Lord, 1997; Rosenberg, 1979), in consequence to the determination of auto-evaluative and behavior permanence could have neglected intra-individual variability, attributed spontaneously to measure error (Marsh and Yeung, 1998).

Studies in social psychology have also excluded understanding of ecological context to characterize measured scores. Some procedures such as artificial task, break of situation during completion and retrospective techniques have isolated variables without contextualization. With disconnection to ecological evolution of studied dimensions, social psychology produced intangible models, sometimes simplistic, incompatible for practice (Kimiecik and Blissmer, 1998; Lawson, 1990; Newell, 1990).

Nomothetic works focused on linear relations in multidimensional or hierarchical structure of self, in other word on direct and proportional links. Nevertheless, the effects in most biological systems are not proportional to values of causes, for example heartbeats (Goldberger, 1999).

Multidimensional or hierarchical model validated by unique measure (except to control reproducibility for questionnaire's validation where a second assessment is generally conducted after one month) are inspired to a thermodynamic rule and a biological principle neglecting time. The rule of energy conservation (invariance and symmetry overtime) and the principle of homeostasis (stationary dynamics, the system tend to reduce variability and to maintain constancy of internal functions) ignores time because of the return to basal level and seems to be obvious (Prigogine, 1994). Whatever time delay, the return seems to be ineluctable. In consequence, the change of psychological dimension's score was considered at worst as measure error (Marsh and Yeung, 1998) or at best as temporary perturbation (Kernis, Grannemann and Barclay, 1989). This functioning supposes a reference value. This basal level is determined during an "at rest" assessment session with a questionnaire. Prigogine (1994) contests elimination of time in classical rules of physics. Studying dissipative structures, he showed that until the system dissipates energy and stay in contact with outside environment, the pattern of behavior is non-equilibrium (Prigogine, 1994). It is the contrast with equilibrium structures such as crystals. Once created, they stay isolated and are inert structures without dissipation of energy (Prigogine, 1994). More the level of complexity increases (chemistry, life, brain), more evident is the effect of time. Thus, the non-equilibrium creates long term correlations. Without theses correlations, we can not have life, or thoughts. The equilibrium becomes a particular state of a more fundamental rule of non-equilibrium (Prigogine, 1994). Moreover, the third thermodynamic rule explains that entropy of a system increases overtime. In that case, the disorder of the system increases overtime. A feeling becomes more and more complex overtime. In consequence, time can not be excluded in social psychology.

The Needs of Dynamical Approach in Social Psychology

Nowak and Vallacher (1998) propose to open social psychology to ecological context, time and complexity. This new area is inspired by several paradigms such as incertitude principles starting with Heisenberg, probabilistic causality starting with Broglie, relativity starting with Einstein, chaos starting with Poincaré and emergency starting with Lewes.

According to Nowak and Vallacher (1998), certain psychological variables can be considered in an ecological context, as the consequence of complex systems submitted to incontrollable and unpredictable impacts. Each value emerges from auto-organization process at t time. Thus, studying separately components of the system can not determine the global functioning. The mind can not be reduced to separate mechanisms without understanding mutual influences and coordination. In consequence, several specific psychological functions operate in parallel to create superior structure susceptible to obtain emergence of a product understandable by all (Varela, Thompson and Rosch, 1993).

The aim of this perspective is to propose a description (1), a characterization (2) and a modelization (3) of behavior of complex system. The description's phase (1) depicts ecological changes of psychological variables in examining « natural » functioning of a subject overtime and in indicating frequency and nature of perturbations and also variables probably implicated to these changes. Then, the researcher extracts regularity, cycle and change of thoughts, emotions and behaviors. The characterization's phase (2) produces an(several) impact(s) (constraint or perturbation) directly on system and qualify/quantify the effects on mean, instability and dynamics of studied variables. The modelization's phase (3) creates pattern of explanation in the one hand using psychology's knowledge and in the other hand using mathematical equation. The model specifies the dynamics overtime in articulate combination constituted by several elements and parameters influencing its different states. Compared to static system, a dynamical system integrates influence of preceding time (y_{t-n}) among parameters characterizing current state (y_t).

A substantial difference with dispositional theories (based on the *true* and *immovable* value of trait) is that dynamical theories include ε_t term in the model. This term does not reflect the distance between true value and observed value indicating measure error. It reflects random and continuous change, favorable or unfavorable (Kenny and Campbell, 1989). In ecological condition, the system evolves continuously overtime. Instead it is the place of minor events more than catastrophes, the chain reactions of all amplitude belong to its dynamics. A same event produces minor consequence or catastrophe. In biology, theses systems rarely attain *steady state*, they function from a metastable state to another (Bak and Chen, 1991).

The advantage of dynamical social psychology is that the researcher examines the trace of psychological variable transcribed in a natural and authentic context. She or he requests to subject to answer frequently and spontaneously, eliminating retrospective biases related to memory. This trace noted *in situ* is related to its context in order to improve sense. In consequence, a minor event can become as well important as major event. If psychologists massively focused on impacts of major events, they often under-estimate consequences of minor life, frequent and low intensity events. First, they considered that participants are not attentive to minor events, thus with weak memorization. Second, participants create adaptive routines to minimize minor events (Hays, 1989). Classifications of life events (positives and negatives) were established excluding in the one hand distinct feelings between subjects and, in the other hand, importance attributed to each event in function of context. Cognitive interpretation and emotional state play major role in the psychological weight assigned to life events. Dynamical social psychology attempts to extract information close to event and his feeling. The prevalence of a particular process, it periodicity, it covariance can emerge within it context, named ecological validity (Brewer, 2000).

Marsh and Yeung (1998) underlined the limits of nomothetic studies to verify application of psychological process with an individual. For example, the undetermined debate between *dispositional* (defender of personality trait), *situationist* (defender of state) or *interactionist* (defender of dynamical equilibrium or homeostasis) theories is tangible proof (Baumeister, 1993; Brown, 1998; Strelau, 2001). The new path of social psychology initiated by Nowak and Vallacher (1998) notifies interest to explore with an intra-individual manner hypotheses let in abeyance by inter-individuals studies.

Limits of Nomothetic Approach to Characterize Self-Esteem

Self-esteem self can function as *trait*, *state*, or *dynamic equilibrium*. A *trait* is stable over time and across situations, whereas in the case of a *state*, circumstances can raise or lower the evaluation of perceived dimensions. The *dynamic equilibrium* model can be a combination between trait and state.

If self-esteem functions as a *trait* (Burke, Kraut and Dworkin, 1984; Coopersmith, 1967; Epstein, 1979; McCrae and Costa, 1994), the inferred model is based on the thermodynamic principle of energy conservation and the homeostatic principle. For example, if a positive or negative event influences self-esteem, then these models emphasize self-conservation, the progressive return to a basal level with weak oscillations (linked exclusively to random variability due to measurement error). Abundant empirical evidence indicates that global self-esteem is resistant to change. According to dispositional theories, a trait is considered to be a relatively stable and individual-specific generalized tendency to behave in a certain way (Strelau, 2001). The literature shows the stability of global self-esteem especially in adults (McCrae and Costa, 1994). In consequence, the correlational literature is replete with evidence of associations between self-esteem level and systematic behaviors or psychological reactions. For example, people with low self-esteem often report depressive episodes (Butler, Hokason and Flynn, 1994). They report more negative emotions and are more sensitive to negative events (Dutton and Brown, 1997; Epstein, 1992). They are more concerned by and with social evaluations (Baumgardner, 1990). Conversely, individuals scoring high in global self-esteem often present a socially conformist image of themselves (Francis, 1997). They are generally characterized by higher levels of sociability, impulsivity, and emotional stability (Francis, 1997).

If self-esteem functions as a *state* (Butler *et al.*, 1994; Leary, 1990), then the perceived dimensions could be considered as short-term histories changing randomly in response to life events. According to situational theories (Leary, Tambor, Terdal and Downs, 1995), changes reflect dependence on endogenous and exogenous variations. Recent research has emphasized the variability of self (Greenier *et al.*, 1999; Kernis, 1993; Nezlek, 2002; Nezlek and Plezko, 2001; Nowak and Vallacher, 1998; Nowak *et al.*, 2000) and subjective well-being (Headey and Wearing, 1989). State self-esteem appears to function as a subjective marker that reflects the individual's social standing in a particular setting (Leary *et al.*, 1995). People with unstable self-esteem, whether low or high, show more extreme emotional and behavioral reactions to events involving other threats to self-esteem. For example, the variability of perceived dimensions reveals central information about depression (Greenier *et al.*, 1999), quality of life changes (Barge-Schaapveld, Nicolson, Berkhof and de Vries, 1999) and behavior (Kernis *et al.*, 1989). Individuals with unstable self-esteem more often experience anger and hostility (Kernis, Grannemann and Mathis, 1991). Stability of self-esteem moderates the relation between level of self-esteem and depression (Kernis *et al.*, 1991).

If self-esteem functions as a *dynamic equilibrium*, then several oscillations around a reference point, though it denotes a tendency to return to a fixed-point attractor on a longer time scale can be observed (Headey and Wearing, 1989; Nowak *et al.*, 2000). Over time, the dynamics of this system tend to cohere into reliable patterns, referred to as attractors. In this particular case, the subject maintains a relatively stable and positive self-evaluation despite a high number of negative elements in his or her self-system (Nowak *et al.*, 2000). She or he concentrates on the positive regions and disregards the negative regions (Pelham and Swann, 1989; Showers, Abramson and Hogan, 1998). Compared to fixed trait, the time needed to return to the reference value can be much longer, and the magnitude of oscillations can be higher. The system may react to endogenous or exogenous influences. The influences tend to be short-lived, however, so that the system quickly returns to its attractor. Occasionally, the reference value will change because of an event judged to be important by the person. At that point, the self-system is pushed to a new equilibrium level, making it difficult to return to its initial state (Nowak *et al.*, 2000)

Dynamical social psychology presents an innovating way to determine psychological processes that regulate evolution of self-esteem (Ninot, Fortes and Delignières, 2001; Nowak *et al.*, 2000). Self-esteem is conceived as an emergent product of multiples interactions in biological and psychological system of one human being. This auto-evaluative dimension can be considered as an order parameter traducing a current state of a system submitted to endogenous constraints (biopsychological) and environmental impacts (physic and social). Moreover, dynamical social psychology offers also perspectives to determine causalities in hierarchical model including self-esteem (Fortes, Ninot, Leymarie and Delignières, 2004) and estimations in short term for a subject (Ninot, Fortes and Delignières, 2005). From psychopathological viewpoint, it can describe process of identity construction and associated troubles (Marks-Tarlow, 1999). Methodologically, this approach needs repeated, frequent and regular measures at human scale to verify all of these functioning hypotheses.

Methodological Aspects

Limits of Classical Approaches

If review of question and meta-analyses emphasize the need of longitudinal studies in social psychology, researchers remain often perplexes to use this kind of protocol design. They wonder if logistic efforts to control parasites variables worth while. The cost of such protocols (subjects, researchers and material) burdens massively the laboratory's resources. Students, concerned to university diploma generally less than three or four years, prefer avoid this kind of protocol. The experimental mortality is important (but rarely specified in psychological publications) for several reasons, sometimes unthinking. This leave affects generalization of results. If longitudinal protocol design theoretically requires need assessment at the same time for each subject, material and organizational constraints will prohibit. In brief, psychologists wonder if parasite factors can not the principal cause of observed significant change. Then, their choice are directed to soft longitudinal (minimizing number of measures or reducing inclusion criterions) and/or *cross-sectional* protocols. Unfortunately, it is at this moment that the micro-variations susceptible to provoke periodic change are lost. The low frequency of acquisition will hide studied process.

In transversal experimental design using questionnaire, strategies for equating groups are neither perfect. Two identical individuals can not be found, including homozygote twins. Therefore, constitution of control group is impossible, as well as determination of median behavior of a group will not reflect an individual behavior (Hanin and Syrjä, 1995).

The selection of persons with specific inclusion criterions often imposes artificial assimilations. Errors of sampling are then possible and can indirectly facilitate hoped result (Bouvard and Cottraux, 1996).

The relevance of general population is required to obtain powerful generalization. In several cases, it is not possible to include enough persons because of several problems (incompatibility of groups, faraway residence of subjects, direct costs...).

The participants may have favorable or unfavorable presumption related to experimental design proposed in function of preliminary information or past experiences. They will have diverse motivations and behaviors. For example, it is well demonstrated that prestige of university or scientific authority influences results of study (Bouvard and Cottraux, 1996). With weak sampling, this constraint generates insoluble biases.

The use of battery of classical questionnaires in longitudinal studies involves fastidious assessment session. The repetition reduces motivation. Participants risk to be bored and to complete improperly.

Attitudes, beliefs and personal convictions of researchers can also influence results within infrequent repeated measures. Double blind protocol is an appropriate methodological opportunity but occasionally take up in social psychology.

An experimented solution, rarely reliable, is retrospective method. Cognitive biases related to memory product several errors in information collection. More time period is prominent, more the studied event looks like to other life events, more that is make sense seems to implicit theory of participant and/or more emotion modifies thought, and more chances to obtain false information are majored.

The Needs of Dynamical Approach in Social Psychology

The dynamical perspective requires idiographic protocol (Runyan, 1983) where data are assessed frequently over a determined period. An idiographic protocol design can be empirical (ecological context) or experimental (laboratory situation controlling variables or simulation).

In ecological situation, the method is named *everyday experience method* (Reis and Gable, 2000). Time unit is chosen in reason of discrete rupture provoked by sleep within biological and psychological rhythms (Williams, Suls, Alliger, Learner and Wan, 1991).

Three types of recording are proposed, (1) programmed, (2) random or (3) conditioned. The first one respects identical, uniform and determined interval of time (Mischel and Shoda, 1998). Interval must have sense theoretically and logically to describe behaviors and/or events appeared since last completion session. The aim of researcher is to optimize acquisition's frequency. A double acquisition's frequency related to studied mechanism is optimal. It avoids measure surcharges due to distraction, pseudo-knowledge without reading question or familiarities with the questionnaire. It improves manifest measurement of variable's change (Mischel and Shoda, 1998). This type of recording facilitates adherence to program research, determination of regularities and opportunity to apply time series analyses. The second type of recording, named *experience sampling method* (ESM) developed by Csikszentmihalyi and Larson (1987), concerns a responses series with random apparitions of signal (fixed interval can be included). This kind of protocol avoids anticipation of response and permits to verify the state of participant during her or his activities. The third type depends of decision of the participant in function of life events defined preliminarily. If interval has sense, the risk remains difficulty to define exactly "events" and detect without ambiguity.

Whatever the type of recording, it is necessary that period and acquisition's frequency reflect an enough number of representative measures. Moreover, except specific study, apparition of major event needs an independent treatment.

Psychometric Aspects

Limits of Classical Approaches

Even if researchers hope to obtain individual time series enough longer, it is impossible to ask to the participant to answer day-to-day to classical questionnaires including near thirty items, still more to a battery. The completion should be too prolonged and fastidious. The number of items systematically superior to four items by scale excludes measurements with restricted interval of time, in consequence, understanding of micro-variations.

The internal validity of a questionnaire used with a specific population is rarely tested and presented in publications. Authors trust validation session, even if they had occasion to check internal validity. It is often that a questionnaire validated with a representative sampling of general population is not structured in a part of this population.

The response's modality of most questionnaires measuring psychological constructs are weakly sensible. The Self-Esteem Inventory of Coopersmith (1967) uses a binary nominal scale. The Physical Self-Perception Profile (PSPP) of Fox and Corbin (1989) and Self-Perception Profile of Harter (1999) propose an ordinal scale with forced choice by tetrad. The French version of PSPP, Physical Self-Inventory (PSI), integrates an ordinal scale with a Likert at six modalities (Ninot, Delignières and Fortes, 2000). The both first modalities are weakly nuanced (figure 1). A sensible participant can have difficulties to determine herself or himself between two criterions, depending to situations.

Psychometric procedures of questionnaire's validation diverge between authors (Bouvard and Cottraux, 1996; Marsh, 1993). Nevertheless, authors consider five main criterions: content validity, internal consistency, external validity, predictive validity, and stability (retest). The third ones are well applied in social psychology (Reid and Judd, 2000).

The predictive validity permits to pronounce a prognostic with results. This procedure is classic in medicine, and very rare in social psychology. The lack of clinical verification limits routinely use of these questionnaires in individuals and can support certain presumptuous postulate apparently supported by retest procedure.

			Seems to me	Does not seem to me
1.	In general, I do not worry	....	☐	☐

Self-Esteem Inventory (Coopersmith, 1967)

Seems to me				Does not seem to me	
really	*a little*			*a little*	*really*
12.	☐	☐	Certain are happy with themselves	*BUT*	other are rarely happy with themselves	☐	☐

Physical Self-Perception Profile (Harter, 1999) and Physical Self-Perception Profile (Fox and Corbin, 1989)

	Seems to me...					
	Not at all	A very little	A little	Enough	A lot	Absolutely
1. I have a good opinion of my self --	--1--	--2---	--3--	--4---	--5--	---6---

Physical Self-Inventory adapted from PSPP of Fox and Corbin (1989)

Figure 1: Responses modalities of questionnaires measuring self-esteem

The retest (or stability coefficient) is a sine qua non condition for psychometric validation of a self-evaluative instrument. The retest relates an identical result between two measures realized in same conditions. The time interval is not fixed. Literature suggests periods from one week to two months. This test is massively criticized. It does not distinguish variability dues to possible change and measurement errors. Marsh (1993) and Schutz (1998) propose a new method based on mean stability corresponding to statistical difference of level score between both measures (with ANOVA for repeated measures and correlation coefficient between times), differential stability corresponding to individuals difference stability overtime with inter-measures correlation coefficient (capacity to an individual to maintain her or his position in the group), and structural stability corresponding to the degree of maintenance of latent variables. The authors justify the use of this last analysis within the postulate that psychological variables are personality's trait, in other word, consistent whatever events and situations. However, the first two parts of this chapter underline that nothing prose that personality dimensions function like that, quite the opposite.

The Needs of Dynamical Approach in Social Psychology

Obtaining time series enough extended is not easy in social psychology. The completion with classical instruments quickly becomes fastidious. Participants declare to have not enough time to assess twice a day using a paper-pencil questionnaire. If they are constrained, they complete automatically in memory of last answer (learning effect), selectively claiming boredom or fatigue, falsely (playing a role), or randomly (to reduce assessment time). These behaviors contribute to invalidate protocols.

Alternatives to these biases are open question (informative on a descriptive plan but with risk of spontaneous comment related to event and not related to studied phenomenon), check-list (quick use for unpredictable event, but limited in other cases) or brief questionnaire including one item per studied dimension (Reid and Gable, 2000).

The brief questionnaire supposes that the lack of internal consistency due to weak number of questions is compensated by repetition of completion. A single item by dimension removes redundancies. It decreases fatigue, frustration and boredom (Robins, Hendin and Trzesniewski, 2001). Spontaneity and promptness to complete eliminates memory biases. Moreover, daily assessment reinforces curiosity of the participant to know her or his data and, in consequence, motivates more than rare occasions.

Ordinal scale constituted by a list of three to six terms organized in intensifying order offers a limited number of responses, thus slight nuance (Jensen, Karoly and Braver, 1986). These scales are weakly sensible and do not detect low variation of intensity. In pain assessment, the signification of term does not necessarily reflect the same intensity between patients. Moreover, variation of pain experience intensity is not identical between scale's terms (Ohnhaus and Adler, 1975). Interval between the selected word and the next or preceding does not represent the same unit. For example, an intensive pain that becomes moderate is not comparable to a weak pain becoming nothing.

To avoid learning effects and response memorization and to increase sensibility of scale, visual analogue scale (VAS) appears to be the best solution (Huskisson, 1974). This scale is easy to administrate and to complete. Severity of pain is perceived only by the subject in trouble with. It is a personal psychological experience to which observer does not play any legitimate role to appreciate accurately. It is now admit that pain is a subjective phenomenon. The patient is the only one judge to determine pain overtime. The complexity of pain phenomenon cannot resume to an only one assessment session. VAS has advantage to be sensible and adapted to repeated measures (Huskisson, 1974).

VAS is a single 10-cm horizontal line without formal indications. For example in social psychology (figure 2), participants are requested to draw a vertical trait on the line anchored by "not at all" (measured 0.0 cm) at the left extremity and "absolutely" at the right (measured 10.0 cm). The researcher then determines the trait's distance from the left extremity and converted the response to a score ranging from 0.0 to 10.0.

Globally, you have a good opinion of yourself		
Not at all		Absolutely

Figure 2: VAS

VAS is a self-evaluative method largely used, diffused and short to assess chronic and acute pain (Jensen et al., 1986). The scale is reliable and reproducible with pain (Huskisson, 1974; Price, McGrath, Rafii and Buckingham, 1983). It reproducibility is better with 10, 15 or 20 cm than 5 cm. The results about pain are not influenced by age, sex or disease. The pain's scores measured with VAS in patients are similar than those completed by clinicians and nurses (Banos, Bosch, Camellas, Bassols and Bigorraa, 1989).

Inconvenient of VAS concerns it misunderstanding score that is 11% for the pain in a general population (Paice and Cohen, 1997) and only 2,7 to 4% for simple verbal scale (Jensen et al., 1986). It use is forbidden in elderly persons (more than 90 years old), young children (before 6 years old) or patients presenting cognitive troubles, spatiotemporal disorientation or linguistic difficulties. Cognitive limits decrease understanding of nuance and self-judgment permitting to traduce personal experience to geometric presentation (Carlson, 1983).

Brief Instrument to Obtain Self-Esteem Time Series

Recent studies validated brief questionnaires measuring one psychological dimension with single item for self-esteem (Robins *et al.*, 2001; Ninot *et al.*, 2001). These instruments using VAS have good balance between practical need and psychometric criterions (Robins *et al.*, 2001). Nevertheless, these tools are not valuable for all psychological dimensions. For example, a multifaceted concept is unconceivable to explore with this kind of tools.

The PSI-6 items, validated in French (Ninot *et al.*, 2001), assesses global self-esteem and physical self components (Fox and Corbin, 1989), physical self-worth, physical condition, sport competence, physical strength, and attractive body (table 1). The questionnaire is completed on single paper, on personal pad or on personal computer using dedicated software. The six items are presented in random order to reduce the likelihood of systematic responses.

For the software version, participants have to move the cursor along a line anchored by "not at all" at the left extremity and "absolutely" at the right (figure 2). The cursor is placed on the left before answer. The software then determines the cursor's distance from the left extremity and converted the response to a score ranging from 0.0 to 10.0.

Participants are also asked to move the cursor to the center of a 10-cm horizontal VAS. This additive item is designated to estimate the measurement error and/or misuse (cognitive troubles, vision problems or fallacious responses) corresponding to the difference between the true value (5 cm, center of the 10-cm line) and the response mark.

Participants were not informed of these numerical scores and were not allowed to consult their previous responses. Last, a commentary zone is created after the VAS completion to offer opportunities to note events and/or everything in relation with the current psychological state (see an example in figure 8).

Table 1: Items of Physical Self Inventory – 6 items

Dimension	Item
Global self-esteem	Globally, you have a good opinion of yourself
Physical self-worth	Physically, you are proud of who you are and what you can do
Physical condition	You would be good in an endurance test
Sport competence	You manage well in all sports
Attractive body	You think that you have a pleasant body to look at
Physical strength	When you come to situations requiring strength, you are among the first to step forward

Time Series Analyses

Limits of Classical Approaches

Classical analyses devoted to repeated measures (t of Student, ANOVA) present several constraints that are sources of interpretation's errors.

To discriminate significant effects on dependent variables, these analyses require important sampling size, sometimes impossible to constitute. In some cases, a non significant result within 15 subjects can become significant with 40. The computation of effect size gives descriptive information but does not solve the problem. Moreover, these analyses can miss significant results because of variance's heterogeneity. Few subjects of the studied population submitted to an inverse effect can provoke a non significance. The exclusion of two or three subjects can be enough to obtain significant result but also to obliterate ethics of researcher.

These analyses can show significant time effect without clinical perception of subjects. This kind of results needs the development of clinical threshold, from which it is a real impact on life.

In experimental design, a person can answer with very weak score at four of five items for the same dimension. The last item can have a medium score. Even if the participant attributes more importance to the last item, the mean or cumulated score will mask the last response and alter ANOVA (Kimiecik and Blissmer, 1998).

To an intra-individual level, analyses of variances reveal anything on time stability of a series of repeated measures (Marsh, 1993; Schutz, 1998).

Often, researchers use ANOVA to examine a series of consecutive observations. Nevertheless, a postulate of ANOVA is that the residuals of measures are not correlated. It is not the case if the score at t time is linked to the previous score at t-1 time, in other word if data are auto-correlated.

The post-hoc tests present a different sensibility. For example, the Newman-Keuls test discriminates more than the Scheffé test. Here again, the researcher's ethics is overstress in case of doubtable result.

Last, an analysis of variance for repeated measures traduces a mean change of a group. The discussion is then about the change of a mean subject who stay absolutely artificial.

In consequence, new analyses are necessary, not well known in social psychology, time series analyses (Shumway and Stoffer, 2000).

The Needs of Dynamical Approach in Social Psychology

The *mean level* of time series (mean of consecutive observations) takes sense if the period is enough longer and in case of stationary process. The first condition requires same intervals between measures over the studied period. To our experience, the minimum unit is 14 for bi-daily measures to obtain acceptable value of self-esteem, in other words a week. The second condition is more complex. A stationary process suggests that any trend can be discovered on the time series. However, a decrease or an increase can appear in a time series because of clinical change (see figure 1). Then, computation of *mean level* reveals few indications for the studied subject, and limits some conclusions of nomothetic studies about the significance of a single level score.

The *standard-deviation* is an instability indicator of time series used by several authors in social psychology (see 1.1.3.). It application to time series is restricted. This indicator derives from Gaussian statistic's hypothesis based on normal and random distribution of data around mean. Then, data are supposed non-correlated overtime. However, most of psychological time series present significant autocorrelations (Gilden, 2001; Slifkin and Newell, 1998), excluding the meaning of Gaussian's hypothesis.

We can propose other indicators of psychological instability overtime, such as *range* (difference between minor and major values over the studied period) and *mean absolute difference* (mean of absolute differences between two consecutive observations, in other word, the series is differenced, transformed in absolute values, and the mean of this new series is calculated).

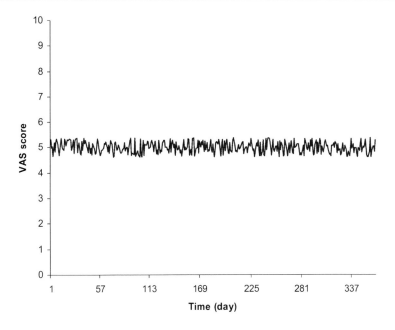

Figure 3: Simulation of stationary time series

Nevertheless, these descriptive indicators reveal a poor image of psychological functioning, because its ignore order in which data were collected. Time series analyses overlook these limits in producing information about dynamics, in other words, about the manner of variability is built observation after observation. Time series analyses aim to determine individual functioning (Slifkin and Newell, 1998).

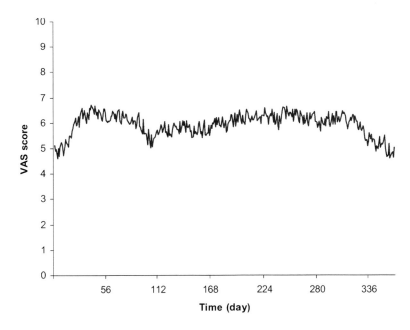

Figure 4: Simulation of non stationary time series

A common analysis consists to compute *autocorrelation function* (ACF) of the series. The ACF is a Bravais-Pearson correlation coefficient from time series correlated with itself. This correlation is computed creating progressive lags. For lag 1, ACF is computed with pairs $(y_t; y_{t+1})$. The ACF describes the historicity of time series (Shumway and Stoffer, 2000).

In certain case, ACF reveals no significant coefficients. This indicates that no relation can be found between successive observations. This result is typical of white noise process, random succession of observations, and thus completely unpredictable. If mean, standard deviation and superior order moments are unchangeable and accompanying non significant ACF, then the studied time series is stationary. An example of classic stationary process is state equilibrium or *steady state* (homeostasis). The variable randomly oscillates around stable reference value overtime (figure 3).

This result remains nevertheless quite exceptional in psychology and biology devoted to ecological context. Habitually, researchers observe significant autocorrelations, which tend to decrease gradually little by little that lag increases. In other words, the observation at t time is particularly dependent to preceding observation t-1, un little bit less at observation t-2, etc. Time series analyses aim to forecast nature of this relation. The non stationary time series present to the opposite more or less important changes overtime (figure 4).

For a non stationary series, ACF must be significant from the first lag to high number of lags. The figure 5 shows ACF graph with significant lags from 1 to 28 (data from time series show in figure 4). A stationary series do not present significant lags or very rarely.

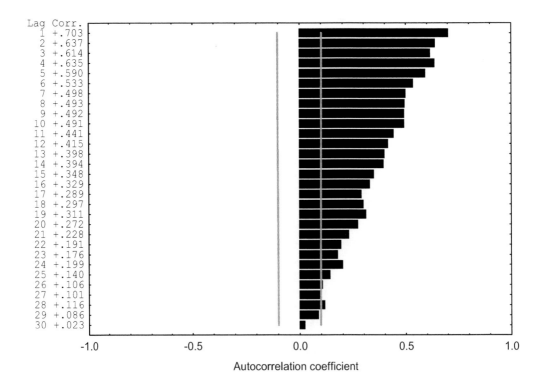

Figure 5: Graph of autocorrelation function

In case of researches of causality between two psychological dimensions in a multidimensional model, the computation of *cross-correlation* coefficient traduces the dependence degree between two time series. It is a correlation including successive couples of synchronic values in two time series (x_t and y_t). The *cross-correlation* coefficient is then computed with the introduction of time lags between both series. This function determines lag corresponding to maximal dependence between two variables, suggesting influence of a series to the other with a certain time lag. The sign indicates the direction of this influence. If evolution of time series X precedes similar evolution of series Y, then the conclusion is that changes of Y depends change of X. The figure 6 presents a cross-correlation graph from two time series without lag because the higher coefficient (.60) is obtained at lag 0 (Shumway and Stoffer, 2000). These series can be windowed to determine certain causalities during certain periods of time series (Boker, Xu, Rotondo and King, 2002; Gernigon, d'Arripe-Longueville, Delignières and Ninot, 2004).

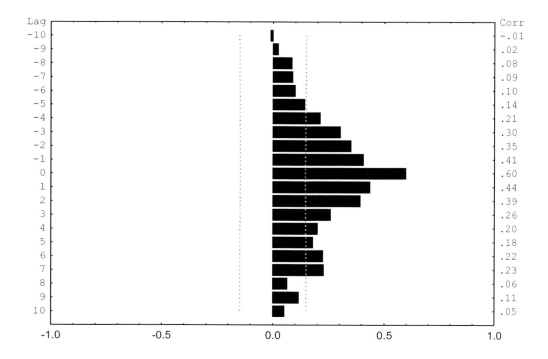

Figure 6: Graph of cross-correlation function

To determine the dynamics of a time series of 50 to 500 observations, *Auto-Regressive Integrated Moving Average* (ARIMA) procedures are proposed by Box and Jenkins (1976). These procedures aim to establish how each value in the series depends on preceding values (iterative pattern) and then to tentatively infer psychological processes underlying the time evolution of the series (Spray and Newell, 1986; Fortes, Ninot and Delignières, 2005). ARIMA procedures constitute a very basic and commonly used time series analysis method especially in econometrics, and are available in most statistical packages (Shumway and Stoffer, 2000). Nevertheless, the method remains unfamiliar to many psychologists. The aim of these procedures is to model the dynamics of time series in form of iterative equation:

$$y_t = f(y_{t-1}) \tag{1}$$

where y_t represent the value observed at time t.

These procedures are based on the study of ACF and partial autocorrelation functions (PACF), which inform about the temporal dependence in the series. An ARIMA model is composed of the potential association of three types of mathematical process: auto-regressive (AR), integrated (I) and moving average (MA) processes. The model is labeled as (p,d,q) where p indicates the number of auto-regressive terms, d the number of differentiations, and q the number of moving average terms.

The first step in ARIMA procedures is the determination of the number of differentiations to include in the model in order to account for the general trends of the series. The determination of the number of differentiations to include is based on the examination of the ACF of the original series.

If the original series is stationary (i.e., presents a constant mean over time), no differentiation is necessary. The ARIMA model (0,0,0) constitutes a dynamics characterized by the following equation:

$$y_t = \mu + \varepsilon_t \tag{2}$$

where μ represents the mean of the time series. This process characterizes random oscillations around a reference value over time. The series appears quite choppy because of the uncorrelated adjacent points. This process is stationary since the mean of the series is constant and does not depend on time. A white noise model has sometimes been encountered in motor learning research. This model was found to represent some series of successive motor task performances with knowledge of results (Spray and Newell, 1986). Psychological interpretation of such models lies on the stationarity of the mean which suggests that individuals develop a stable reference around which responses randomly fluctuate. As previously explained, the personality *trait* hypothesis related to self-esteem suggests that its functioning would be characterized by a (0,0,0) model as the stable referenced value associated with weak and random fluctuations. Similarly, the time series of measurement error item should evolve around a mean whose value should correspond to the center of the line.

The presence of positive and persistent autocorrelations (up to 10 lags, for example) implies the need to introduce at least one differentiation term in the model. Then, the ACF of the differenced series (i.e., the series of successive differences in the original series) is examined. The persistence of significant autocorrelation in this differenced series suggests that a second differentiation term might need to be introduced in the model. Conversely, the appearance of one significant negative autocorrelation at the first lag suggests that the series has been over-differenced. This first step allows the estimation of parameter d of the ARIMA model. A differentiation of order 1 accounts for a linear trend in the series, noted (0,1,0), can be expressed as follows:

$$y_t = y_{t-1} + \mu + \varepsilon_t \tag{3}$$

where y_t is the value observed at time t, μ is a constant that represents the average difference between adjacent values in the original series, and ε_t is a white Gaussian noise. More complex trends may be modeled by a second-order differentiation. As previously explained, the (0,1,0) model without significant constant characterizes psychological *state* functioning over time. This model is typical of time series that exhibit sensitivity to local events (immediate experience). The current value is determined by the preceding value (y_{t-1}), plus the current disturbance (ε_t) or local event (or random shock) that impacts either positively or negatively. The process is a dependency to change. The process leads to a substantial evolution in the local mean of the series under the influence of life events.

The second step aims at identifying the autoregressive and moving average terms to include in the model, through examination of the ACF and PACF of the (stationarized) series. An AR process suggests that the current value is determined by a weighted sum of the preceding values. For example, an AR process (1,0,0) obeys the following equation:

$$y_t = \mu + \phi \, y_{(t-1)} + \varepsilon_t \tag{4}$$

where μ is a constant, ϕ is the auto-regressive coefficient, and ε_t is the error associated with the current value. The typical signature of an AR process is a slow decay of the ACF and a sharp cut-off of the PACF, which presents a limited number of significant peaks. The number of significant correlations in the PACF indicates the number of AR terms to include in the model. If μ is not significant, the model (1,0,0) is related to constant adaptation to events over time. The autoregressive model characterizes psychological *dynamical equilibrium* functioning over time. This model with significant constant is typical of time series that exhibit homeostasis functioning. The current value is determined by a constant μ that represents the average of the original time series (referenced value), the preceding weighted value (y_{t-1}), and the local disturbance (ε_t). The amplitude of oscillation is given by ϕ. The functioning is stable associated with random fluctuations and relaxation oscillations.

A moving average (MA) process suggests that the current value is determined by the weighted average of the preceding values. When the series is considered to be stationary, this process can also be defined as the sum of the mean of the series plus the weighted sum of the errors associated with the preceding values. Thus an MA process of order 1 obeys the following equation:

$$y_t = \mu - \theta \, \varepsilon_{(t-1)} + \varepsilon_t \tag{5}$$

where μ is the mean of the series, θ is the moving average coefficient and ε_t is the error associated with the value at time t. The typical signature of an MA process is a slow decay of the PACF and a sharp cut-off of the ACF. The number of significant correlations in the ACF indicates the number of MA terms to include in the model.

The resulting models are constituted from the combination of the basic equations previously presented. For example, an ARIMA model (0,1,1) obeys the following equation:

$$y_t = \mu + y_{(t-1)} - \theta \, \varepsilon_{(t-1)} + \varepsilon_t \tag{6}$$

which contains one differentiation term and one moving average term. Such a model allows the description of the progressive evolution of the series and an inference concerning the underlying psychological functioning. The obtained models are submitted to a multi-criteria evaluation: (1) each coefficient in the model should be statistically significant, (2) the residuals should represent a white noise process without any time dependence, and (3) the standard deviation of the residuals should be lower than the standard deviation of the original series (Box and Jenkins, 1976).

The application of the ARIMA procedures provided interesting statistical results, and a quite reasonable model of the psychological processes underlying the dynamics (Fortes *et al.*, 2005). Nevertheless, this approach tends to focus on short-term correlations in the series, and is unable to reveal more complex dynamics, as for example longer-term time dependencies.

Fractal analysis methods are devoted to determine long term correlations, for time series more than 1024 observations. The duration of assessment is decided to optimize spectral analyses, which work on the basis of series with lengths that are powers of 2. The methods detect the presence of fractal processes underlying the dynamics of time series. A number of methods have been proposed for assessing the scaling exponent of fractal series (Eke, Herman, Bassingthwaighte, Raymond, Percival, Cannon, Balla and Ikrényi, 2000; Scheppers, van Beek, and Bassingthwaighte, 1992). Eke *et al.* (2000) proposed methodological principles to apply these analyses. The methods are explained in details in our specific paper (Delignières, Fortes and Ninot, 2004).

A DYNAMICAL APPROACH TO DETERMINE SELF-ESTEEM FUNCTIONING

Example of Self Esteem Time Series

An idiographic protocol can be a daily measurement of self-esteem over a two months period. It permits to obtain a time series of 60 consecutive observations. The researcher will determine not only the nature of events but also median level (*mean* during the period), instability (*standard-deviation, range, mean of absolute difference* between two consecutive days) and the dynamics. An illustration is presented with a young woman with moderate anorexia particularly unstable and with a dynamic with a low process of preservation (figure 7).

Functioning of Self-Esteem

Mean and Instability

The first hypothesis was that the means but not the instability such as standard deviations of self-esteem measured twice a day would be similar over two consecutive periods of six months in healthy adults (Ninot, Fortes, Delignières and Maïano, 2004). Each participant completed a PSI twice a day between 7:00 and 9:00 am and between 7:00 and 9:00 pm over one year period. Each inventory included one item for self-esteem, and one for the measurement error. The individual time series presented 728 observations. The figures 8 and 9 respectively show two times series of man aged of 42 years and woman aged of 29 years.

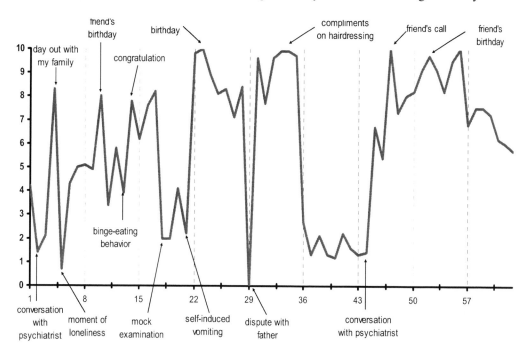

Figure 7: Daily change of self-esteem in a young anorexic adult (0 *not at all* and 10 *absolutely*)

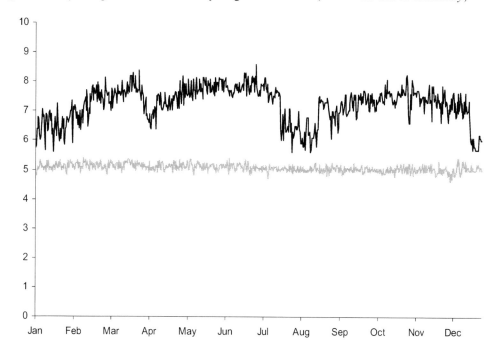

Figure 8: Bi-daily change in self-esteem (upper curve) and measurement error item (lower curve) in a man over the year 2001

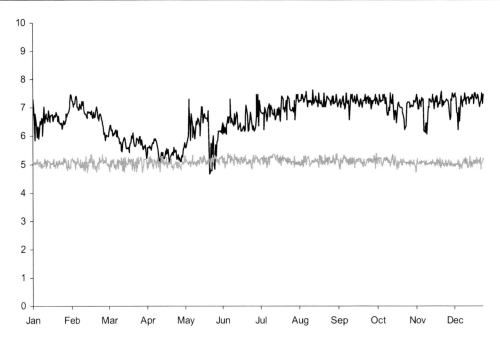

Figure 9: Bi-daily change in self-esteem (upper curve) and measurement error (lower curve) in a women over the year 2001

Table 2 presents the descriptive results over the two consecutive periods of six months. The paired *t*-test reveals no differences in the mean score of self-esteem between the two semesters. The paired *t*-test reveals standard deviation of self-esteem significantly higher for semester 1 compared to semester 2 ($p < .05$).

Table 2: Descriptive values of global self-esteem and physical self over two consecutive semesters

			A(M)	B(M)	C(M)	D(M)	E(W)	F(W)	G(W)	H(W)	*p*
ME	Sem 1	M	5.08	5.07	5.07	5.08	5.10	5.08	5.08	5.08	
		SD	0.12	0.12	0.16	0.12	0.13	0.12	0.13	0.12	
	Sem 2	M	5.04	5.04	5.01	5.06	5.05	5.04	5.09	5.04	0.50 ($t = 0.70$)
		SD	0.11	0.11	0.16	0.11	0.11	0.10	0.12	0.11	0.11 ($t = 1.77$)
GSE	Sem 1	M	9.11	8.36	7.24	7.43	5.18	7.49	6.67	6.25	
		SD	0.47	0.84	0.60	0.53	1.08	0.54	0.66	0.85	
	Sem 2	M	9.37	8.66	7.10	7.49	5.37	7.10	7.13	5.58	0.95 ($t = -0.06$)
		SD	0.29	0.75	0.59	0.54	0.69	0.44	0.28	0.25	0.03 ($t = 2.84$)

W = woman; M = man; ME = measurement error item; GSE = global self-esteem; Sem = semester.

Adults present stable mean scores of self-esteem between two consecutive periods of six months. The individual systems of self-perception maintained globally their scores over a period of one year.

However, graphs and descriptive data showed global and local instabilities of self-esteem, more than measurement error item. The significant difference in the standard deviation of self-esteem scores indicated that these adults reduced their fluctuations during the second semester. The presence of instabilities of self-esteem tied to specific external events such as success or failure. The results support fluctuations evidenced by Kernis and his collaborators in self-esteem ratings (Kernis, 1993; Kernis and Waschull, 1995; Greenier et al., 1999). Self-esteem appears to be sensitive to daily events (Nezlek and Plesko, 2001), and its instability reflect the reactivity of each individual to these events. Individuals tend to experience slight variations rather than dramatic shifts in their self-evaluations (Kernis, 1993; Kernis et al., 1989; Kernis et al., 1991).

More generally, *standard-deviation, range, mean of absolute difference* are sensitive to different features of variability in the time series and our results showed that they represent quite independent characteristics (Fortes, Delignières et Ninot, 2004b; Ninot et al., 2004). The *standard deviation* reflects the global sensibility of the series. The *range* is related to the excursion to extreme values during self-assessments. The *mean absolute difference* informs on the local sensitivity to daily disturbances. Each subject seemed to be characterized by a particular combination of these three properties. This suggests the hypothesis of a type of individual dynamic invariant that would consistently underlie self-evaluative behavior.

Nevertheless, the descriptive indicators of variability were insufficient to determine the psychological process that produces self-esteem perception.

Short Term Dynamics

One of our study assessed intra-individual dynamics of self-esteem in healthy adults over a six-month period (Ninot et al., 2005). The purpose was to examine over time the suppositions offered by nomothetic researches about the dynamics of self-esteem (see 1.1.3). The hypothesis was that the self-esteem functions as a *trait* over a six-month period in adults.

The participants were eight adults, four women and four men (mean age: 29.4 years; SD: 7.9; SEM: 2.8). They were all employed, came from middle-class backgrounds, and none lived alone. None had pharmacologically treated psychiatric disorders or severe medical illness and none had recently undergone major negative life events that would have affected psychological functioning over the six-month period. All gave informed written consent to participate.

All time series of global self-esteem present long-trend ACF. Each of them exhibits significant and progressive decline in ACF coefficients from lag 1 to the maximal significant lag ($p < .05$). This assumes that the original series are non-stationary and have a constant average trend. Moreover, the better and significant ACF coefficient is always found at lag 1. Conversely, ACF and partial ACF of each measurement error item time series do not exhibit for any lag significant coefficients. Thus, the best ARIMA model for measurement error item time series is systematically a (0,0,0) model which is characterized by the equation (2).

To determine the best fitted ARIMA model for self-esteem time series, differencing procedures were performed for all series to make them stationary. Time series presenting a long-trend ACF underwent a first order differencing. The lag 1 autocorrelation of the differenced series satisfied requirements, thus indicating that no further differencing was necessary. As a result, all the models were (p,1,q) models, suggesting that the original series were not stationary and had constant average trends. No significant constants were found and the standard deviations were reduced, indicating that the trends had been completely eliminated. The autocorrelation function of the differenced series displayed a sharp cutoff while the partial ACF decayed slightly (i.e., had significant spikes at higher lags), thus suggesting a MA signature. The MA model (0,1,1) without significant constant was systematically obtained for all of the differenced time series ($p < .001$). All the time series presented the same MA dynamics with specific θ coefficient from 0.47 to 0.81, thus characterizing the time functioning as not stationary, and with short-term autocorrelation. The time series must not be considered as white noise fluctuations around a stable value.

The *trait* hypothesis was that self-esteem dynamics were only related to measurement error, suggesting that individuals actively resist to change and return to a reference value. The results showed clearly that the eight self-esteem time series fluctuated over the six-month period, more than the time series resulting from the measurement error item. The self-esteem time series were not stationary or random. The significant autocorrelation, including a progressive decrease, indicated that the process of self-esteem functioned with a short-term history for each participant. Using repeatedly a sensitive instrument over a long period showed that self-esteem can be considered as a complex dynamical system subjected to internal and environmental constraints (Nowak *et al.*, 2000). It cannot be considered as white noise fluctuations around a stable value.

The ARIMA procedures showed systematically MA model associated with first order differencing and a non-significant constant (0,1,1) characterized by equation 6 without significant constant ($\mu = 0$). The system did not oscillate around one reference value, and/or it did not tend to come back to this reference after a perturbation. The system exhibited noisy fluctuations around a slowly varying mean.

Conversely, the (0,0,0) model, characterized by random fluctuation around a reference value corresponding, was systematically obtained for measurement error item ($\mu = 5$). In a closed room without stimulation over a period of four hours and 15 minutes (completion each 5 minutes), we obtained 88% of self-esteem times series related to white noise fluctuations around a defined value and 12% of the time series functioned as an MA (0,1,1) model (Ninot *et al.*, 2004). This suggests that individuals actively resist change and return to a local reference value under conditions of a confined environment with no interruption.

In ecological context, the *trait* hypothesis had to be rejected. Self-esteem cannot be an attractor that functions as *trait* over time. Self-esteem measured over time did not function as a real *state* or *dynamic equilibrium*.

The pattern (0,1,1) of self-esteem emerges from an organic system confronted by several constraints. The time series has a specific sense over a short time period. The assessment at time t is characterized by an error term (ε_t), mathematically considered as a random disturbance. Psychologically, this disturbance should be considered as the resultant (perceptible and/or imperceptible) of all the recent (good or bad) events likely to affect the assessed dimension. The value at time t is modeled as the preceding observed value (y_{t-1}) minus a fraction of its own disturbance ($\theta\varepsilon_{t-1}$). In other words, the value at time t tends to absorb the preceding disturbance. The amplitude of the correction is given by θ, and the restoration should be complete with a θ value close to 1. This correction underlies the preservation process, which limits the influence of the perturbations, and ensures the stability of the series.

Mathematically, the first part of the MA equation ($y_t = y_{(t-1)} + \varepsilon_t$) proposes individual iterative functioning based on history over a short period that generates adaptation to the impact of preceding and current events. The second part of the MA equation ($-\theta\varepsilon_{(t-1)}$) is related to preservation function, corresponding to a fraction of the measurement error emerging from the previous auto-evaluation (a sort of correction of previous adaptation).

Psychologically, this model suggests that the dynamics of self-esteem could be underlain by the combination of two opposite processes: an *adaptation* process, which tends to inflect the series in the direction of the perturbation, and a *preservation* process, which tends to restore the previous value after disturbance (functioning as a resistance to the influence of daily events). For *adaptation* process, the inclusion of incoming information is well-known (Butler, Hokanson and Flynn, 1994; Nezlek and Plesko, 2001; Rosenberg, 1979). For *preservation* process, the importance of maintaining relatively stable and positive self-evaluation despite a high number of negative events that may affect stability of self has been clearly demonstrated in the literature (Sedikides and Skowronski, 1997; Tesser and Campbell, 1983).

The ARIMA model (0,1,1) was obtained in several occasions (Fortes *et al.*, 2004b; Delignières *et al.*, 2004; Ninot *et al.*, 2004). The combined effects of these two processes led to a local reference value that evolved slowly under the influence of life events. These results indicate that a *dynamic adjustment* governs changes in global self-esteem. According to Marks-Tarlow (1999), self-esteem can be viewed as a continuous flow that is beyond contextual, social, and cultural factors. This global self-perception emerges from a system possessing enough stability to maintain consistent functioning, but sufficient randomness to ensure adaptability and creativity. The analysis of its historical evolution is essential to understanding it (Marks-Tarlow, 1999).

The coefficient θ is generally far from 1. We reported values ranging from 0.40 to 0.86, and as such a residual fraction of the previous disturbance remains in the current expected value. In other words, each disturbance tends to leave a persistent trace in the dynamics of the series. The moving average coefficient θ determines the balance between these two opposite processes. We evidenced a high consistency between the coefficients obtained for the different time series of a given participant (Fortes *et al.*, 2004b; Ninot *et al.*, 2004). This suggested a kind of individual characteristic related to the stability of self-esteem and its resistance to the influence of daily events. From a clinical point of view, the closer the θ coefficient was to 0, the less conservative the system was and the less it resisted to environmental stimuli. The low θ coefficient reflected low historical consistency, which can be interpreted as unstable self-esteem, fragile and vulnerable self-worth, an over-dependence on the love and approval of significant others, a heightened tendency to be ego-involved in every day activities, excessive dependency needs, over-reliance on the evaluations of others, and an impoverished self-concept (Butler et al., 1994; Kernis *et al.*, 1989; Rosenberg, 1979; Tennen and Affleck, 1993; Greenier *et al.*, 1999).

More interestingly, we applied the same ARIMA procedure to the hierarchical structure of physical self (figure 10) in many healthy adults. We obtained the same common dynamics (0,1,1) over different periods (Delignières et al., 2004; Fortes et al., 2004b; Ninot et al., 2004). This homogeneous dynamics in the physical self and global self-esteem suggests that the different dimensions in the model share a common dynamics. This suggests that an invariant individual dynamics would consistently underlie self-evaluative behavior. Biological systems are often characterized by spontaneous behaviors having a high level of stability and reproducibility (Kelso, 1995). The similar pattern suggests that the intra-individual dynamics of self-perceptions were stable over time. This tendency reveals the presence of attractors linked to the dynamics of self. Research is needed to explore this hypothesis within specific impacts (Marks-Tarlow, 1999; Ninot *et al.*, 2004; Nowak *et al.*, 2000).

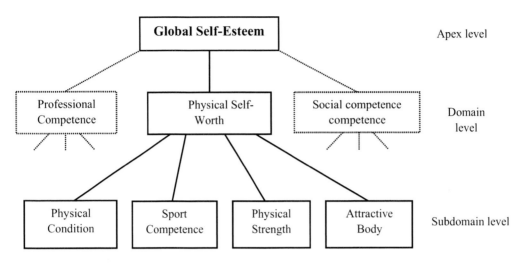

Note: Fox and Corbin (1989) proposed a hierarchical model for the physical domain of competence that has been empirically supported by studies throughout the Western world (e.g., Sonstroem, Speliotis, and Fava, 1992). The median level of the physical self is occupied by physical self-worth, which can be seen as a general feeling of happiness, satisfaction, pride, respect, and confidence in the physical self. The most specific level is composed of four sub-domains: physical condition, sport competence, physical strength, and attractive body. Physical condition represents the perception of one's physical condition, fitness and stamina, one's ability to maintain exercise, and one's confidence in the exercise and fitness settings. Sport competence corresponds to the perception of sport and athletic ability, ability to learn sport skills, and confidence in the sport environment. Physical strength is related to perceived strength, muscle development, and confidence in situations requiring strength. Finally, attractive body corresponds to the perceived attractiveness of the body, the ability to maintain an attractive body and confidence in one's appearance.

Figure 10: Hierarchical model of self-esteem within physical domain particularly developed (Fox and Corbin, 1989)

The application of the ARIMA procedures provided interesting statistical results and a quite reasonable model of the psychological processes underlying the dynamics of self-esteem. The system exhibited noisy fluctuations around a slowly varying mean. Nevertheless, this approach tends to focus on short-term correlations in the time series and is unable to reveal longer-term dependencies, which could be indicative of the presence of fractal processes in the time series. Investigating self-esteem as an emergence of a complex dynamical system leads to a variety of insights regarding self-structure and self-process.

Long Term Dynamics

Several theoretical and empirical arguments lead to put forward the hypothesis of the presence of chaotic or fractal processes underlying self-esteem time series. Most of the contemporary models of self-esteem consider this construct as multidimensional. Marks-Tarlow (1999) argued that each level of the self is formed through interactions and complex feedbacks loops occurring at various physiological, psychological, and social levels. Each level possesses an emerging dynamics, and is embedded in the next, giving rise to fractal properties such as self-similarity. In the same vein, Nowak *et al.* (2000) considered self-esteem as an emergent property of a complex dynamical system, composed of a myriad of specific and interconnected self-thoughts. From this viewpoint, the emergence of self as a coherent structure and its maintenance facing incongruent elements can be understood as the result of a process of self-organization, on the basis of the multiple interactions acting within the system. The macroscopic behavior of such complex dynamical systems was frequently proven to exhibit fractal properties (Bak and Chen, 1991; Gilden, 2001; West and Shlesinger, 1990).

The examination of the ACF of self-esteem series and physical self, in previous studies (Fortes *et al.*, 2004b; Ninot *et al.*, 2001; 2004; 2005), reveals the persistence of significant autocorrelation over a wide range of lags (up to 100 lags in some time series with more than 500 observations). These results suggest the presence of long-term time dependencies in the time series.

Another argument relates to the inherent stability of such fractal processes. A number of biological and psychological time series were recently proven to possess fractal properties. Recent research evidenced this kind of results in continuous uni-manual tapping (Chen, Ding, and Kelso, 2001), in serial reaction time (Gilden, Thomton, and Mallon, 1995), in step duration series during locomotion (Hausdorff, Mitchell, Firtion, Peng, Cudkowicz, Wei, and Goldberger, 1997) or in heartbeats (Goldberger, 1999). When obtained from young and healthy organisms, these time series exhibit a very special case of fractal behavior, called $1/f$ or *pink* noise. "$1/f$ noise" signifies that when considering the power spectrum of these time series, each frequency has power proportional of its period of oscillation. As such, power is distributed across the entire spectrum, and not concentrated at a certain portion. Consequently, fluctuations at some time scale are only loosely correlated with those of another time scale. This relative independence of the underlying processes acting at different time scales suggests that a localized perturbation at one time scale will not necessarily alter the stability of the global system. In other words, $1/f$ noise renders the system more stable and more adaptive to internal and external perturbations (West and Shlesinger, 1990).

One can easily understand why fractal behavior constitutes an appealing hypothesis for modeling the dynamics of self-esteem time series. Four adults volunteered for this study (Delignières *et al.*, 2004). All were employed, and came from middle-class backgrounds. None had pharmacologically treated psychiatric disorders or severe medical illness and none had recently undergone major negative life events that would have affected psychological function over the testing period. They were not paid for their participation. Each participant completed the questionnaire on computer twice a day over a period of 512 consecutive days. Participants were not informed of these numerical scores, and were not allowed to consult their previous responses. We finally obtained 1024-point time series, for each dimension and each participant. The duration of the experiment was determined in order to optimize spectral analyses, which work on the basis of series with lengths that are powers of 2.

The main result is the uncovering of long-range, fractal correlation in self-esteem time series (Delignières *et al.*, 2004). The fractal behavior of the series was proven without ambiguity, with consistent results obtained by different methods, one in the frequency domain, and three in the time domain. The results give a good illustration of the interest of an integrated approach in fractal analysis, by the joint use of different methods, not only for detecting the presence of fractal processes, but also for the estimation of the scaling exponents (Rangarajan and Ding, 2000).

The uncovering of long-range, fractal correlation in self-esteem series led to important theoretical considerations. Such fractal behavior, at a systemic level, is generally considered as the expected outcome of a complex, dynamical system, composed of multiple interacting elements (West and Shlesinger, 1990). Long-range correlations constitute the typical signature of complex systems in critical self-organized state (Bak and Chen, 1991). Multiscaled randomness could under some conditions give rise to such behavior (Hausdorff and Peng, 1996). All these propositions share the idea of the presence of many interacting components acting on different time scales. As such, our results represent an interesting support for the theory proposed by Nowak *et al.* (2000), which considered self-esteem as a self-organized dynamical system.

Interestingly, this fractal behavior was discovered, with similar scaling exponents, for each dimension in the hierarchical model of physical self. On the basis of the principles underlying the hierarchical model of physical self (Fox and Corbin, 1989), one could conceive self-esteem as more complex (i.e. integrating a wider number of elements) than the others dimensions. Our results associated to those with ARIMA analyses suggest that sub-domains behave in a similar way than the higher and more global levels, and should also be considered as complex systems. This result is consistent with the basic principles of self-similarity, each level in the self appearing to contain similar dynamics, while being embedded in the next level (Marks-Tarlow, 1999).

The exponents obtained for each series allowed us to classify them as close to $1/f$ noise. This noise represents a compromise between white noise and Brownian motion. More precisely, $1/f$ noise represents a compromise between the absolute preservation of the mean achieved by white noise (which is characterized by a strictly stationary series, with random fluctuations around a stable mean), and the absolute adaptation of Brownian motion (defined as the cumulative sum of a series of random shocks).

These results have important implications, concerning the way one can conceive functioning of self-esteem. When $1/f$ noise was discovered in a number of young and healthy systems, each frequency of these time series has power proportional of its period of oscillation. Power is distributed across the entire spectrum, and not concentrated at a certain portion. Consequently, fluctuations at some time scale are only loosely correlated with those of another time scale. This relative independence of the underlying processes acting at different time scales suggests that a localized perturbation at one time scale will not necessarily alter the stability of the global system. $1/f$ noise possesses an intrinsic stability, due to the relative independence of the underlying processes acting at different time scales. In other words, $1/f$ noise renders the system more stable and more adaptive to endogeneous and exogeneous perturbations (West and Shlesinger, 1990). This "optimal" fractality appears as the typical signature of young, healthy, and adaptive systems. On the contrary, certain diseases seem associated with a disruption of this "optimal" fractality (West and Shlesinger, 1990). Hausdorff *et al.* (1997) showed that fluctuations in the duration of the gait cycle display $1/f$ behavior in healthy young adults. This fractal dynamics was systematically altered with elderly subjects or with subjects with Huntington's disease. In these cases, fluctuations appeared more random, closer to a white noise process. In the same vein, Goldberger (1999) analyzed beat-to-beat fluctuations in heart rate and showed that a congestive heart failure led to an alteration of the $1/f$ fractality observed for healthy subjects. In these two experiments the amplitude of the alteration was proportional to the severity of the disease.

Implications

Dynamics of Self-esteem

The application of time series analyses to self-esteem and physical self series constitutes only a first step in the characterization of their functioning. Nomothetic researches proposed finally a simplification of intra-individual functioning of self-esteem and quick generalization. Reductionism, determinism and epistemological orientations can explain these simplifications. Dynamical social psychology opens a new perspective in considering self-esteem functioning. Successive ecological constraints are needed to understand psychological processes implicated to self-esteem emergence. These random impacts cannot be ignored as a *trait*, assimilated as a *state*, or fixed to a reference value as a *steady state*. The results did not show an increase of entropy. The constraints are progressively integrated with the process called *dynamic adjustment*. The local mean evolves slowly with random impacts. Everything functions as if equilibrium of self-esteem is found with the disequilibrium caused by ecological constraints, as dissipative structure that needs energy to "exist" (Prigogine, 1994). This functioning differs to a major Piagetian principle that stipulates: equilibrium of life organism is a pseudo-equilibrium dynamic due to multitude of disequilibrium naturally compensated for. The observed process far to the equilibrium needs random impacts and permits a great flexibility without neglecting own history. It is a fundamental condition to create new behaviors. In consequence, studying exclusively the level score a t time is insufficient and very approximate to determine self-esteem of a subject, whatever the final aim. Studying instability and dynamics is indispensable to understand the functioning and provide validity to mean level.

The $1/f$ behavior we evidenced could be conceived as the typical intrinsic dynamics of self-esteem and physical self for healthy, physically and professionally active adults. According to Marks-Tarlow (1999), psychological health resides at the edge of chaos, a transition zone between predictable order and unpredictable chaos. Within this zone, systems possess enough stability for maintaining a consistent functioning, but sufficient randomness to ensure adaptability and creativity. Disabled systems behave away from this edge, in the direction of unpredictable chaos, as in hysterical patients, or in the opposite direction of deterministic order, as in obsessive-compulsive patients. Marks-Tarlow (1999) predicts that for such patients, specific alterations of fractality should be observed, in the direction of Brownian motion in the first case, and in the direction of white noise in the second. Gottschalk, Bauer and Whybrow (1995) evidenced such results in the close domain of mood variation. They analyzed long-term daily mood records in bipolar disorder and normal subjects, and observed in both groups a $1/f$-type noise in the collected series. ß exponents were significantly higher in bipolar disorder patients, suggesting that self-rated mood in such patients was more organized, and characterized by a loss of complexity.

One of the most important results is the demonstration of the non-stationary nature of self-esteem over time. Such non-stationary processes could be characterized by a number of features, including changes in the dynamics, or bifurcations. Such phenomena could be especially expected in chronic disease patients (Ninot, Fortes, Leymarie, Brun, Poulain,

Desplan and Varray, 2002). But, some specific episodes could entail local changes of self-esteem dynamics in healthy persons (see figure 9 and 10).

Our studies support to the conception of the self as a complex dynamical system (Nowak et al., 2000; Vallacher et al., 2002). The fractal behavior reflects intrinsic dynamics of self-esteem and physical self of healthy adults, and its inherent properties could explain some macroscopic, commonly recognized features, such as stability, preservation, or adaptation. Further studies are needed with ecological and experimental viewpoint in different individuals to detail combination of processes.

Functioning of Multidimensional Models

Theoretical conceptualizations of self-esteem have changed markedly. Self-esteem was first conceived as a one-dimensional and global construct (Coopersmith, 1967; Rosenberg, 1979), namely the individual's overall sense of worth as a person. More recently, multidimensional models were developed on the basis of evaluative statements, with self-esteem seen as the combination of distinct self-assessments relative to specific domains of competence (Harter, 1985). These models were then enriched by the introduction of hierarchical conceptions (Fox and Corbin, 1989; Marsh and Shavelson, 1985) that allowed direct focus on mechanisms of change in the self-system. Several domains of competence seem to be implicated in self-esteem enhancement, particularly the physical domain (Fox and Corbin, 1989; Marsh and Yeung, 1998; Sonstroem et al., 1992). According to these hierarchical conceptions, global self-esteem is at the apex of the structure and is then linked to first-order facets (e.g., academic self-concept, physical self-concept), themselves composed of second-order facets (e.g., math competence or sport competence).

(In)stability in self-perception hierarchical structure remained unknown. According to several authors (Buckworth and Dishman, 2001; Fox, 1990), (in)stability of global self-perception reflects self-consistency, with the development of feelings of unity, independence, predictability, and control. The lowest levels will undergo stronger variations resulting from situational experiences than the higher levels. The assumption is that meaningful changes in self-esteem from an activity might be difficult to detect because the global scale lacks the necessary sensitivity. Changes would be detected at the specifically relevant subscale. Other authors (Amorose, 2001; Brown, 1998; Marsh and Yeung, 1998) found that responses to global self-concept scores were unstable in comparison with specific physical scales. Global self-evaluations are more affected by mood and immediate experiences, and therefore are likely to vary more over time (Brown, 1998). The assumption is that the lowest level would be the most specific and stable because specific abilities cannot radically change in just a few days. Conclusions of these studies were based on theoretical supposition or longitudinal protocols with fewer than six measures performed over unequal periods (3 weeks to 18 months). Moreover, some studied adolescents, who are considered to be less stable than adults (Rosenberg, 1979).

Descriptive indicators of (in)stability and cross-correlation function allowed us to test this hypothesis concerning the relative stability of each dimension in the hierarchical model. The results did not reveal any evidence of a higher or lower (in)stability for the apex level as compared with the more specific dimensions (Fortes et al., 2004a; Ninot et al., 2004). This intra-individual homogeneity was evidenced for the three indicators of instability (standard deviation, range, and mean absolute difference) and cross-correlation function (Fortes et al., 2004a). Each participant were characterized by a particular combination of these three properties whatever the hierarchical level. A maximum centered on lag zero of cross-correlation function was obtained. (In)stability appeared quite consistent for each subject among dimensions, whatever the position of these dimensions in the hierarchical model of physical self. This homogeneous (in)stability in the self-concept system constitutes a surprising result and suggests that the different dimensions in the model share common dynamics. This also suggests a strong coupling between the dimensions, characterized by a synchronic evolution over time.

Causal Flow in Hierarchical Models

The conception of self as a hierarchical structure led researchers to question the mechanisms of change across the self-system. Based on individual-environment interactionism and situation-specific constructs, hierarchical self-concept was thought by some to generalize from situation-specific experiences. This perspective emphasizes the role of cognitive processes, with self-esteem seen as the result of judgments about one's qualities in various domains (Harter, 1999). Thus, hierarchical models are assumed to be crossed by pathways whereby life experiences first affect specific levels of the hierarchy and then modify more global elements. The lowest and most specific levels are assumed to be the most sensitive to environmental influences and thus the least stable. The highest and most general level, on the other hand, is the most stable and least sensitive to specific experiences. In contrast, other psychologists suggested that self-esteem mainly derives from affective processes (Brown, 1998). This approach is consistent with the evidence that many attitudes are affectively based. According to Brown (1993), "specific beliefs about one's competencies and attributes are considered as consequences rather than antecedents of global self-esteem and are used to buttress and sustain feelings of self-worth" (p. 32). Thus, the apex of the self structure would be the most sensitive to mood variations and the most stable level. Although self-concept as a hierarchically organized construct is now well established, the processes that would explain the changes in self-esteem still need to be identified.

These opposite theoretical conceptualizations of self-concept (i.e., cognitive vs. affective) led to several hypotheses about the causal influences among the elements of the hierarchical structure. Based on the assumption of predominantly cognitive functioning, the *bottom-up* hypothesis suggests that influences diffuse from the lowest elements at the base of the self structure to higher-level dimensions (Fox, 1990; Harter, 1999; Sonstroem *et al.*, 1994). For example, high satisfaction with a given physical strength task reinforces the feeling of competence in the corresponding sub-domain, then enhances physical self-worth and finally global self-esteem. According to self-enhancement theory (Sonstroem *et al.*, 1994), physical self-efficacy is the primary cognitive link between physical measures and higher-order psychological constructs. This suggests that behavioral outcomes influence self-efficacy beliefs, which in turn contribute to determine more global constructs of competence and self-esteem. The *bottom-up* hypothesis has been widely tested empirically and currently seems to be the most agreed upon. Conversely, the *top-down* hypothesis, which assumes the predominance of affective functioning, suggests that causal flow is directed from the apex of the structure to the lower-level dimensions (Brown, 1993; 1998). In other words, global self-esteem is massively submitted to emotions and mood change (Greenier *et al.*, 1999) and a sudden depreciation due to negative emotions, for example, would irradiate to subjacent domains, such as the physical domain, and then modify the corresponding sub-domains. However, this perspective is fairly speculative and lacks empirical support and refinement.

Bottom-up and *top-down* hypotheses are not utterly opposed in that they both acknowledge that global self-esteem and self-evaluations in specific domains are related, with only the direction of causal flow being inverted. Some authors have considered the possibility of simultaneous cognitive and affective routes of causal flow and suggested a third hypothesis, the *reciprocal* (Marsh and Yeung, 1998) or bi-directional (Feist, Bodner, Jacobs, Miles, and Tan, 1995) model. According to this hypothesis, diffusion processes follow both directions. Finally, Marsh and Yeung (1998) and Kowalski and his colleagues (Kowalski, Crocker, Kowalski, Chad, and Humbert, 2003) used structural equation modeling to test the direction of causal flow in the physical self structure based on two assessment moments separated by a period of one year. They used respectively the Physical Self Description Questionnaire and the Physical Self Perception Profile and concluded in favor of a fourth hypothesis of causal flow: the *horizontal effects* model. This model emphasizes the stability of each component over time and suggests that the current value for a perceived dimension depends mainly on its previous value. This perspective offers weak support to the hierarchical conception of the self-structure because it assumes the independent functioning of the structural elements.

Despite the interesting work of Marsh and Yeung (1998) and Kowalski *et al.* (2003), little has been established regarding the direction of causal flow in the physical domain. Heuristic speculations about the *bottom-up* hypothesis introduced by Fox (1990) or the *reciprocal* influences remain to be empirically supported. Two main objections may be addressed to these studies. First, two assessment moments are not sufficient to capture changes between dimensions. Although researchers have generally insisted on the need for longitudinal data collection to test causal flow hypotheses (Amorose, 2001; Marsh and Yeung, 1998), few attempts have been made to fully analyze the time-evolutionary properties of the hierarchical structure. Instead, most studies have focused on the contextual determinants of self-esteem fluctuations and have borrowed static rather than dynamic methodological approaches. The second objection to previous attempts to demonstrate causal influence is that the approaches have been nomothetic rather than idiographic.

Intra-individual studies need to be highly pertinent to provide a formal framework for identifying causal flow in the physical self structure. The hierarchical model of physical self and global self-esteem developed by Fox and Corbin (1989) can be considered as such a framework: a complex system subjected to several constraints over time that produces the same causal flow (Harter, 1999; Ninot *et al.*, 2001; Nowak, Vallacher, Tesser, and Borkowski, 2000; Robins *et al.*, 2001). For example, the *bottom-up* hypothesis would be supported if, for each individual, a systematic change in the physical strength sub-domain altered the physical self-worth level after a time delay, and if this change was in turn followed by a delayed change in global self-esteem.

Intra-individual studies are needed to verify whether which causal flows underlie the functioning of the self system over time. It is assumed that the causal flow direction would correspond to specific patterns in the results emerging from time series analyses. From now, our studies considered the collected series separately, and neglected to examine their interactions. The assessed dimensions are conceived as the interconnected components of a hierarchically organized system, but the way by which one dimension could influence its neighbors in the model remains an open question.

Relation with other Variables

Accuracy between abilities and perceived competence is a good predictor of mental health (Harter, 1999), especially for mood and dynamism. Nevertheless, few studies propose intra-individual protocol measuring both biological and psychological variables. Authors explain this situation using psychological arguments such as inexperience, lack of expertise, positive cognitive biases, auto-handicap strategies, overgeneralization, modesty or social desirability, and methodological arguments such as time limited protocols (see 1.2) or the fact to studying too global dimensions (Buckworth and Dishman, 2002).

For example, the accuracy between endurance variables and perceived physical dimensions should be an important indicator of training improvement. Endurance athletes hope to become professional and are therefore intensely focused on their daily physical condition. The accurate perception serves to motivate training, support their life projects, and improve their well-being (Sonstroem *et al.*, 1994).

Applications

On practical plan, psychological survey of a participant can be useful during certain life phases such as reeducation, learning session and behavioral change attempt. Personality questionnaires, enclosing subjects in restrictive categories or level, are susceptible to obstruct future psychological interventions. The repeated completion of brief tools and the comprehension of individual dynamics will permit to improve participation to any psychological intervention.

Determination of MA (0,1,1) coefficient or, in some case, of nature of dynamics, indicates the manner of using *adaptation* and *preservation* processes. With a certain paradox, *trait* or *state* functioning will appear respectively too rigid or too environment dependant to cope with efficacy to ecological constraints. From a psychopathological viewpoint, researchers will observe dynamical diseases (McKey et Milton, 1995) due to self-perception troubles.

If we worked massively on ecological context, observation of specific impacts on self-esteem using experimental design or simulation protocols will be very interesting. For example, we can study the consequences of an event on relaxation time, causal flow and/or change in the hierarchical structure.

In contrast to personality psychology, dynamical social psychology tries to understand recent behavior. Auto-correlation, omnipresence of MA (0,1,1) model and probable non-linear functioning open a new comprehension of human complexity for less than two years. This perspective opens great perspective to understand life transition periods such as disease, damage, mourning, retirement, or specific moments such as momentum, flow…

Several nomothetic studies failed to produce accurate prevision of exacerbations in chronic disease patients or optimal performance in athletes. Self-esteem conceived as a complex system submitted to random constraints can not be predicted over a long period. Conversely, prevision over a short term period with intra-individual survey can be possible with an associated probability coefficient. For example, ARIMA procedures are dedicated to obtain this coefficient.

The computer version of brief questionnaires can be useful in education, prevention or reeducation situations. Items (objective and/or subjective) can be added to observe specific and/or individualized symptoms. The automatic transcription to PDA can enhance care motivation in chronic disease patients. The development of Internet transfer data can inform clinician of compliance and health behaviors.

Individual curves offer opportunities to researcher and clinician to exchange with the user of a brief instrument. The comments of these curves will have determinant sense. The curves are support for interview, a kind of "relationship mediator". It is an occasion to point out changes, perturbations, oscillations, cyclic events… Verbalize within a curve traducing our own history is an opportunity to take distance, to observe recursive changes, and eventually understand differently. This strategy can have therapeutic virtues within the work of a psychologist. This can help the person to relive differently events. For a chronic disease patient, the visualization of curve can help to change behaviors and to detect causes producing symptoms exacerbations.

CONCLUSION

Nowak and Vallacher (1998) have opened social psychology to dynamical approach. Nevertheless, few authors from now have prolonged analogies or computer simulations (such as cellular automata) with empirical or experimental protocols. To the past, other authors, convinced of heuristic power of intra-individual survey, were stay on hypothesis phase (Mischel and Shoda, 1998).

The difficulties of intra-individual protocols, the lack of brief instruments, the need to use time series analyses rarely at the program of psychological studies and skepticism of review's expert with innovation were constraints to the advent of empirical or experimental proofs. Now, all theoretical methodological elements are ready to study the functioning of social psychology variables in a field quasi-unexplored.

REFERENCES

Allport, G.W. (1985). The historical background of social psychology. In G.Lindzey and E.Aronson (Eds.). The Handbook of social psychology (third edition, vol. I). New York: Random House.

Amorose, A.J. (2001). Intraindividual variability of self-evaluations in the physical domain: prevalence, consequences, and antecedents. *Journal of Sport and Exercise Psychology, 23,* 222-244.

Bak, P., and Chen, K. (1991). Self-organized criticality. *Scientific American, 264,* 46-53.

Banos, J.E., Bosch, F., Canellas, M., Bassols, A., and Bigorra, J. (1989). Acceptability of visual analogue scales in the clinical setting: A comparison with verbal rating scales in post-operative pain. *Method Finding Experimental Clinical Pharmacology, 11*(2), 123-127.

Barge-Schaapveld, D.Q., Nicolson, N.A., Berkhof, J., and de Vries, M.W. (1999). Quality of life in depression: Daily life determinants and variability. *Psychiatry Research, 88,* 173-189.

Baumeister, R.F. (1993). Understanding the inner nature of self-esteem. In R.F. Baumeister (Ed.), *Self-esteem: The puzzle of low self-regard* (pp. 201-218). New York: Plenum Press.

Baumgardner, A.H. (1990). To know oneself is to like oneself: Self-certainty and self-affect. *Journal of Personality and Social Psychology, 58*, 1062-1072.

Boker, S.M., Xu M., Rotondo, J.L., King, K. (2002). Windowed cross-correlation and peak picking for the analysis of variability in the association between behavioral time series. *Psychological Methods, 7*(3), 338-355.

Bouvard, M., and Cottraux, J. (1996). Protocoles et échelles d'évaluation en psychiatrie et en psychologie [Protocols and scales for psychiatry and psychology]. Paris: Masson.

Box, G.E., and Jenkins, G.M. (1976). *Time series analysis: forecasting and control*. Oakland: Holden-Dag.

Brewer, M.B. (2000). Research design and issues validity. In Reis, H.T., and Judd, C.M. (Eds.). *Methods in social and personality psychology* (pp. 3-16). Cambridge: Cambridge University Press.

Brown, J. D. (1998). *The Self*. Boston: McGraw-Hill.

Brown, J.D. (1993). Self-esteem and self-evaluation: Feeling is believing. In J. Suls (Ed.), *Psychological perspectives on the self* (vol. 4, pp. 27-58). Hillsdale: Erlbaum.

Buckworth, J., and Dishman, R.K. (2002). *Exercise psychology*. Champaign: Human Kinetics.

Burke, P.A., Kraut, R.E., and Dworkin, R.H. (1984). Traits, consitency, and self-schemata: What do our methods measure. *Journal of Personality and Social Psychology, 47*, 568-579.

Butler, A.C., Hokason, J.E., and Flynn, H.A. (1994). A comparison of self-esteem liability and low trait self-esteem as vulnerability factors for depression. *Journal of Personality and Social Psychology, 66*, 166-177.

Carlson, A.M. (1983). Assessment of chronic pain. Aspects of the reliability and validity of visual analogue scale. *Pain, 16*, 87-101.

Chen, Y., Ding, M., and Kelso, J.A.S. (2001). Origins of timing errors in human sensorimotor coordination. *Journal of Motor Behavior, 33*, 3-8.

Coopersmith, S. (1967). *The antecedents of self-esteem*. San Francisco: W.H. Freeman.

Csikszentmihalyi, M., and Larson, R. (1987). Validity and reliability of the experience sampling method. *Journal of Nervous and Mental Disease, 175*, 526-536.

Delignières, D., Fortes, M., and Ninot, G. (2004). The fractal dynamics of self-esteem and physical self. *Nonlinear Dynamics, Psychology, and Life Sciences, 8*, 479-510.

Demo, D.H. (1992). The self-concept over time: Research issues and directions. *Annual Review of Sociology, 18*, 303-326.

Dutton, K.A., and Brown, J.D. (1997). Global self-esteem and specific self-views as determinants of people's reactions to success and failure. *Journal of Personality and Social Psychology, 73*, 139-148.

Eke, A., Herman, P., Bassingthwaighte, J.B., Raymond, G.M., Percival, D.B., Cannon, M., Balla, I., and Ikrényi, C. (2000). Physiological time series: Distinguishing fractal noises from motions. *Pflügers Archives, 439*, 403-415.

Epstein, S. (1979). The stability of behaviour: On predicting most of the people much of the time. *Journal of Personality and Social Psychology, 37*, 1097-1126.

Feist, G.J., Bodner, T.E., Jacobs, J.F., Miles, M., and Tan, V. (1995). Integrating top-down and bottom-up structural models of subjective well-being: A longitudinal investigation. *Journal of Personality and Social Psychology, 68*, 138-150.

Fortes, M., Ninot, G., Leymarie, S., and Delignières, D. (2004a). The hierarchical structure of the physical self: An idiographic and cross-correlational analysis. *International Journal of Sport and Exercise Psychology*, *2*, 119-132.

Fortes, M., Delignières, D., and Ninot, G. (2004b). The dynamics of self-esteem and physical self: Between preservation and adaptation. *Quality and Quantity*, *38*, 735-751.

Fortes, M., Ninot, G., and Delignières, D. (2005). ARIMA procedures: Interests for APA. *Adapted Physical Activity Quarterly*, *22*, 221-236.

Fox, K.H., and Corbin, C.B. (1989). The Physical Self Perception Profile: Development and preliminary validation. *Journal of Sport and Exercise Psychology*, *11*, 408-430.

Fox, K.R. (1990). *The Physical Self-Perception Profile manual*. DeKalb: Office of Health Promotion.

Francis, L.J. (1997). Coopersmith's model of self-esteem: Bias toward the stable extravert? *Journal of Social Psychology*, *137*, 139-142.

Gernigon, C., d'Arripe-Longueville, F., Delignières, D., and Ninot, G. (2004). Dynamics of goal involvement states and of their relationships in sport: A quantitative and qualitative idiosyncratic study. *Journal of Sport and Exercise Psychology*, *26*, 572-596.

Gilden, D.L. (2001). Cognitive emissions of $1/f$ noise. *Psychological Review, 108*, 33-56.

Gilden, D.L., Thomton, T. and Mallon, M.W. (1995). 1/f noise in human cognition. *Science, 267*, 1837-1839.

Goldberger, A.L. (1999). Non linear dynamics, fractals, and chaos theory: Implication for neuroautonomic heart rate control in health and disease. In C.L. Bolis and J. Licino (Eds.), *The autonomic nervous system* (pp. 43-52). Geneva: WHO.

Gottschalk, A., Bauer, M.S., and Whybrow, P.C. (1995). Evidence of chaotic mood variation in bipolar disorder. *Archives of General Psychiatry, 52*, 947-959.

Greenier, K.D., Kernis, M.H., McNamara, C.W., Waschull, S.B., Berry, A.J., Herlocker, C.E., and Abend, T.A. (1999). Individual differences in reactivity to daily events: Examining the roles of stability and level of self-esteem. *Journal of Personality, 67*, 185-208.

Hanin, Y.L., and Syrjä, P. (1995). Performance affect in junior ice hockey players: An application of the individual zones of optimal functioning model. *The Sport Psychologist, 9*, 169-187.

Harter, S. (1985). Competence as dimensions of self-evaluation: Toward a comprehensive model of self-worth. In R. L. Leahy (Ed.), *The development of the self* (pp. 55-122). San Diego, CA: Academic Press.

Harter, S. (1999). The construction of the Self: A Developmental Perspective. New York: The Guilford Press.

Hausdorff, J.M., Mitchell, S.L., Firtion, R., Peng, C.K., Cudkowicz, M.E., Wei, J.Y., and Goldberger, A.L. (1997). Altered fractal dynamics of gait: reduced stride-interval correlations with aging and Huntington's disease. *Journal of Applied Physiology, 82*, 262-269.

Hays, R.B. (1989). The day-to-day functioning of close versus casual friendships. *Journal of Personality and Social Psychology*, *48*, 428-434.

Headey, B., and Wearing, A. (1989). Personality, life events, and subjective well-being: Toward a dynamic equilibrium model. *Journal of Personality and Social Psychology*, *57*, 731-739.

Huskisson, E.C. (1974). Measurement of pain. *The Lancet*, *2*, 1127-1131.

Jensen, M.P., Karoly, P., and Braver, S. (1986). The measuremnt of clinical pain intensity: A comparison of six methods. Pain, 2(7), 117-126.

Kelso, J. A. (1995). Dynamic patterns: the self-organization of brain and behavior. Cambridge: MIT Press.

Kenny, D.A., Campbell, D.T. (1989). On the measurement of stability in over-time data. *Journal of Personality, 57*(2), 445-481.

Kernis, M. H. (1993). The role of stability and level of self-esteem in psychological functioning. In R. F. Baumeister (Ed.), *Self-esteem: The puzzle of low self-regard* (pp. 167-182). New York: Plenum Press.

Kernis, M.H., Grannemann, B.D., and Barclay, L.C. (1989). Stability and level of self-esteem as predictors of anger arousal and hostility. *Journal of Personality and Social Psychology, 56*, 1013-1022.

Kernis, M.H., Grannemann, B.D., and Mathis, L.C. (1991). Stability of self-esteem as a moderator of the relation between level of self-esteem and depression. *Journal of Personality and Social Psychology, 61*, 80-84.

Kimiecik, J.C., and Blissmer, B. (1998). Applied exercise psychology: Measurement issues. In J.D. Duda (Ed.), *Advances in sport and exercise psychology measurement* (pp. 447-460). Morgantown: Fitness Information Technology.

Kowalski, K.C., Crocker, P.R., Kowalski, N.P., Chad, K.E., and Humbert, M.L. (2003). Examining the physical self in adolescent girls over time: Further evidence against hierarchical model. *Journal of Sport and Exercise Psychology*, 25, 5-18.

Lawson, H. (1990). Beyond positivism: Research, practice, and undergraduate professional education. *Quest, 42*, 161-183.

Leary, M.R., Tambor, E.S., Terdal, S.K., and Downs, D.L. (1995). Self-esteem as an interpersonal monitor: The sociometer hypothesis. *Journal of Personality and Social Psychology, 68*, 518-530.

Lord, C.G. (1997). *Social psychology*. Fort Worth: Hartcourt Brace College Publishers.

Marks-Tarlow, T. (1999). The self as a dynamical system. *Nonlinear Dynamics, Psychology, and Life Sciences*, 3, 311-345.

Markus, H. (1977). Self-schemata and processing information about the self. *Journal of Personality and Social Psychology*, 35, 63-78.

Marsh, H.W. (1993). Stability of individual differences in multi-wave panel studies: Comparison of simplex models and one-factor models. *Journal of Educational Measurement, 30*, 157-183.

Marsh, H.W., and Shavelson, R. (1985). Self-concept: Its multifaceted hierarchical structure. *Educational Psychologist, 20*, 107-123.

Marsh, H.W., and Yeung, A.S. (1998). Top-down, bottom-up, and horizontal models: The direction of causality in multidimensional, hierarchical self-concept models. *Journal of Personality and Social Psychology, 75*, 509-527.

McCrae, R.R., and Costa, P.T. (1994). The stability of personality: Observations and evaluations. *Current Directions in Psychological Science, 3*, 173-175.

McKey, M.C., and Milton, J.G. (1995). Dynamical diseases. In J. Bélair, L. Grass, U.A. Der Heiden and J. Milton (Eds.), *Dynamical disease: Mathematical analysis of human illness*. Woodbury: Aip Press.

Mischel, W., and Shoda, Y. (1998). Reconciling processing and personality dispositions. *Annual Review of Psychology*, 49, 229-258.

Newell, K. (1990). Physical activity, knowledge types, and degree programs. *Quest, 42,* 243-268.

Nezlek, J.B. (2002). Day-to-day relationships between self-awareness, daily events, and anxiety. *Journal of Personality, 70,* 249-275.

Nezlek, J.B., and Plesko, R.M. (2001). Day-to-day relationships among self-concept clarity, self-esteem, daily events, and moods. *Personality and Social Psychology Bulletin, 27,* 201-211.

Ninot, G., Delignières, D., and Fortes, M. (2000). L'évaluation de l'estime de soi dans the domaine corporel [Assessment of self-esteem in physical domain]. *STAPS, 53,* 35-48.

Ninot, G., Fortes, M., and Delignières, D. (2001). A psychometric tool for the assessment of the dynamics of the physical self. *European Review of Applied Psychology, 51,* 205-216.

Ninot, G., Fortes, M., Leymarie, S., Brun, A., Poulain, M., Desplan, J., and Varray, A. (2002). Effects of an intensive period inpatient rehabilitation program on the perceived physical self in moderate COPD patients. *International Journal of Rehabilitation Research, 25,* 51-55.

Ninot, G., Fortes, M., Delignières, D., and Maïano, C. (2004). The dynamic adjustment of physical self in adults overtime. *Individual Differences Research, 2,* 137-151.

Ninot, G., Fortes, M., and Delignières, D. (2005). The dynamics of self-esteem in adults over a six-month period: An exploratory study. *Journal of Psychology, 139,* 315-330.

Nowak, A., and Vallacher, R.R. (1998). *Dynamical social psychology.* New York: The Guilford Press.

Nowak, A., Vallacher, R. R., Tesser, A., and Borkowski, W. (2000). Society of self: the emergence of collective properties in self-structure. *Psychological Review, 107,* 39-61.

Ohnhaus, E.E., and Adler, R. (1975). Methodological problem in the measurement of pain: A comparison between the verbal rating scale and the visual analogue scale. *Pain, 1*(4), 379-384.

Paice, J.A., and Cohen, F.L. (1997). Validity of a verbal administered numeric rating scale to measure cancer pain intensity. *Cancer Nurse, 20*(2), 88-93.

Price, D.D., McGrath, P.A., Rafii, A., and Buckingham, B. (1983). The validation of visual analogue scales as ratio scale measures for chronic and experimental pain. *Pain, 17,* 45-46.

Prigogine, I. (1994). *Les lois du chaos* [rules of chaos]. Paris: Flammarion.

Rangarajan, G., and Ding, M. (2000). Integrated approach to the assessment of long range correlation in time series data. *Physical Review E, 61,* 4991-5001.

Reis, H.T., and Gable, S.L. (2000). Event-sampling and other methods for studying everyday experience. In : Reis, H.T., and Judd, C.M. (eds.). *Methods in social and personality psychology* (pp. 190-222). Cambridge: Cambridge University Press.

Reis, H.T., and Judd, C.M. (2000). *Methods in social and personality psychology.* Cambridge: Cambridge University Press.

Robins, R.W., Hendin, H.M., and Trzesniewski, K.H. (2001). Measuring global self-esteem: Construct validation of a single-item measure and the Rosenberg self-esteem scale. *Personality and Social Psychology Bulletin, 27,* 151-161.

Rogers, C. R. (1959). A theory of therapy, personality, and interpersonal relationships, as developed in the client centered-framework. In S. Koch (Ed.). *Psychology: A study of science* (Vol. 3, pp. 184-256). New York: McGraw-Hill.

Rosenberg, M. (1979). *Conceiving the self.* New York: Basics Books.

Runyan, W.M. (1983). Idiographic goals and methods in the study of lives. *Journal of Personality, 51,* 413-437.

Schepers, H.E., van Beek, J.H.G.M., and Bassingthwaighte, J.B. (1992). Four methods to estimate the fractal dimension from self-affine signals. *IEEE Engineering in Medecine and Biology, 11,* 57-71.

Schutz, R.W. (1998). Assessing the stability of psychological traits and measures. J.D. Duda (Ed.), *Advances in sport and exercise psychology measurement* (pp. 393-408). Morgantown: Fitness Information Technology.

Sedikides, C. (1995). Central and peripheral self-conception are differentially influenced by mood: Tests of the different sensitivity hypothesis. *Journal of Personality and Social Psychology, 69,* 759-777.

Shumway, R.H., and Stoffer, D.S. (2000). *Time series analysis and its applications.* New York: Springer-Verlag.

Slifkin, A.B, and Newell, K.M. (1998). Is variability in human performance a reflection of system noise? *Current Directions in Psychological Science, 7,* 170-177.

Sonstroem, R.J., Harlow, L.L., and Josephs, L. (1994). Exercise and self-esteem: Validity of model expansion and exercise associations. *Journal of Sport and Exercise Psychology, 14,* 207-221.

Sonstroem, R.J., Speliotis, E.D., and Fava, J.L. (1992). Perceived Physical Competence in Adults: An examination of the Physical Perception Profile. *Journal of Sport and Exercise Psychology, 14,* 207-221.

Spray, J.A., and Newell, K.M. (1986). Times series analysis of motor learning: KR versus no-KR. *Human Movement Science, 5,* 59-74.

Strelau, J. (2001). The concept and status of trait in research of temperament. *European Journal of Personality, 15,* 311-325.

Tennen, H., and Affleck, G. (1993). The puzzles of self-esteem, a clinical perspective. In R. F. Baumeister (Ed.), *Self-esteem: The puzzle of low self-regard.* New York: Plenum Press.

Tesser, A., and Campbell, J. (1983). Self-definition and self-evaluation maintenance. In J. Suls and A.G. Greenwald (Eds.), *Psychological perspectives on the self.* Hillsdale: L.E.A.

Vallacher, R.R., Nowak, A., Froehlich, M., and Rockloff, M. (2002). The dynamics of self-evaluation. *Personality and Social Psychology Review, 6,* 370-379.

Varela, F., Thompson, E., Rosch, E. (1993). *L'inscription corporelle de l'esprit* [The body inscription of mind]. Paris: Seuil.

West, B.J., and Shlesinger, M.F. (1990). The noise in natural phenomena. *American Scientist, 78,* 40-45.

Williams, K.J., Suls, J., Alliger, G.M., Learner, S.M., and Wan, C.K. (1991). Multiple role juggling and daily mood states in working mother: an experience sampling study. *Journal of Applied Psychology, 76,* 664-774.

In: The Concept of Self in Education, Family and Sports
Editor: Anne P. Prescott, pp. 153-177

ISBN 1-59454-988-5
© 2006 Nova Science Publishers, Inc.

Chapter 6

INFLUENCES OF DISTAL AND PROXIMAL FAMILY ENVIRONMENT VARIABLES ON PRE-ADOLESCENTS' SELF-CONCEPT

Bea R. H. Van den Bergh
Department of Psychology, University of Leuven

ABSTRACT

The socialization of the self in the family was investigated in 315 boys and 277 girls of the fourth, fifth and sixth grade (mean age = 10.5 years). Self-concept was measured with Harter's Self- Perception Profile (SPPC) for children. A LISREL-model was tested in which the following variables were included: (1) *Moderator variables*: gender and age of the pre-adolescents, number of children in the family; (2) *Distal family environment variables*: structural family features such as: socioeconomic status (parental educational level and family income), and mothers' and fathers' time in employment; (3) *Proximal variables related to the parents*: parents cognition (i.e. measured perception) on conditions that alter parenting behavior such as: personal resources of the parents (financial problems), child characteristics (temperament), and contextual sources of stress (marital distress and conflict), (4) *Proximal variables related to the pre-adolescents*: pre-adolescents' cognition (i.e. measured perception) of family processes and relations, and of the family as a unit, and (5) the six SPPC-subscales, one measuring Global Self-worth and the other five assessing the child's perception of domain specific competencies or adequacies namely Scholastic Competence, Social Acceptance, Athletic Competence, Physical Appearance, Behavioral Conduct. The model tested different hypotheses with regard to the mediating influence of the proximal variables on the distal family environment variables. The fit of the model was satisfactory and 5 to 18% of the variance in each SPPC-subscales was explained. These results highlight the importance of the supportive parent-child relation, and of pre-adolescents cognition and affect in the socialization of self-concept. Pre-adolescents who feel positively reinforced in the communication with their parents have a positive metacognition. This positive metacognition enhances their global self-worth and their perceptions of competence on specific domains. These results can be seen as an empirical verification of the looking-glass self notion (Cooley).

INTRODUCTION

Considering oneself as a competent and worthy person is an important aspect of the optimal development of children and adolescents. Lack of sufficient self-esteem often underlies psychological problems and can interfere with successful development in adult years (Van den Bergh and Marcoen, 1999). In this chapter we give a short overview of the empirical study of the self and formulate and test hypotheses about the influences of distal and proximal variables on pre-adolescents' self-concept. Self-concept was measured with Harter's Self- Perception Profile for Children (SPPC) in 592 pre-adolescents with a mean age of 10.5 year. The SPPC contains six subscales; one measures Global Self-Worth and the other five assess the child's perception of domain specific competencies or adequacies namely Scholastic Competence, Social Acceptance, Athletic Competence, Physical Appearance and Behavioral Conduct.

EMPIRICAL STUDY OF THE SELF: SHORT OVERVIEW

The development of 'the self' has been studied from different perspectives and different constructs have been used (see e.g. Bracken, 1996; Byrne, 1996; Damon and Hart 1988; Erikson, 1950/1963; Harter, 1983, 1998; Hattie, 1992; Kegan, 1982; Markus and Kitayama, 1991; Marsh, Trautwein, Lüdke, Köller and Baumert, 2005; Wylie, 1989). For the early symbolic interactionists (Cooley, Mead and Baldwin) the self is viewed as a '*social construction*' or 'looking-glass self' (Cooley, 1902); the self represents the reflected appraisals of significant others (see e.g. Harter, 1983, 1998 for an overview). Consistent with these theories of the self, developmental theorists emphasize the growth of self-awareness as a socially constituted process (Thompson, 1998) and specified or modified the looking-glass self notion (see e.g. Cook and Douglas, 1998; Killeen and Forehand, 1998). Many theorists have also forcefully argued that the self is a *cognitive construction* (Epstein, 1991; Kelly, 1955; Markus and Kitayama, 1991). From a neo-Piagetian perspective the self is viewed as one particular domain of knowledge where the level of development may differ from that in other domains (Harter, 1998). Concepts from social cognition (e.g. Fiske and Taylor, 1991; Leekam, 1993; Nelson, 1981) and attribution theories (e.g. Bugental, Johnston, New and Silvester, 1998; Fincham, Beach, Arias, and Brody, 1998) are framed within a developmental perspective (Bugental and Goodnow, 1998). It is also recognized that the *affectional connection*, established with caregivers in the first years provide a foundation for the child's emergent understanding of the self (Thompson, 1998). Finally, there has also been increasing emphasis on the integration of social, cognitive and affective processes and their impact on the development of the self (Harter, 1998). This trend of integration is characteristic, not only for the development or socialization of the self, but for all socialization processes (Bugental and Goodnow, 1998; Grusec and Goodnow, 1994; Parke and O'Neil, 1999).

In mutual exchange with this integration of social, cognitive and affective processes new trends emerged in empirical research field of the self. *First,* the need to study dyads in stead of the individuals alone (Sears, 1951; Hartup and Lempers, 1973), and the need to study bidirectional influences in socialization (Bell, 1968, 1979; Clarke-Stewart, 1988; Lerner and Spanier, 1978; Maccoby, 1992) was recognized. *Second,* the study of socialization, evolved beyond the point of emphasizing the need to study the reciprocal relations of the developing person (Kreppner and Lerner, 1989). It was recognized that the person is embedded in a multilevel context, with the most proximal being the family (Bronfenbrenner, 1979, 1986). With the rise of system theories the family became conceptualized as a social system with interdependent subsystems (Belsky, 1981; Belsky and Fearon, 2004). Family members influence each other directly and indirectly and moreover, the family unit itself is also seen as a contributor to children's socialization (Brody, Pillegrini, and Sigel, 1986; Parke and Buriel, 1998). A variety of factors have been proposed as potential mediators of the relation between the subsystems, for instance between the marital and the parent-child or parenting subsystem (Belsky and Fearon, 2004), including gender of parent, gender of child, age of child, birth order and/or number of children (Parke and Buriel, 1998). *Third,* the literature shows that individual differences in sociopersonality functioning from infancy into later years are maintained not only by emerging personality processes -associated with social expectations, self-understanding, and working models of relationships - but also by continuity in relational experiences and support over time (Thompson, 1998) (e.g. Buri, Murphy, Richtsmeier, and Komar, 1992). This reveals a need to identify the role of protective and risk factors in the broader social ecology. Parke and Buriel (1998) point to the influence of socioeconomic status and women's and men's employment patterns on socialization in the family. Protective and risk factors can also be found in conditions that alter parenting behavior such as personal resources of the parents (e.g. income), child characteristics (e.g. temperament) and contextual sources of stress and support (e.g. marital conflict)(Belsky, 1984). *Fourth,* comprehensive models, linking family factors and processes and social, cognitive and affective processes to child and adolescent self-concept esteem, have begun to emerge (Harter, 1998). The heuristic model of Feiring and Taska (1996) is build upon attachment theory. They reviewed isolated findings consistent with pieces of the model, but observe that there is relatively little research that comprehensively addresses many of the issues in their model (Harter, 1998). Hattie (1992) presents a model which includes structural features (e.g. social status) and family process characteristics, family activities and interests. These models can be linked to the 'developmental impingement perspective' outlined by Gottfried, Gottfried, Bathurst, and Killian (1999). This perspective is proposed as an interpretive and heuristic framework with which to understand family functioning; it links distal to proximal family environment factors. According to the developmental impingement perspective maternal and paternal employment and other distal variables, such as socioeconomic status are expected to play a role in parenting and in children's development and well-being only to the extent that they are related to more proximal variables (Estes, 2004; Gottfried et al., 1999). Proximal environment consists of the social, cognitive, affective and physical stimulation provided to the children by the family interpersonal relationships. While maternal employment categorises mothers on the basis of employment status it however conveys no information regarding the nature or quality of the environment that impinges on children's development (Gottfried, et al., 1999: 15). The developmental impingement perspective can explain why children's and adolescents' development is significantly and consistently related to the quality of home environment and family processes across socio-economic status, as is indicated by an extensive literature.

In the remaining paragraphs of the introduction we describe one general and several concrete hypotheses relating distal and proximal family variables to the self-concept of the pre-adolescent. These hypotheses were tested by means of a Linear Structural Relation (LISREL).

H1: GENERAL HYPOTHESIS

We formulated the general hypothesis of our current project against the backdrop of an emphasis on the integration of social, cognitive and affective processes and in line with the heuristic framework of the developmental impingement perspective. It states that the effect of distal family environment variables is mediated by proximal variables, namely the social, cognitive and affective processes that take place in the interaction between the family members. The following variables were included: (1) *Moderator variables*: gender and age of the children, number of children in the family; (2) *Distal family environment variables*: structural family features such as: socioeconomic status (parental educational level, family income), and mothers' and fathers' time in employment (or work time); (3) *Proximal variables related to the parents*: parents cognition (i.e. measured perception) on conditions that alter parenting behavior such as: personal resources of the parents (financial problems), child characteristics (temperament), and contextual sources of stress (marital distress and conflict), and (4) *Proximal variables related to the pre-adolescents*: pre-adolescents' cognition (i.e. measured perception) on family processes and relations, and of the family as a unit.

H2: THE RELATIONSHIPS BETWEEN DISTAL VARIABLES RELATED TO PARENTS' EMPLOYMENT, PROXIMAL VARIABLES RELATED TO THE PARENTS AND TO THE PRE-ADOLESCENT AND SELF-CONCEPT OF THE PRE-ADOLESCENT

We hypothesized that maternal and paternal educational level and the number of hours worked are positively associated with family income and that family income is negatively associated with financial problems (see e.g.Hemström, 2005; Weeden, 2005). Having financial problems may lead to conflicts in the marital relationship.

There is convincing evidence that marital distress and conflict are associated with a wide range of deleterious effects on the child, including inter alia poor academic and social competence, withdrawal, depression, health problems and many conduct-related difficulties (Crockenberg and Forgays, 1996; Emery, 1982; Hetherington, 1989; Schudlich, Shamir, and Cummings, 2004; Vandewater and Lansford, 1998). Clearly, there are different mechanisms by which different forms of marital conflict may affect the many facts of children's social and emotional development (Katz and Gottman, 1993). We hypothesized *first* that the effects of conflicts between parents on the self-concept (e.g. the appraisal of its behavioral conduct) may be mediated by the child's cognition and appraisal of these conflicts, e.g. via the mechanism of internalizing (Christie-Mizell, 2003; Crockenberg and Forgays, 1996; Grych, 1998). *Second*, several associations between the child's temperament and family relationships have been established (Bates and Wachs, 1994; Calkins, Hungerford and Dedmon, 2004; Kochanska, Friesenborg, Lange, and Martel, 2004). Rutter (1987) has noted that the increased risk of the temperamentally difficult child is partly attributable to transactions with the parents. It has been found that parents who experience enduring stress (conflicts) in interpersonal relationships more often have a child with a difficult temperament or more often perceive their child as having a difficult temperament (Bates, 1986; Hetheringon, 1989; Swets-Gronert, 1986; Van den Bergh, 1992; Vaughn et al., 1987). Hetherington (1989) found convincing evidence for the notion of Rutter (1987) that temperamentally difficult children are likely to be the target of their parents' aversive responses and are at the same time less able than temperamentally easy children to cope with this abusive behavior from parents when it occurs; this can have a negative influence on the self-concept of the child. *Third*, having a difficult temperament, or being perceived as having a difficult temperament, has some stability over time (Bates, 1986; Guerin, Gottfried; and Thomas, 1997). We therefore hypothesized that the perception that the child was difficult to handle when it was a baby is associated with the parents' perception of having a pre-adolescent with a difficult temperament. *Forth*, in line with the symbolic interactionist view it is possible that a child that is perceived by his parents as being difficult has the 'metaperception' (i.e. perception of a perception; see e.g. Cook and Douglas, 1998) of being a difficult child, which can influence the self-concept of the pre-adolescent.

Much of the research of the past 25 years on the work-family interface has focused on the construct of work-family conflict (e.g. Greenhaus and Powell, 2003) and their antecedents (including occupational structure, work organization, work-family support, personality) and consequences (including career success, psychological distress, burnout, family relationships (e.g. Behson, 2005; Huston and Rosenkrantz Aronson, 2005; Karasek and Theorell, 1990; Kirchmeyer, 2005; Marchand, Demers, and Durand, 2005; Nycklicek and Pop, 2005; Siegrist, 1996). Of the studies focusing on consequences of work-family conflict for family relationships (e.g. Crouter, 1997; Gottfried et al., 1999; Hoffman et al., 2989; Parke and Buriel, 1998) almost no studies investigated children directly. This means for instance that the relationship between relevant aspects of parents' employment (such as work time) and children's perception of family relationships and functioning was not investigated. We hypothesized, *first* that mothers' time in employment has an influence on children's perception and satisfaction with mothers' time with them, *second* that fathers' time in employment has an influence on children's perception and satisfaction with fathers' time with, *third* that it is the satisfaction with mothers' and fathers' time that influences children's satisfaction with the gainful employment of their parents (Van den Bergh and Van Ranst, 1997) and fourth, that the latter satisfaction influences the self-concept op the pre-adolescent.

H3: The Relationships between Moderator Variables (Gender, Age and Number of Children in the Family) Proximal Variables Related to the Pre-adolescent and Self-concept of the Pre-adolescents

Meta-analyses on gender effect studies with regard to self concept reported small but significant size effects, favoring males (see Ruble and Martin, 1998). With regard to the SPPC, one of the more consistent findings is boys scoring higher than girls, especially on Athletic Competence and Physcial Appearance but also on Scholastic competence and Global Self-worth, and girls scoring higher on Behavioural Conduct.

Age effects are less frequently observed in the group of 8 to 12 year olds (Marsh, Craven, and Debus 1998; Marsh, Trautwein, Lüdtke, Köller, and Baumert, 2005). In general, older children score lower than younger children on Global Self-worth and Behavioural Conduct (Harter, 1985, 1998; Van den Bergh and Marcoen, 1999). We therefore hypothesize that gender has an effect on Global Self-worth and on several specific competences and that age has an effect on Global Self-Worth and Behavioural Conduct.

In some studies the number of children in the family has been found to influence various developmental outcomes, favouring only children for e.g. intellectual abilities and academic achievement and character (Polit and Falbo, 1987) and disfavouring them with regard to self-monitoring (Musser and Browne, 1991) and peer evaluations of independent thinking, persistence, behavioral control, cooperation with peers (Jiao et al., 1986). However, in the study of Meredith, Abbott and Ming (1992) in China, comparisons of siblings and only children showed no differences of number of children on self-concept. Evans and McCandless (1978) hypothesized that with increasing numbers of siblings, authoritarian parental control strategies become more evident. We hypothesized that, the effect of the number of siblings on self-concept is mediated by the level of autonomy experienced (e.g. the right to decide for oneself how to dress, hair fashion, contacts with friends...) and, moreover that autonomy is negatively effected by the number of children in the family e.g. because of the enhanced use of authoritarian parental control strategies in large families.

H4: The Relationships between Proximal Variables Related to the Pre-adolescent and Self-concept of the Pre-adolescent

H4a: The Family Unit: Pleasantness and Openness of the Family

The family unit can be seen as a contributor to children's socialization (Parke and Buriel, 1998). The child's perception of two family processes, namely pleasantness (the child likes the family interactions, likes to be at home) and openness (the relatedness of the family to the outside-world; social contacts of the family) were hypothesized to be important contributors to the feelings of competence of the child (e.g. Parke and Buriel, 1995; Parke and O'Neil, 1999).

H4b: Positive and Negative Regard from Parents

Positive interactions between caregiver and child coupled with a warm and reliable relationship will foster positive self representations within the family context as well as more global self-evaluations that transcend family relationships (Demaray and Malecki, 2002; Feiring and Taska, 1996). We hypothesized that the child's perception of positive and negative regard from the parents had a direct influence on self-concept, as well as an indirect one, i.e. mediated by child's cognition of his parents' opinion about him or her.

Parents' allocation of time to their children may reflect their own characteristics and priorities. Huston et al. (2005, p. 469) indicate for instance that mothers who are more sensitive to their children's needs may spend more time with them. We therefore hypothesized that children's perception of positive regards from mother and father is positively related to the children's satisfaction with mother's and father's time with them.

H4c: The Looking-glass Self Notion

Finally, and most importantly, we aimed to empirically validate the looking-glass self notion (Cooley, 1902; Harter, 1983) and hypothesized that the child's cognition of its parents' opinion about him or her influences its global self-worth and perception of competences and adequacies on the five specific domains.

In sum, the main aims of this study are to formulate and test a LISREL-model that links distal family factors and proximal social, cognitive and affective processes in the family to self-concept in 8-to-12- year olds. This test includes an empirical verification of Cooley's (1902) looking-glass-self notion that the self-concept represents the reflected appraisals of significant others. The proposed model is broadly defined and testing the fit of it can only be seen as an exploratory effort, which clearly needs further confirmation in other research.

METHOD

Participants

Data were collected from 592 primary school children between 8 and 12 years old ($M = 9.91$, $SD = 0.91$) and from their parents. There were 315 boys and 277 girls. The data were part of a large-scale investigation into the nature and quality of the living conditions and competence of 6- to 12-year old children, conducted in a representative sample of 68 primary schools of the Flemish Community (Belgium). Only children whose parents had given informed consent participated in this study (85.4 % permission rate). The response rate of the children was 84 % and the parents' response was 58 %. 95.4% of the children lived in a two-parent family. In 67% of the families both parents were gainfully employed, in 23% only the father, in 2.4% only the mother and in 3% none of the parents were gainfully employed. (*remark*: in the text we use the words 'child' and 'pre-adolescent' without distinction to indicate the 8-to-12-year old children of our sample)

Instruments

Predictor Variables

Four group of variables were operationalized *moderator variables*.1) Gender of the child (1 = boy, 2 = girl); 2) Age of the child; 3) Number of children in the family.

distal family environment variables.1 and 2) Time in employment: total number of hours the child's mother/father spends on paid labor or studying during one week (commuting time included); 3 and 4) Educational level of mother/father: six educational levels were distinguished, level 1 being primary school and level 6 university degree; 5) Family income: twelve levels of total monthly net income of the family were distinguished, level 1 being less than $ 285 and level 12 more than $ 4,285.

proximal variables related to the parents: the parents' cognition (i.e. measured perception) of: 1) Financial problems: one item on a 5-point scale probing financial problems; 2) Marital distress and conflicts: composite of the scores on three items probing the degree of satisfaction with the relationship and the frequency of marital quarrels; 3) Difficult temperament of child: one item on a 5-point scale probing whether the parents perceive the child as being difficult; 4) Difficult temperament when baby: one item on a 5-point scale probing whether the parents perceived their child as being difficult when it still was a baby.

proximal variables related to the pre-adolescent: the pre-adolescent's cognition (i.e. measured perception) of: 1) Pleasantness of the family: composite of the scores on two items probing the degree to which the child likes the family and the home; 2) Openness of the family: composite of the scores on two items measuring the frequency of visiting others and of receiving visitors at home; 3 and 4) Mother's/father's time with child: one item measuring the child's satisfaction with the time mother/father spend with him or her; 5 and 6) Child's perception of positive regard from mother/father: composite of the scores on three items probing the perceived presence of positive emotions in the relationship with mother and father; 7 and 8) Child's perception of negative regard from mother/father: composite of the scores on two items probing the perceived presence of negative emotions in the relationship with mother and father; 9) Conflicts between parents: composite of the scores on two items probing the perceived quality of the relationship between the parents; 10 and 11) Child's satisfaction with work situation of mother/father: one item measuring the child's satisfaction with the fact that its mother/father is either gainfully employed or housewife/houseman; 12) Level of autonomy: one item measuring the degree of freedom to make its own decisions; 13) Child's positive impression of parents' opinion about his/her self: composite of the scores on two items measuring the perceived parents' view of the child.

Dependent Variables

The self-concept was studied with a Dutch version (Veerman et al., 1997) of the Self-Perception Profile for Children (Harter, 1985). The SPPC is a 36-item scale subdivided into six subscales, each subscale being composed of six items. Five of these scales measure self-perception on a discrete domain of competence or adequacy. These domains are

Scholastic Competence, Social Acceptance, Athletic Competence, Physical Appearance, and Behavioral Conduct. The sixth scale measures Global Self-Worth. For each item the score can range from 1 to 4, a high score reflecting a higher degree of perceived competence. The scores on the items were summed to calculate the scores on the subscales. The internal consistency of the Dutch SPPC varied somewhat per scale in the Flemish sample, ranging from $\alpha = .73$ (Behavioral Conduct) to $\alpha = .82$ (Physical Appearance). With regard to the construct validity, the factor structure of the five scales of domain specific perception of competence was replicated (principal component analysis with varimax rotation). Confirmatory factor analysis performed with LISREL8 (Jöreskog and Sörbom, 1993) revealed a reasonable good fit of the model with five correlated specific factors: $c^2/df = 2.36$, GFI = .92, NFI = .87 and RMSEA = .040 (Van den Bergh and Marcoen, 1999; Van den Bergh and Van Ranst, 1998; Veerman et al., 1997). In Table 1 an overview is given of means and standard deviations of all predictor and dependent variables.

Table 1. Means and standard deviations of the predictor and the dependent variables

	M	*SD*
Moderator variables		
Gender	1.47	0.50
Age	9.91	0.91
Number of children	2.51	1.10
Distal family environment variables		
Time in employment (hours worked) M	28.53	19.47
Time in employment (hours worked) F	50.85	16.62
Educational level of Mother	3.57	1.57
Educational level of Father	3.63	1.73
Family Income	8.76	1.95
Proximal variables related to the parents		
P's perception of financial problems	1.99	0.80
P's perception of marital distress and conflict	5.11	1.29
P's perception of difficult temperament of child	2.51	0.84
P's perception of difficult temperament when baby	2.31	1.03
Proximal variables related to the pre-adolescent		
Child's perception of pleasantness (nice family)	7.26	1.09
Child's perception of openness (open family)	4.61	1.04
Child's satisfaction with mother's time with child	2.84	0.81
Child's satisfaction with father's time with child	2.51	0.80
Child's perception of positive regard from M	9.11	1.63
Child's perception of positive regard from F	8.97	1.76
Child's perception of negative regard from M	3.33	0.87
Child's perception of negative regard from F	3.43	1.00
Child's perception of conflicts between parents	3.05	0.96
Child's satisfaction with work/being housewife M	2.93	0.99
Child's satisfaction with work/being houseman F	2.83	0.95
Child's experienced level of autonomy	2.22	0.66
Child's positive impression of parents' opinion about him or her	6.44	1.23
Scholastic Competence	16.12	3.76

Table 1. Continued

	M	SD
Proximal variables related to the pre-adolescent		
Social Acceptance	17.65	3.83
Athletic Competence	17.25	3.90
Physical Appearance	18.64	4.20
Behavioral Conduct	16.95	3.08
Global Self-worth	18.56	3.53

M = Mother; F = Father, P = Parents

Procedure

Trained research assistants administered the Dutch version of the SPPC to the children in class sessions in their regular classrooms. The administration of the SPPC in itself lasted about half an hour and passed off smoothly; administration of all questionnaires of the large-scale investigation lasted about two hours. Most pre-adolescents liked to participate in the study.

Statistical Analysis

To evaluate a model of structural relationships between distal and proximal variables in the direct family environment on the one hand and the self-concept of the child on the other hand, we used LISREL 8 (Jöreskog and Sörbom, 1993). The successive models were tested using covariance matrices and the maximum likelihood method of estimation. The assessment of the overall model fit was based on several criteria: the χ^2-test, the p value, the χ^2/df ratio, the Goodness-of-Fit Index (GFI), the Adjusted Goodness-of-Fit Index (AGFI), and the standardized Root Mean Square Residuals (RMR). The χ^2-test measures the discrepancy between the sample covariance matrix and the fitted covariance matrix. Small χ^2 values (and accompanying large p values) indicate a better fit. However, the χ^2 will nearly always be statistically significant, even when there is a reasonably good fit to the data, in models in which there are many variables and many degrees of freedom. Therefore, the χ^2/df ratio is a more representative index of fit (Tanaka, 1987). While the value of χ^2 depends on the sample size, the value of GFI does not explicitly. The GFI measures how much better a model fits as compared to no model at all. The AGFI is the GFI adjusted for the degrees of freedom. The standardized RMR with a value of 0.05 or smaller indicates a close fit to the model. To establish a well-fitting model, the original model was modified by theory trimming and by means of the modification indices (MI). Theory trimming indicates that non-significant paths are deleted from the model. Next, we looked at the biggest MI, suggesting relaxing a parameter. These suggestions only were followed, if added parameters were acceptable in light of the theoretical assumptions.

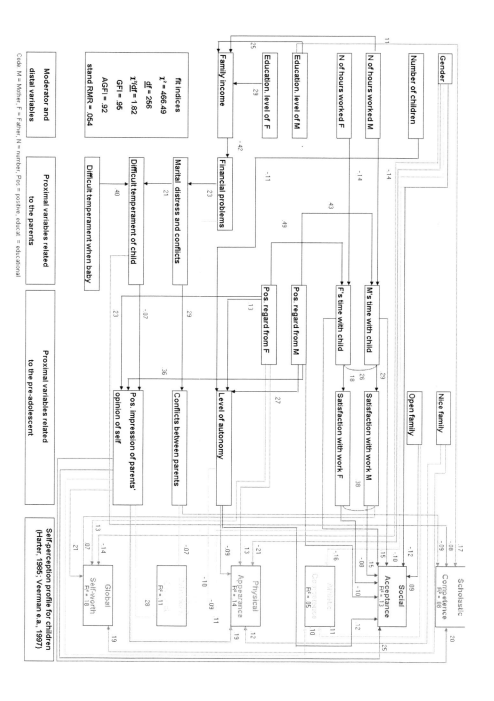

Figure 1. The interrelatedness of the independent and dependent variables in the final LISREL-model.

Code: M = Mother, F = Father, N = number, Pos = positive, educat = educational

RESULTS AND DISCUSSION

In the introduction one general and several concrete hypotheses were formulated. In this section we describe in the first paragraphs the testing of the successive LISREL-models by which these hypotheses were tested. In the next four paragraphs we describe whether the general hypothesis and the concrete hypotheses were confirmed. The general model and all significant paths of the LISREL-model are described in the order in which they appeared in the hypotheses outlined in the introduction. These significant paths indicate possible ways in which the distal and proximal variables are linked to each other. Only for the most complex paths this description is followed by a discussion, i.e. for the paths formulated in hypothesis 2 which link self-concept to parents' employment via proximal variables related to parents and pre-adolescents. Finally, in the sixth paragraph we give some limitations of the study. We want to stress that, due to shortcomings of our study, these results can only be seen as preliminary, or as having a heuristic value. They clearly need confirmation in other research.

Table 2. Progression of the testing of the successive models

	χ^2	vg	p	GFI	AGFI	RMR
1. Theoretical model	1226.82	190	.00	.87	.67	.096
2. Trimmed model (equivalence M/F)	1235.55	263	.00	.86	.77	.098
3. Path added from "Pos. regard M" (MI = 155.4) and from "Pos. regard F" to "Child's impression of parents' opinion of his/her self"	1027.95	261	.00	.89	.81	.087
4. Path added from "Pos. regard F" to "F's time with child" (MI = 151.3) and from "Pos. regard M" to "M's time with child"	724.77	259	.00	.92	.87	.064
5. Errorcov. added between "Satisfaction with work M" and "Satisfaction with work F" (MI = 93.9)	621.91	258	.00	.93	.89	.061
6. Path added from "Pos. regard M" (MI = 76.4) and from "Pos. regard F" to "Level of autonomy"	533.92	256	.00	.94	.90	.052
7. Errorcov. added between "M's time with child" and "F's time with child" (MI = 64.9)	464.47	255	.00	.95	.91	.050
8. Trimmed model	457.56	253	.00	.95	.92	.053
9. Trimmed model	466.49	256	.00	.95	.92	.054

Note. GFI = Goodness-of-Fit Index (GFI); AGFI = Adjusted Goodness-of-Fit Index; RMR = standardized Root Mean Square Residuals;
M = Mother; F = Father, pos.= positive.

Testing of Successive Models

In Table 2 an overview is given of the fit measures of successively tested models. In the initial model the errors between the six dependent variables were allowed to covariate, indicating that the dependent variables still can correlate after the effects of the predictor variables are removed. While the fit of the initial model was unsatisfactory (step 1), the model was trimmed (step 2). However, we kept the equivalence between mother and father. This means that e.g. when the path from "Educational level of mother" to "Scholastic competence" was significant but that from "Educational level of father" to "Scholastic competence" was not, this last path was kept in the model. Age and child's perception of negative regard from mother and father were omitted because they had no effect and were not affected themselves. In step 3 till step 7 the model was modified several times by adding new paths or error covariances. These adjustments of the initial model were done following the suggestions given each time by the largest modification index. When a modification index suggested relaxing a path between two variables we kept the equivalence between mother and father. Finally, the model was trimmed twice (step 8 and step 9), deleting all non-significant paths and error covariances.

The final model is shown in Figure 1 and Table 3. The fit of this model was satisfactory: $\chi^2 = 466.49$, $df = 256$, $\chi^2/df = 1.82$, GFI = .95, AGFI = .92, and stand. RMR = .054. All paths were significant ($p < .05$); the path coefficients were standardized. The R^2 of the dependent variables varied between $R^2 = .05$ (Athletic competence) and $R^2 = .18$ (Global self-worth).

H1: The General Hypothesis

With regard to our general hypothesis, it is important to note that the fit of the final model was satisfactory and moreover, that all distal variable except one had an indirect effect - i.e. mediated by proximal variables - rather than a direct one. Only one distal variable - educational level of the mother- had a direct effect, namely on Scholastic Competence ($\beta = -.12$). 5 to 18% of the variance in the SPPC-subscales was explained by the variables included in the model. These findings lend support to our general hypothesis.

H2: The Relationships between Distal Variables Related to Parents' Employment, Proximal Variables Related to the Parents and to the Pre-adolescent, and Self-concept of the Pre-adolescent

In general the observed relationships between the distal and proximal variables confirm hypothesis 2.

Educational level of mother ($\beta = .25$) and father ($\beta = .29$) and mother's time in employment ($\beta = .11$) have a positive effect on family income. Family income is negatively associated with having financial problems ($\beta = -.42$)(cfr. Hemström, 2005; Weeden, 2005). The finding that father's time in employment does not affect family income may be explained by the fact that in most families father is full-time employed and brings in the biggest part of the family income. Having financial problems mediates the effect of income on parents'

Table 3. Standardized path coefficients of the direct paths between the independent variables and the dependent variables

Independent Variables	SC	SA	AC	PA	BC	GSW
Moderator variables						
Gender		-.12	-.16	-.21		-.14
Number of children						
Distal family environment variables						
Time in employment (hours worked) M						
Time in employment (hours worked) F						
Educational level of M	.17					
Educational level of F						
Family income						
Proximal variables related to the parents						
P's perception of financial problems					-.10	
P's perception of marital distress and conflicts						
P's perception of difficult temperament of child	-.08					
P's perception of difficult temperament when baby						
Proximal variables related to the child						
Child's perception of pleasantness (nice family)		.09		.12		.19
Child's perception of openness (open family)		-.10	.11			
Child's satisfaction with mother's time with child		.15				
Child's satisfaction with father's time with child		-.10				
Child's perception of positive regard from M						
Child's perception of positive regard from F				.13		.13
Child's perception of conflicts between parents	-.09				-.07	
Child's satisfaction with work/being housewife M		.15			.11	.07
Child's satisfaction with work/being houseman F		-.08				
Child's experienced level of autonomy		.12		-.09	-.09	
Child's positive impression of parents' opinion about him or her	.20	.25	.10	.19	.28	.21
R^2	.08	.13	.05	.14	.11	.18

Note. SC = Scholastic Competence; SA = Social Acceptance; AC = Athletic Competence; PA = Physical Appearance; BC = Behavioral Conduct; GSW = Global Self-worth; M = Mother; F = Father.

perception of marital distress and conflicts (β = .23). These results confirm our hypothesis. The direct effect of educational level of the mother on Scholastic Competence (see figure 1, and Table 3) can be explained in different ways. First, children of highly educated women can be brighter students on genetic grounds and therefore make better school achievements and feel more competent. Second, highly educated mothers may encourage children or enhance children's feelings of Scholastic Competence more then less-educated women do.

Convincing evidence is also found for our hypotheses on the relationships between parents' perception of marital distress and conflict and the self-concept of the child. *First* the child's perception of conflicts between parents seems to be an important mediating factor between marital distress and conflict on the one hand and Behavioral Conduct (β = -.07) and Scholastic Competence (β = .-.09) on the other hand. *Second*, the parents' perception of marital distress and conflicts (β = .21) influences the parents' perception of how difficult the pre-adolescent's behaviour is. *Third*, the perception that the child was difficult to handle when it was a baby influence their perception of the pre-adolescent having a difficult temperament (β = .40). *Fourth*, the parents' perception of being a pre-adolescent with a difficult temperament influences the pre-adolescent's perception of Scholastic Competence negatively (β = -.08) and also has a negative effect on his or her cognition of its parents' opinion about him or her (β = -0 07). Having a positive metacognition about oneself influences all domain specific perceptions of competence and Global Self-Worth in a positive way (β between .10 and .28).

The results concerning the paths relating parents' cognition of marital distress and conflicts to child's temperament and self-concept are important for different reasons. It has for instance repeatedly been shown that high levels of interparental distress and conflict are associated with adjustment problems in children, independently of whether couples are married or divorced (e.g. poor academic outcome, behavioral problems (e.g. Katz and Gottman, 1993; Long, Forehand, Fauber and Brody, 1987; Vandewater and Lansford, 1998). Our results illustrate one possible mechanism of how marital distress and conflict can have an impact and the child's behavior and development, namely by influencing the child's self-concept. Marital conflict can have profound implications for children's felt emotional security (Davies and Cummings, 1994, 1998; Harold, Shelton, Goeke-Morey, and Cummings, 2004). Moreover, being temperamentally difficult seems to be a high risk factor for children whose parents display a negative marital interaction pattern. Temperamentally difficult children are likely to be the target of their parents' aversive reactions during marital conflict and are less able than temperamentally easy children to cope with this abusive behavior from parents when it occurs (Hetherington, 1989, p. 4). On the other hand, a temperamentally difficult child elicits more arousal and distress from caregivers and may put strain on the marital relationship (Bates, 1986). It is possible that 'difficult' children are less able to meet the socialization goals set by their parents because they fail to show the usual gains in self-regulatory ability in toddler hood (Kopp, 1982), are less receptive to particular parental approaches to socialization (Kochanska, 1993) and elicit increasingly coercive strategies from parents. Finally, as a result of these mutual interactions, these children show more behavioral problems and perceive themselves as being a 'difficult child'. This metacognitions influences their perception of Scholastic competence and Behavioural conduct, as is shown in the LISREL-model. Children incorporate into their self-understanding the varieties of attributions, inferences concerning motives and abilities, and values that characterize how parents regard them. Parental reactions to the child's behavior are crucial because the emotional attachment between parent and child enhance the significance of the parent's reaction (Thompson, 1998). However, we want to stress that, to really understand the differences in children's adjustments to marital conflicts, we need more information on variables such as the parents' behavior and hostility during marital conflicts, the children's history of exposure to conflict in the family, the children's appraisal of interparental conflict and children's emotional reactions (see e.g. Grych, 1998; Nathan-Ailor, Crockenberg and Langrock, 1996). Notice that while the influence of financial problems -a proximal variable related to the parents- on self-concept was mediated by proximal variables such as marital distress and conflicts, this variable also had a direct link with Behavioral Conduct ($\beta = -.10$). More information on the nature of the financial problems and their familial context is needed to explain this link.

Although much research has been conducted on the construct of work-family conflict (e.g. Behson, 2005; Crouter, 1997; Greenhaus and Powell, 2003, Gottfried et al., 1999; Hoffman et al., 1989; Huston and Rosenkrantz Aronson, 2005; Karasek and Theorell, 1990; Kirchmeyer, 2005; Marchand, Demers, and Durand, 2005; Nycklicek and Pop, 2005; Parke and Buriel, 1998), almost no studies investigated the impact on children directly, with measures obtained from the children. Our LISREL-model reveals that there was no direct effect of the work situation of the mother or of the father on the self-concept of the child (cfr Gottfried et al., 1999) and that the mediated effects were related to the gender of the parent (cfr. Boyum and Parke, 1995; Parke and Buriel, 1998). Our results indicate that parents' time in employment has a negative effect on the child's satisfaction with their parents' time with them ($\beta = -.14$ for both parents). The child's satisfaction with mother's and father's time with the child is positively associated with the child's satisfaction with the work situation (i.e. whether the parent is gainfully employed or is housewife/houseman) of mother ($\beta = .29$) and father ($\beta = .18$). The child's perception of father's time with the child has a positive effect on Social Acceptance ($\beta = .15$) while the satisfaction with the father's work situation has a negative effect on it ($\beta = -.08$). For the mother the opposite is true: the child's perception of mother's time with the child has a negative effect on Social Acceptance ($\beta = -.10$) and the child's satisfaction with mother's work situation has a positive effect ($\beta = .15$). While we can explain the positive effects, it is difficult to understand the negative effects.

It is possible that children who have many friends learned from their parents the importance of sharing time with someone. Possibly their parents gave them the feeling that they are worth full and that is it is nice to spend time with them. The child's perception of mother's time with the child has a negative effect on the child's social competence and this is also the case for the child perception of a positive regard from mother ($\beta = -.10$)(see below). These results are difficult to understand. One possible explanation holds that children, who are satisfied with their mother's time availability and who feel positive regarded by her, are overprotected by their mother, so that they don't feel the need to have friends. The finding that children who are satisfied with the work situation of their father score low on Social Acceptance is even more difficult to understand. These findings clearly need more exploration in other research before definitive statements can be made.

It is also important to note that the satisfaction with the work situation of the mother has a positive effect on the child's perception of Behavioral Conduct ($\beta = .11$) and of Global Self-Worth ($\beta = .07$).

H3: The Relationships between Moderator Variables (Gender, Age and Number of Children in the Family) Proximal Variables Related to the Pre-Adolescent, and Self-concept of the Pre-adolescents

Age had no effect on self-concept in this study. The effect of gender on the self-concept is pronounced. Boys score higher on Social Acceptance, Athletic Competence, Physical Appearance and Global Self-worth. Our results are similar though not identical to results found in other studies with the SPPC (see Harter, 1998; Van den Bergh and Marcoen, 1999; Veerman et al., 1997). Because of the equivalence of structure of the underlying concept for boys and girls in the Dutch SPPC-version (Van den Bergh and Van Ranst, 1998), we may interpret gender differences in the present study as real. Boys in general really perceive themselves as more competent. These findings indicate that gender stereotypes are internalized in pre-adolescents.

Number of children in the family has no direct effect on self-concept; the effect is mediated by the child's perception of his or her level of autonomy as was hypothesized. Children in larger families have a lower level of autonomy (β =-.11). This might be explained by the use of authoritarian parental control in larger families (Evans and McCandless, 1978). These interpretation is strengthened by the fact that the child's perception of positive regard from mother (β =.27) and from father (β =.13) - possibly resulting from more democratic parental strategies - both have a positive effect on the feelings of autonomy. Feelings of autonomy have an effect on different dimensions of perceived competence, namely on Social Acceptance (β =.12) on Physical Appearance (β =-.09) and on Behavioral Conduct (β =-.09). Children who can decide themselves about things that are important for them (e.g. about their clothes and hair, sleeping time, friends) feel more socially accepted, but are less satisfied with there physical appearance and perceive themselves as having more problems than children who can't decide about those things.

H4: The Relationships between Proximal Variables Related to the Pre-Adolescent and Self-concept of the Pre-adolescent

H4a: The Family Unit: Pleasantness and Openness of the Family

The child's perception of pleasantness at home has a direct effect on Physical Appearance (β =.12) and on Global Self-worth (β =.19). The child's perception of openness in the family has a direct effect on Social Acceptance (β = .09) and on Athletic Competence (β =.11). These results confirm hypothesis H4a.

H4b: Positive and Negative Regard from Parents

Positive regards from father have a direct effect on the child's perception of Physical Appearance (β =.13) and on Global Self-worth (β = .13), whereas positive regard from mother have a negative effect on the child's perception of Social Acceptance (β =.-.10). An important finding is that the child's metacognition of oneself is influenced by the child's perception of positive regard from mother (β =.36) and father (β =.23). These results confirm hypothesis H4B and lend support to the findings that positive interactions with the caregivers foster positive self representations in the family context (Demaray and Malecki, 2002; Feiring and Taska, 1996), and helps to explain individual differences in sociopersonality functioning from infancy into later years (Thompson, 1998).

Children's perception of positive regards from mother and father were positively related to the children's satisfaction with respectively mother's (β =.43) and father's time with them (β =.49); these results lend support to (β =.436) to the idea that parents' allocation of time to their children may reflect parental attitudes, characteristics and priorities (Huston et al., 2005; Van den Bergh and Van Ranst, 1997). According toe Thompson (1998) allocation of time to the children may be regarded as a protective factor in the family environment.

H4d. The Looking-glass Self Notion

The child's impression of its parents view on him or her is the most important predictor variable. It is the only variable that has a direct effect on all aspects of perceived competence and on Global Self-worth and, moreover, standardized β-weights are high for almost all aspects of perceived competence (β 's between .10 (Athletic competence) and .28 (Behaviour conduct). This result lends empirical evidence to the looking-glass self notion that children's self-perception reflects how they think they are viewed by their parents: i.e. they perceive themselves as being viewed by their parents (Cooley, 1902; Harter, 1998; Shrauger and Schoeneman, 1979).

A final remark on significant paths in the LISREL model holds that, of all specific self perceived competences, Social Competence was influenced by most of the proximal family environment variables related to the child, included in the model. This can be seen as an indication that the child's affect and cognition are important mediating factors in the family-peer linkages (Parke and O'Neil, 1999).

Limitations of our Study

Our study shows some major limitations, therefore it can at this point only be seen as an exploratory effort. *First*, there is a conceptual limitation. Although there are already many proximal variables in the model, other variables might have been added such as the relationships with siblings and peers (Harris, 1995), the teacher and the school (Harter, 1998). In future research on the self-concept, the parent-child relationship and the family could even be studied more broadly, namely as components of the larger developmental and contextual system of which they are part (Kreppner and Lerner, 1989; Parke and O'Neil,1999). *Second*, due to the large amount of variables there were limitations in the operationalization of the variables. The independent variables tapping the parents' and the child's cognition are only measured with one, two or three items. Clearly, before firm conclusions can be reached, research is needed with more elaborated measures. *Third*, there is a methodological limitation. A latent variable model could have been a solution for the problem of equivalence between the model of the mother and the father. In such a model father and mother could be included as indicators on the same variables or, the equivalence between a model for mother and a model for father could have been tested.

CONCLUSION

Our general hypothesis, that the effect of distal family environment variables on the self-concept of 8-to-12- year olds is mediated by proximal variables - namely the social, cognitive and affective processes that take place in the interactions between the family members – was confirmed. This confirmation lends support to the developmental impingement perspective (Gottfried et al., 1999). Our final LISREL-model proved to have a good fit with the data and 5 to 18% of the variance in the SPPC-subscales was explained. This model can be seen as one concrete form of the heuristic framework with which to understand how family functioning can influence the development and socialization of the self in 8-to- 12-year olds. Many of the specific hypotheses, outlined in the introduction were confirmed; the significant paths in the model indicate possible ways in which the distal and proximal variables are linked to each other. Because of the lack of research in which integrated models are tested (Hattie, 1992; Feiring and Taska, 1996), the testing and adequate fit of our LISREL-model can be seen as an important progress in the research field on self-concept. Importantly, we empirically verified Cooley's notion on the looking-glass self in 8-to-12-year olds. Children who feel positively reinforced in the communication with their parents have a positive metacognition. This positive metacognition enhances their global self-worth and their perceptions of competence on specific domains. These results highlight the importance of the parent-child relation, namely of the positive emotional regard from the parents and of the children's cognition and affect when interacting with their parents. Although development is increasingly viewed as "a consequence of social interactions that are shaped by contextual factors and characteristics of all participants in the interaction" (Eisenberg, 1998, p. 20), Bugenthal and Goodnow (1998) have noted that there has been relatively little attention directed to the role of children's individual attributions or self-efficacy in socializing relationships. Our results indicate that the pre-adolescent's cognition and affect are important mediating factors in the socialization of self-concept. It may be important to study these factors more in depth in the socialization of the self in the family in future research.

ACKNOWLEDGEMENTS

The greatly acknowledges Dr. Marc Callens for his help with the sampling procedure and Dr. Nancy Van Ranst for statistical analyses. This study was conducted as part of a project funded by the Population and Family Study Centre of the Flemish Government, Brussels, in collaboration with the Centre for Developmental Psychology of the University of Louvain. The author thanks the heads of these centers (Professor Emeritus R. Cliquet and Professor Emeritus A. Marcoen) for their encouragement, the secretary of the Population and Family Study Centre for her help in several parts of the study, and all children, parents, teachers, school directors, and students for their cooperation.

REFERENCES

Bates, J. E. (1986). On the relation between temperament and behavior problems. In G.A. Kohnstamm (Ed.), *Temperament discussed: Temperament and development in infancy and childhood* (pp. 181-189). Lisse: Swets and Zeitlinger.

Bates, J. E., and Wachs, T. D. (Eds.) (1994). *Individual differences at the interface of biology and behavior.* Washington, D.C.: American Psychological Association.

Behson, S.J. (2005). The relative contribution of formal and informal organizational work-family support. *Journal of Vocational Behavior, 66*, 487-500.

Bell, R.Q. (1968). A reinterpretation of direction of effects of studies in socialization. *Psychological Review, 75*, 81-95.

Bell, R.Q.(1979). Parent, Child and Reciprocal Influences. *American Psychologist, 34*, 821-826.

Belsky, J. (1981). Early Human Experience: A Family Perspective. *Developmental Psychology, 17,* 3-23.

Belsky, J. (1984). The determinants of parenting: A process model. *Child Development, 55,* 83-96.

Belsky, J., and Fearon, R.M.P. (2004). Exploring marriage-parenting typologies and their contextual antecedents and developmental sequelae. *Development and Psychopathology, 16*, 501-523.

Boyum, L.A, and Parke, R.D. (1995). The role of family emotional expressiveness in the development of children's social competence. *Journal of Marriage and the Family, 57*, 593-608.

Bracken, B.A. (Ed.)(1996). Handbook of Self-Concept. Developmental, Social and Clinical Considerations. New York: Wiley.

Brody, G.H., Pilligrini, A.D., and Sigel, I.E. (1986). Marital quality and mother-child and father-child interaction with school-aged children. *Developmental Psychology, 22*, 291-296

Bronfenbrenner, U. (1979). *The ecology of human development.* Cambridge, MA: Harvard University Press.

Bronfenbrenner, U. (1986). Ecology of the family as a context for human development.: Research perspectives. *Developmental Psychology, 22*, 723-742.

Bugental, D.B., and Goodnow, J.J. (1998). In W. Damon (Series Ed.) and N. Eisenberg (Volume Ed.). *Handbook of Child Psychology (Fifth Ed). Vol 3: Social, Emotional and Personality Development* (pp. 389-462). New York: J.Wiley.

Bugental, D.B., Johnston, Ch., New, M., and Silvester, J. (1998). Measuring parental attribution: Conceptual and Methodological Issues. *Journal of Family Psychology, 12*, 459-480.

Buri, J.R., Murphy, P., Richtsmeier, L.M., and Komar, K.K. (1992). Stability of parental nurturance as a salient predictor of self-esteem. *Psychological Reports, 71*, 535-5172.

Byrne, B. M. (1996). *Measuring self-concept across the life span: Issues and instrumentation.* Washington, DC: American Psychological Association.

Calkins, S.D, Hungerford, A., and Dedmon, S.E. (2004). Mothers' interaction with temperamentally frustrated infants. *Infant Mental Health Journal, 25*, 219-239.

Christie-Mizell, C.A.(2003). Bullying: The consequences of interparental discord and child's self-concept. *Family Process, 42*, 237-251.

Clarke-Stewart, K.A. (1988). Parents' effects on children's development: A decade of progress? *Journal of Applied Developmental Psychology, 9*, 41-84.

Cook, W.L., and Douglas, E.M. (1998). The looking-glass self in family context: a social relations analysis. *Journal of Family Psychology, 12*, 299-309.

Cooley, C.H. (1902). *Human nature and the social order*. New York: Charles Schribner's Sons.

Crockenberg, S. and Acredolo, C. (1983). Infant temperament ratings: A function of infants, of mothers, or both? *Infant Behavior and Development, 6*, 61-72.

Crockenberg, S., and Forgays, D. K. (1995). The role of emotion in children's understanding and emotional reactions to marital conflict. *Merrill-Palmer Quarterly, 42*, 22-47.

Crouter, A.C. (1997). Development of a typology of dual-earner families: a window into differences between and within families in relationships, roles and activities. *Journal of Family Psychology, 11*, 65-75.

Damon, W., and Hart, D. (1982). The development of self-understanding from infancy through adolescence. *Child Development, 53*, 841-864.

Davies, P.T., and Cummings, E.M. (1994). Marital conflict and child adjustment: An emotional security hypothesis. *Psychological Bulletin, 116*, 387-411.

Davies, P.T., and Cummings, E.M. (1998). Exploring children's emotional security as a mediator of the link between marital conflicts and child adjustment. *Child Development, 69*, 124-139.

Demaray, M.K., and Malecki, C.K. (2002). Critical levels of perceived social support associated with student adjustment. *School Psychology Quarterly, 1*, 213-141.

Eisenberg, N. (1998).Introduction. In W. Damon (Series Ed.) and N. Eisenberg (Volume Ed.), *Handbook of Child Psychology (Fifth Ed). Vol 3: Social, Emotional and Personality Development* (pp.1-24). New York: Wiley

Emery, R. E. (1982). Interparental conflict and the children of discord and divorce. *Psychological Bulletin, 92*, 310-330.

Epstein (1991). Cognitive-experiential self theory: Implications for developmental psychology. In M.R. Gunnar and L.A. Sroufe (Eds*.) Self processes and development: The Minnesota Symposium on Child Development* (Vol 23, pp. 111-13). Hillsdale, NJ: Erlbaum.

Erikson, E. H. (1950/1963). *Childhood and society (2nd ed.)*. New York: Norton.

Estes, S.B. (2004). How are family-responsive workplace arrangements family friendly? Employer accommodation, parenting, and children's socio-emotional well-being. *Sociological Quarterly, 45*, 637-661.

Evans, E.D. and McCandless, B.R. (1978). *Children and youth. Psychosocial Development*. New York: Holt, Rinehart and Winston.

Feiring, C., and Taska, L.S. (1996). Family self-concepts: Ideas on its meaning. In B. Bracken (Ed.). *Handbook of self-concept* (pp. 317-373). New York: Wiley.

Fincham, F.D., Beach, S.R.H., Arias, I., Brody, G.H. (1998). Children's attributions in the family: the children's relationship attribution measure. *Journal of Family Psychology, 12*, 481-493.

Fiske,W.T. and Taylor, S.E. (1991). *Social cognition*. New York: Mc Graw-Hill.

Gottfried, A.E., Gottfried, A.W., Bathurst, K., and Killian, C. (1999). Maternal and Dual-Earner Employment. Family Environment, Adaptations and the Developmental Impingement Perspective. In Lamb, E. (Ed.) *Parenting and child development in "nontraditional" families* (pp. 15-38). Mahwah, NJ: Erlbaum.

Greenhaus, J.H., and Powell, G.N. (2003). When work and family collide: deciding between competing role demands. *Organizational Behavior and Human Decisions Processes, 90*, 291-303.

Grusec, J.E., and Goodnow, J.J. (1994). Impact of parental discipline methods on the child's internalization of values: a reconceptualization of current point of vies. *Developmental Psychology, 30*, 4-19.

Grych, J.H. (1998). Children's appraisal of interparental conflict: situational and contextual influences. *Journal of Family Psychology, 12*, 437-453.

Guerin, D.W., and Gottfried, A.W., and Thomas, C.W. (1997). Difficult temperament and behaviour problems: A Longitudinal Study from 1.5 to 12 years. *International Journal of Behavioral Development, 21*(1), 71-90.

Harold, G.T., Shelton, K.H., Goeke-Morey, M.C., and Cummings, E.M. (2004). Marital conflict, child emotional security about family relationships and child adjustment. *Social Development, 13*, 350-376.

Harris, J.R. (1995). Where is the child's environment? A group socialization theory of development. *Psychological Review, 102*, 458-489

Harter, S. (1983). Developmental perspectives on the self-esteem. In E. H. Hetherington (Ed.), *Handbook of child psychology (Vol 4): Socialization, personality, and social development* (pp. 275-385). New York: Wiley.

Harter, S. (1985). Manual for the Self-Perception Profile for Children. Denver: University of Denver.

Harter, S. (1998). The development of Self-Representations. In W. Damon (Series Ed.) and N. Eisenberg (Volume Ed.), *Handbook of Child Psychology (Fifth Ed). Vol 3: Social, Emotional and Personality Development* (pp. 553-617). New York: Wiley.

Hartup, W.W. and Lempers, J. (1973). A problem in life-span development: The international analysis of family attachments. In P.Baltes and K.W. Schaie (Eds.), *Life-span developmental psychology: Personality and socialization* (Vol 3, pp. 235-252). New York: Academic Press.

Hattie, J. (1992). *Self-concept*. Hillsdale, NJ: Erlbaum.

Hemström, O. (2005). Health inequalities by wage income in Sweden: the role of work environment. *Social Science and Medicine, 61*, 637-647.

Hetherington, E. M. (1989). Coping with family transitions: Winners, losers and survivors. *Child Development, 60*, 1-14.

Hoffman, L. W. (1989). Effects of maternal employment in the two-parent family. *American Psychologist, 44*, 283-292.

Huston, A.C. and Rosenkrantz Aronson, S. (2005). Mothers' time with infant and time in employment as predictors of mother-child relationships and children's early development. *Child Development, 76*, 467-482.

Jiao, S., Ji, G., and Jing, Q. (1986). Comparative study of behavioural qualities of only children and sibling children. *Child Development, 57*, 357-361.

Jöreskog, K., and Sörbom, D. (1993), LISREL8: Structural equation modeling with the SIMPLIS command language. Hillsdale, NY: Erlbaum.

Karasek, E.K. and Theorell, T.(1990). Healthy work: stress, productivity, and the construction of the working life. New York: Basis Books.

Katz, L. F., and Gottman, J. M. (1993). Patterns of marital conflict predict children's internalizing and externalizing behaviors. *Developmental Psychology, 29*, 940-950.

Kegan, R. (1982). *The evolving self: Problem and process in human development.* Cambridge, Mass.: Harvard University Press.

Kelly, G. A. (1955). *The psychology of personal constructs.* New York: Norton

Killeen, M.R., and Forehand, R. (1998). A transactional model of adolescent self-esteem. *Journal of Family Psychology, 12*, 132-148.

Kirchmeyer, C. (2005). The different effects of family on objective career success across gender: A test of alternative explanation, in press

Kochanska, G. (1993). Toward a synthesis of parental socialization and children's temperament in early development of conscience. *Child Development, 64*, 325-347.

Kochanska, G., Friesenborg, A.E., Lange, L.A., and Martel, M.M. (2004). Parents' personality and infants' temperament as contributors to their emerging relationship. *Journal of Personality and Social Psychology, 86*, 744-759.

Kopp, C.B. (1982). Antecedents of self-regulation. A developmental perspective. *Developmental Psychology, 18*, 199-214.

Kreppner, K. and Lerner, R.M. (1989). *Family systems and life-span development.* Hillsdale: Lawrence Erlbaum Associates.

Leekam, S. (1993). Children's understanding of mind. In M. Bennett (ed.). *The child as psychologist: An introduction to the development of social cognition.* Hemel Hempstead: Harvester Wheatsheaf.

Lerner, R.M., and Spanier, G.B. (1978). Child influences on marital and family interactions: A life span perspective. New York: Academic Press.

Long, N., Forehand, R., Fauber, R., and Brody, G. (1987). Self-perceived and independently observed competence of young adolescents as a function of parental marital conflict and recent divorce. *Journal of abnormal Child Psychology, 15,* 15-27.

Maccoby, E. E. (1992). The role of parents in the socialization of children: an historical overview. *Developmental Psychology, 28*, 1006-1017.

Marchand, A.,Demers, A. and Durand, P.(2005). Does work really cause distress? The contribution of occupational structure and work organization to the experience of psychological distress. *Social Science and Medicine, 61*, 1-14.

Markus, H.M. and Kitayama, S. (1991). Culture and the self: Implications for cognition, emotion and motivation. *Psychological Review, 98*, 234-253.

Marsh, H.W., Craven, R., and Debus, R. (1998). Structure, stability and development of young children's self-concepts: a multicohort-multioccasion study. *Child Development, 69*, 1030-1053.

Marsh, H.W., Trautwein, U., Lüdtke, O., Köller, O., and Baumert, J. (2005). Academic Self-concept, interest, grades, and standardized test scores: reciprocal effects models of causal ordering. *Child Development, 76,* 397-416.

Meredith, W. H., Abbott, D. A., and Ming, Z. F. (1992). Self- concept and sociometric outcomes: A comparison of only children and sibling children from urban and rural areas in the People's Republic of China. *Journal of Psychology, 126,* 411-419.

Musser, L. M., and Browne, B. A. (1991). Self-monitoring in middle childhood: Personality and social correlates. *Developmental Psychology, 27,* 994-999.

Nathan-Ailor, J., Crockenberg, S., and Langrock, A. (1996, August). *Predicting children's adjustment form marital conflict behavior and children's emotions.* Poster presented at the XIVth Biennial Meetings of the International Society for the Study of Behavioral Development, Quebec City, Canada.

Nelson, K. (1981). Social cognition in a script framework. In J.H. Flavell and Ross (eds.) *Social cognitive development: Frontiers and possible futures.* Cambridge: Cambridge University Press.

Nycklicek, I. and Pop, V.J. (2005). Past and familial depression predict current symptoms of professional burnout. *Journal of Affective Disorders*, in press

Parke, R.D., and Buriel, R.(1998). Socialization in the family: ethnic and ecological perspectives. In W. Damon (Series Ed.) and N. Eisenberg (Volume Ed.). *Handbook of Child Psychology (Fifth Ed). Vol 3: Social, Emotional and Personality Development* (pp. 463-552). New York: J.Wiley.

Parke, R.D., and O'Neil, D. (1999). Social Relationships Across Contexts: Family-Peer Linkages. In Collins, W.A. and Laursen, B. (Eds.). *Relationships as developmental contexts. The Minnesota Symposia on Child Psychology.* Vol 30 (pp. 211-240). Mahwah (NJ): Lawrence Erlbaum Associates Publishers.

Polit, D. F., and Falbo, T. (1987). Only children and personality development: A qualitative review. *Journal of Marriage and the Family, 49,* 309-325.

Ruble, D.N., and Martin, C.L. (1998). Gender Development. In W. Damon (Series Ed.) and N. Eisenberg (Volume Ed.), *Handbook of Child Psychology (Fifth Ed). Vol 3: Social, Emotional and Personality Development* (pp. 933-1016). New York: Wiley.

Rutter, M. (1987). Psychosocial resilience and protective mechanisms. *American Journal of Orthopsychiatry, 57,* 316-331.

Schudlich, T.D.D.R., Shamir, H., and Cummings, E.M. (2004). Marital conflict, children's representations of family relationships, and children's dispositions towards peer conflict strategies. *Social Development, 13,* 171-192.

Sears, R.R. (1951). A theoretical framework for personality and social behavior. *American Psychologist, 6,* 46-483.

Shrauger, J. S., and Schoeneman, T. J. (1979). Symbolic interactionist view of self-concept: Through the looking glass darkly. *Psychological Bulletin, 86,* 549-573.

Siegrist, J. (1996). Adverse health effects of high-effort/low-reward conditions. *Journal of Occupational Health Psychology, 1,* 27-41.

Swets-Gronert, F. (1986). Temperament, taalcompetentie en gedragsproblemen van jonge kinderen: een longitudinaal onderzoek bij kinderen van een half tot vijf jaar. [Temperament, Linguistic Competence and Behavioural Problems of Young Children: a Longitudinal Study among Children from Six Months to Five Years Old]. Lisse: Swets and Zeitlinger.

Tanaka, J. S. (1987). "How big is big enough ?": Sample size and goodness of fit in structural equation models with latent variables. *Child Development, 58,* 134-146.

Thompson, R.A. (1998). Early sociopersonality development. In W. Damon (Series Ed.) and N. Eisenberg (Volume Ed.), *Handbook of Child Psychology (Fifth Ed). Vol 3: Social, Emotional and Personality Development* (pp. 25-104). New York: Wiley.

Van den Bergh, B. (1992). Maternal emotions during pregnancy and fetal and neonatal behaviour. In J. G. Nijhuis (Ed.), *Fetal Behaviour. Developmental and Perinatal Aspects* (pp. 157-178). Oxford: University Press.

Van den Bergh, B. R. H., and Marcoen, A. (1999) Harter's Self-Perception Profile for Children: Factor structure, reliability and convergent validity in a Dutch-speaking Belgian sample of fourth, fifth and sixth graders. *Psychologica Belgica, 39*, 29-47

Van den Bergh, B. R. H., and Van Ranst, N. (1998), Self-concept in children: Equivalence of measurement and structure across gender and grade of Harter's Self-Perception Profile for Children, *Journal of Personality Assessment, 70,* 564-582.

Van den Bergh, B.R.H., and Van Ranst, N. (1997). Welzijn van het kind in het gezin: LISREL-analyse van objectieve en subjectieve factoren uit de directe gezinsomgeving. [The child's well-being within the family: LISREL-analysis of objective and subjective factors in the direct family environment]. *Bevolking en Gezin,* 1997/1, 43-74.

Vandewater, E.A., and Lansford, J.E. (1998). Influences of family structure and parental conflict on chidren's well-being. *Family Relations, 47,* 323-330.

Vaughn, B.E., C.F. Bradley, L.S. Joffe, R. Seifer, and P. Barglow (1987). Maternal characteristics measured prenatally are predictive of ratings of temperament "difficulty" on the Carey Temperament Questionnaire. *Developmental Psychology, 23,* 152-161.

Veerman, J. W., Straathof, M. A. E., Treffers, Ph. D. A., Van den Bergh, B.R.H. and ten Brink, L.T. (1997). *Handleiding Competentiebelevingsschaal voor Kinderen CBSK.* [Manual for the Dutch version of the SPPC]. Lisse: Swets and Zeitlinger.

Weeden, K.A. (2005). Is there a flexiglass ceiling? Flexible work arrangements and wages in the United States. *Social Science Research, 34,* 454-482.

Wylie, R. C. (1989). *Measures of self-concept.* Lincoln: University of Nebraska Press.

In: The Concept of Self in Education, Family and Sports ISBN 1-59454-988-5
Editor: Anne P. Prescott, pp. 179-189 © 2006 Nova Science Publishers, Inc.

Chapter 7

THE SELF-CONCEPT BELIEFS: SELF-REFERENTIAL AND COMPARATIVE FRAMES OF REFERENCE

Antonella D'Amico, *Floriana Carmeci and Maurizio Cardaci*

Dipartimento di Psicologia – Università degli Studi di Palermo

ABSTRACT

Different frames of reference may contribute to the self-concept construal, influencing in turn the academic and working careers, the social fitness or the life satisfaction. In the present study we will focus on two particular frames of reference, defined as self-referential or internal frame of reference and comparative or external frame of reference (i.e. D'Amico and Cardaci, 2003; Marsh, Walker and Debus, 1991; Skaalvik and Skaalvik, 2002). The self referential frame leads people to evaluate their own capabilities using a personal and subjective framework (e.g. I'm quite handsome), or an internal comparison between different competency domains (e.g I'm better to play volleyball than football). The external frame of reference judgments, on the contrary, is based on comparisons with other people (e.g. I'm better than my friend in maths).

Previous studies involving adolescents, demonstrated that the different frames of reference may vary as a function of gender, and influence the self efficacy beliefs (Bong and Clark, 1999; D'Amico and Cardaci, 2003) or the scholastic and academic self concept (Pajares and Miller, 1994; Skaalvik and Skaalvik, 2002). In the present study, we are interested in investigating if this "dual frame of reference" is stable over time, also appearing in the self-concept construal of older people. Moreover, we aim to study if the self-referential or the comparative frames of reference influence, to a different extent, the perceptions of social well-being and life satisfaction. To this aim, about one hundred adults will be involved in the research. We are going to measure their self-referential and comparative self-esteem beliefs (using a 10 item scale adapted from Battle, 1996), social well-being (Keyes, 1998) and life satisfaction (Diener, Emmons, Larsen and Griffin, 1985). Results will be discussed.

* For correspondence, please contact: Antonella D'Amico, Dipartimento di Psicologia, Viale delle Scienze, Edificio 15, Palermo. Italy. e-mail: adamico@unipa.it; Voice: 0039 91 485738; Fax: 0039 91 6521010

Key words: self-esteem, self-referential esteem, comparative self-esteem, well-being, life satisfaction.

INTRODUCTION

Since early James' foundation of psychology (James, 1890), a huge literature recognizes to self-concept a crucial importance in understanding how the individual perceives him/herself and gives a sense to his/her own experience.

A variety of theories has in turn depicted the construct either as the subject's global, generalized self-representation of him/herself (e.g. Snygg and Combs, 1949; Rogers, 1959), or as a hierarchical/differentiated system with a number of specific sub-components (e.g. academic vs. non-academic self) that people draw from different areas of their life (e.g. Wells and Marwell, 1976; Wylie, 1979; Shavelson, Hubner and Stanton, 1976; Scheirer and Kraut, 1979; Marsh and Shavelson, 1985).

In spite of these heterogeneous conceptions that make difficult to find a universal theoretical agreement on the nature of the self-concept, it can be strictly associated to self-esteem (Wylie, 1974, 1979; Strein, 1993). If we define self-esteem as "a person's perception of himself" (Shavelson, Hubner and Stanton, 1976), these two constructs tend to overlap. Actually, many scholars, without assimilating self-esteem to self-concept directly, conceive self-esteem, broadly speaking, as the evaluative dimension of the self. In this framework, Coopersmith (1967) conceives self-esteem as the outcome of a series of self-evaluation that individuals form in different areas of experience. Moreover, Harter (1986) stresses that self-esteem is dependent both on social support and perceived competence in domains viewed as important by individuals. As long as self-esteem derives from subjective processes of self-evaluation, it also involves affective states related to perceived personal value. In other words, self-esteem is "a judgment of self-*value*, a personal evaluation of one's self that includes the feelings of self-worth that accompany that evaluation" (Pajares, 2000). According to Marsh, Walker and Debus (1991) self-esteem judgments basically rely on a dual source, having to do both with social comparisons (i.e. "I'm better than my friend in Math") and self-comparisons (i.e. "I'm better at English than at Mathematics). This convincing distinction, that reasonably emphasizes the different role of internal vs. external frames of reference in building up self-judgments, starts supporting by various empirical investigations. For instance, Singelis (1994) found two self-esteem factors, respectively named *independent self-construal and interdependent self-construal factor*: the former is defined as a "bounded, unitary, stable self separate from social context", the latter as a "flexible and variable self", influenced by the social environment and other people. Furthermore, studies mainly involving adolescents demonstrated that these two frames of reference are also differently associated to the self-efficacy beliefs and might be modified as a function of some variables, as gender (Bong and Clark, 1999; D'Amico and Cardaci, 2003) or academic self-concept (Pajares and Miller, 1994; Skaalvik and Skaalvik, 2002).

According to Diener and Fujita (1997), the role of others as point of reference is prevalent in school, because students are implicitly required to judge their performances/outcomes by comparisons with peers, specifically with those showing similar characteristics (Marsh, 1984a; 1984b; 1987). Besides, as a number of authors points out, these comparisons with peers are extremely important in giving valid criteria to evaluate one's abilities (Marshall and Weinstein, 1984; Goethals and Darley, 1987; Covington, 1992; Marsh, 1993; Marsh, Kong, and Hau, 2000).

Although the research offers some empirical evidence of a dual source in self-evaluation (self-referential vs. comparative frame of reference) in preadolescence and adolescence, little information is available, to our knowledge, in adults or elder people. Indeed, we don't know if people use the dual frame in judging themselves in adulthood and middle age too. In any case, the exploration of self-esteem structures after the adolescence could throw light on the perceptions of social wellbeing and life satisfaction as correlates of broader self-concept construal. Indeed, it is reasonably to assume that the way the individuals perceive and judge themselves influences (or is associated to) their feeling of personal wellbeing/satisfaction in life. Intuitively, it's not impossible that positive vs. negative self-evaluations affect thoughts, emotions, sensations, and so on, concerning ones' level of wellbeing.

Once more, we would like to stress that not even the relationship between self-esteem and wellbeing has been adequately investigated. Only specific self-esteem items have been included in some wellbeing scales (e.g. "Berne Questionnaire of Subjective Well Being", in Grob, 1995), consistently with the assumption that self-esteem is an indicator (i.e. dependent variable) of subject's psychological state. Nevertheless, Jourard and Landsaman (1980) mentioned *a positive self-opinion* together with other components of wellbeing (e.g. ability to care about others, open mind, capability of loving, creativity, pragmatic approach to reality).

Summarizing main trends of literature on wellbeing, we can find that people's evaluations about the quality of their life seem to involve a twofold frame again. On the one hand, the person uses an internal frame represented by his/her self-concept, thoughts and feeling associated to self-referential judgment, on the other hand he/she refers to a series of environmental and interpersonal variables such as social adjustment/ community integration/interpersonal support (Diener et al., 1985; Pavot and Diener, 1993; Mc Dowell and Newell ,1987; Keyes ,1998).

In the present study, we are hence interested in offering empirical evidences that this "dual frame of reference" is stable over time, also appearing in the self-concept construal of elder people. Moreover, we aim to verify if the self-referential or the comparative frames of reference influence, to a different extent, the perceptions of social wellbeing and life satisfaction.

METHOD

Subjects

One hundred twelve (49 Males, 62 Females) of mean age 50 years (SD= 7,74, range 40-60) were involved in the present research. The subjects were drawn from populations of different instructional levels; twelve of them held a middle school certificate, sixty-seven a school leaving certificate and thirty-two a degree certificate.

Materials and Procedure

A twenty-four items questionnaire was administered to subjects in order to investigate different aspect of Self-Esteem and Well-Being. In particular, 8 items explored the individuals' self-esteem and were inspired to the Battle's "Culture Free Self Esteem Inventory for Children" (1996); in particular, as evidenced in the above mentioned D'Amico and Cardaci's research (2003), 4 items investigated how the subject evaluates him/herself using a self-referential frame of reference, and 4 items investigated how the subject evaluates himself using a social frame of reference.

The remaining 16 items explored different aspect of the Well-Being feeling; in particular 11 items were drawn from the social well-being questionnaire by Keyes (1998), that explores the individuals' social integration (5 items), social confidence (3 items) and social contribution (3 items), while 5 items were drawn form the Life Satisfaction scale by Diener et al. (1985).

The subjects were requested to complete each questionnaire choosing among four alternatives (not true at all, not true, true, truest) corresponding to their degree of agreement with each statement. The four alternatives were then converted in scores ranging from 0 to 3; low scores indicate either lower agreement degree. The scores of items expressed in negative form were inverted. The administration of the questionnaire took about 15 minutes.

RESULTS

Psychometric Properties of the Self-Esteem and Well-Being Scales

Two separate factor analyses were conducted to explore the psychometric properties of the Self-Esteem and Well-Being scales. The first factor analysis was performed on the 8 Self-Esteem items, while the second factor analysis was performed on the 16 items tapping the different aspects of Well-Being.

For both the analyses we used the principal component method with Varimax rotation. After Varimax rotation, only items with factor loadings greater than .30 were considered, accounting for variance of 5% or more.

Two principal components emerged from the analysis involving the Self-Esteem items, accounting for 57% of total variance. The first component (42.2% of total variance) was named Self-Referential Esteem (SRE), because the items loading this factor explored how the subject evaluates himself without any explicit comparisons with others. The second component (14.8% of total variance) was named Comparative Self-Esteem (CSE) because included items explored how the subject evaluates himself through comparisons with other individuals.

To examine the internal reliability of each factor, Cronbach's alpha values (1960) were calculated, obtaining $\alpha=.77$ for the Self-Referential Esteem and $\alpha=.62$ for the Comparative Self-Esteem. In Table 1 are showed the items and their loadings in each factor.

**Table 1. Factorial weighs of each item after Varimax rotation.
Only scores statistically significant (r>.30) are reported, followed by means and
standard deviations of each factor**

	Self-Referential Esteem	Comparative Self-Esteem
I have no confidence in myself. [*]	.48	.36
I feel almost always unsatisfied with what I do. [*]	.86	
I easily become discouraged and sad. [*]	.76	
If I could, I'd change many aspects of myself. [*]	.82	
I'm good-looking as the most of people.		.65
I'm strong and healthy as the most of people.		.85
I feel to be important as the most of people.	.57	.37
I'm clever as the most of people.	.46	.48

[*] the score of the item has been inverted.

**Table 2. Factorial weighs of each item after Varimax rotation. Only scores statistically
significant (r>.30) are reported, followed by means and standard deviations of each
factor**

	Life Satistaction	Social contribution	Social Integration	Social Confidence
If I live again, I do not change anything	.30	.52		
The condition of my life are very good	.72			
I'm satisfied of my life	.82			
My real life is quite similar to my ideal life	.74			
So far, I obtained the important things I desired	.84			
I think my work gives important contributions to the society		.71		
My behavior influences the other people of my community	.46	.69		
I have time and energies for giving something to my community		.61		.30
I feel close to other people of my community			.80	
I believe that other people consider me a worth person	.38		.60	
I feel to be integrated in my community			.86	
If I have something to say, I believe my community to follow me			.20	
I consider my community as a source of wellness	.56		.31	
I believe people to think only to themselves [*]			.35	.70
I think other people to be unreliable [*]				.76
Today, I believe people to be more and more dishonest [*]				.77

[*] the score of the item has been inverted.

Four principal components emerged from the analysis involving the Well-Being items; the four components accounted for 63.9% of total variance. Although 6/16 items showed a spurious pattern of factorial weights (see Table 2), the factorial solution obtained seems to fit with the hypothesized dimensions of the Keyes (1998) and Diener et al. (1985) questionnaires. In particular, the first component was saturated by all the Life Satisfaction items (LS), and accounted for the 37.5% of total variance. The second component (10.9% of total variance) comprised all the Social Contribution items; the third Component was saturated by all the Social Integration items and explained the 8.3% of the total variance; the fourth component was saturated by the Social Confidence items and explained the 7.1% of the total variance.

The internal reliability (Cronbach's alpha values) was α=.81 for the Life Satisfaction , α=.58 for the Social Contribution, α=.81 for the Social Integration , and α=.65 for the Social Confidence.

All items and their loadings in each factor are showed in Table 2.

The following step in the data analysis was to calculate the intercorrelation between the Self-Esteem and the Well-Being variables. To this aim, means and standard deviations were calculated for each of the factors emerged in the previous phases of analysis, by averaging the raw scores of the items included in each factor (see Table 3).

Table 3. Means and Standard Deviations of all variables studied

	M	SD
Self-Referential Esteem	2.94	.61
Comparative Self-Esteem	2.94	.41
Life Satisfaction	2.59	.55
Social Contribution	2.68	.56
Social Integration	2.84	.49
Social Confidence	2.38	.58

The principal correlation analysis revealed and high level of correlation between all the variables considered (see Table 4). In particular, the Self-Referential Esteem was correlated to various degrees with all the Well-Being variables, while the Comparative Self-Esteem was correlated with Life Satisfaction, Social Contribution and Social Integration, but not with Social Confidence.

These results support the existence of a reciprocal influence between Self-Esteem and Well-Being, even if these variables involve different aspects of beliefs about themselves. However, as self Referential and Comparative Self-Esteem was correlated each other (r=. 56 p<.001), is quite difficult to distinguish the influence of each of them on the Well-Being variables. Thus, we retained necessary to calculate the partial correlation values of Self-Referential Esteem and the four Well-being variables after that the influence of the Comparative Self-Esteem was accounted for. The same analysis allowed us to calculate the association between Comparative Self-Esteem and the four Well-being variables after that the influence of Self-Referential Esteem was accounted for.

As showed in the table 5, the partial correlation analysis reveal a slightly different pattern of results: indeed, Self-Referential Esteem is significantly correlated only to Life Satisfaction (r=.39), Social Integration (r=.20) and Social Confidence (r=.26), while the Comparative Self-Esteem is correlated only with Life Satisfaction (r=.27), Social Contribute (r=.51) and Social Integration (r=.54). The implication of such pattern of association is discussed in the conclusive part of this article.

Table 4. Correlation between all the variables studied

	Self-Referential Esteem	Comparative Self-Esteem	Life Satisfaction	Social Contribution	Social Integration	Social Confidence
Self-Referential Esteem	1.00	.56[†]	.57[†]	.45[†]	.50[†]	.28[†]
Comparative Self-Esteem	-	1.00	.50[†]	.63[†]	.67[†]	.11
Life Satisstaction			1.00	.59[†]	.65[†]	.19[*]
Social Contribution				1.00	.65[†]	.13
Social Integration					1.00	.25[†]
Social Confidence						1.00

[†]=p<.01; [*]=p<.05

Table 5. Partial Correlation between Self Referential Esteem, Comparative Self-Esteem and the other variables

	Life Satisstaction	Social Contribution	Social Integration	Social Confidence
Self Referential Esteem (controlled for CSE)	.39[†]	.14	.20[*]	.26[†]
Comparative Self Esteem (Controlled for SRE)	.27[†]	.51[†]	.54[†]	-.05

The last step in the data analysis, was the study of the differences due to Gender and instructional level in the various dimensions of Self-Esteem and Well-Being. No gender differences were found between males and females in Self-Referential Esteem ($F_{(1)}$=2.19 p>.10) and Comparative Self-Esteem ($F_{(1)}$=0.46 p>.50). As regard to the Well being variables, no gender differences were found in Social Integration ($F_{(1)}$=.07 p>.50), and Life Satisfaction ($F_{(1)}$=2.94 p>.05) while the gender differences in Social Contribution ($F_{(1)}$=7.19 p<.01) and Social Confidence ($F_{(1)}$=6.68 p>.01) were both statistically significant. All the differences indicated that the Well-Being levels were higher in females than in males.

A similar analysis was performed using the Instructional Level (middle school, high school and degree) as independent variables. Results revealed significant differences due to instructional level in Comparative Self-Esteem ($F_{(2)}$= 2.98 p<.05), Life Satisfaction ($F_{(2)}$=3.76 p<.05), Social Contribution ($F_{(2)}$=10.65 p<.001) and Social Integration ($F_{(2)}$= 4.92 p<.01); no differences were found in Self-Referential Esteem ($F_{(2)}$= 2.7 p>.05) and in Social Confidence ($F_{(2)}$=.61 p>.50).

Post hoc comparisons (Bonferroni) revealed that individuals with middle school certificate did not differ significantly from individuals with high school or degree certificates; on the contrary, the differences between individual with high school certificate and degree certificate revealed that graduate people have higher Comparative Self-Esteem beliefs (p<.05) than individual that interrupted their educational careers to the high school. Analogous results were found as respect to the Life Satisfaction (p<.05), Social Contribution (p<.001) and Social Integration (p<.05) feelings.

CONCLUSION

In conclusion, the present study demonstrated quite clearly that the "dual frame of reference" (self-referential or comparative) is stable over time, also appearing in the self-concept construal of adult people. The emerging of two components of self esteem demonstrated indeed that individuals come to the formulation of self-judgments both in a self-referential frame and by comparisons with peers, according to what claimed by many authors (Singelis, 1994; Marsh, Walker and Debus, 1991; D'Amico and Cardaci, 2003).

The self-referential or the comparative frames of reference influence, to a different extent, different aspects of social well-being. In particular, the partial correlation analyses revealed that the Self-Referential frame of reference is correlated to the Life Satisfaction more than Comparative self esteem. This result may indicate that the Self-Referential Esteem, basically for its independence from the context and from the social judgment, produces generally better levels of life satisfaction, that are more stable over time.

Only the Comparative Self-Esteem is correlated to the Social Contribution feelings, while no significant correlations emerged between Self-Referential Esteem and Social Contribution. This result is again consistent with the existence of a frame of reference that is more and more independent from the context. People that use this self construal does not use the social feedbacks to develop their self images. Their Self-Esteem level is independent from the extent to which their perceive themselves as useful for the society. On the contrary, the high correlation between Social Contribution and Comparative Self–Esteem demonstrates that people that perceive themselves as important for the society tend to develop higher Self-Esteem levels that are based on comparisons with others. Similar observations may be done for the relationships between Comparative Self-Esteem and Social integration and between Self-Referential Esteem and Social integration. Indeed, people that base their self-image on comparisons with others perceive themselves as more integrated in the community than self-referential people.

Finally, no relationship emerged between Comparative Self-Esteem and Social Confidence, while the Self-Referential Esteem of people varies proportionally with this dimension. The reasons of such relationship are not so intuitive. In our perspective, this result reflects the individuals' level of optimism/pessimism; in other words, it may be that people with low Self-Esteem feelings project their negativity in the social environment, that become for them less acceptable and confident; conversely, people with high self esteem feelings tend to see the world in a more optimistic way, attributing to it more confidence.

Others interesting outcomes refers to the study of the gender differences; results revealed that Self referential or Comparative Self-Esteem levels are not significantly different in men and women. This result is somewhat in contrast with the literature on adolescent, since it reports self-esteem levels generally lower in females than in males (Blyth, Simmons e Carlton Ford, 1983; Nottelmann, 1987). D'Amico and Cardaci (2003), in particular, found that there are no gender differences in the Comparative Self-Esteem, while females show lower Self-Referential Esteem levels than males. These results are generally attributed to the worries, typically feminine, about physical and sexual development. In this perspective, is possible to hypothesize that, as years go by, the women acquire more sureness, overcoming all the adolescent uncertainties. This in turn determines an increasing of their Self-Esteem feelings, which become similar to the men's ones.

As regard to the Well-Being variables, the results revealed that females perceive themselves and their role more important for the community than males, and at the same time declare a higher level of acceptance and confidence in the community. These results appear consistent with those obtained by Ryff (1989) in a previous study, and confirm the stereotypical gender-roles, indicating that females are more oriented for the social relationships than males.

The influence of instructional level on self-esteem and well-being was the last aspect investigated in the present research; our results revealed that the Self-Referential Esteem is not influenced by the instructional level, evidencing again that people's Self-Referential Esteem is independent from their social-cultural level. On the contrary the Comparative Self-Esteem showed to be influenced by the instructional level, but only in individuals that have reached high instructional level. Quite interestingly, indeed, no differences have been found between middle school people and others: we retain this result to reflect the different social framework of reference of these two populations. Indeed (at least in Italy) people that held only a middle school certificate belong to communities were the social status (and presumably the self esteem) is definitely not influenced by factors such as instruction and culture, but probably by attitude to physical works, to get rich, to obtain the leadership, etc. In the previous research of D'Amico and Cardaci (2003), for instance, it was demonstrated that the Comparative Self-Esteem of adolescents belonging to lower social cultural levels was affected more by their ability in sport and other practical activities than by their school achievement in linguistic or scientific matters. People that held a high school certificate or a degree certificate, on the contrary, belong often to the same social community and they compare each other quite usually; in this perspective, the difference in Comparative Self-Esteem between high school certificated and degree certificated people could express the feeling of regret of people that have interrupted their educational careers at the high school, perceiving themselves as less efficient and persistent than people that hold a degree. Moreover, the holding of a degree is perceived as an opportunity to a more satisfying work and a more comfortable life. This interpretation is corroborate by results referring to Life Satisfaction, Social Contribution and Social Integration, that in the degree certificated are higher than in people with high school certificate.

As mentioned in the introduction, the most of the studies performed so far have investigated the interaction between the adolescents' dual frame of reference and their life context, mostly represented by the scholastic, academic or sport environment (Perry and Marsh, 2003); in the present research we have demonstrated that adults, as well as adolescents, use both self-referential and comparative frame of reference to make judgments about their own value. Moreover, each frame of reference influences (and is presumably influenced by) the way in which people perceive their own life, in terms of life satisfaction, social contribute, social integration and social confidence. Starting form these results, further researches could be oriented at investigating how the adults' self-referential or comparative esteem vary as a function of the social context in which they live or work.

REFERENCES

Battle, A. D. (1996) Culture Free Self-esteem Inventory for Children. In Tressoldi P.E. and Vio C. (Eds.), *Diagnosi dei disturbi dell'apprendimento scolastico*, 145-147. Trenton, NJ: Erickson.

Bong, M., and Clark, R. E. (1999). Comparison between self-concept and self-efficacy in academic motivation research. *Educational Psychologist, 34*, 139–154.

Coopersmith, S. (1967). *The antecedents of self-esteem.* San Francisco: Freeman.

Covington, M. V. (1992). *Making the grade: A self-worth perspective on motivation and school reform.* New York: Cambridge University Press.

D'Amico A., and Cardaci M. (2003). Relations among perceived self efficacy, self esteem, and school achievement. *Psychological Reports, 92*, 745-754.

Diener E., Emmons R. A., Larsen, R. J., Griffin S. (1985). The Satisfaction with Life Scale. *Journal of Personality Assesment, 49*, 71-5

Diener, E., and Fujita, F. (1997). Social comparison and subjective well-being. In B. P. Buunk and F. X. Gibbons (Eds.), *Health, coping, and well-being: Perspectives from social comparison theory*, 329–358. Mahwah, NJ: Erlbaum.

Goethals, G. R., and Darley, J. M. (1987). Social comparison theory: Self-evaluation and group life. In B. Mullen and G. R. Goethals (Eds.), *Theories of group behaviour*, 21–47. New York: Springer-Verlag.

Grob A. (1995). Subjective Well-being and Significant Life-Events across the Life Span. *Swiss Journal of Psychology, 54 (1)*, 3-18

Harter, S. (1986). Processes underlying the construction, maintenance, and enhancement of self-concept in children. In S. Suhls and A. Greenwald (Eds.), *Psychological perspectives of the self, 3*, 136–182. Hillsdale, NJ: Erlbaum.

James W. (1890). *The principles of Psychology*, Vols. 1 and 2. New York: Holt

Jourard S. M., Landsaman T. (1980). Health Personality: an Approach from the Viewpoint of Humanistic Psychology. Macmillian, New York

Keyes C. L. M. (1998). Social Well-being. *Social Psychology Quarterly, 61 (2)*, 121-40.

Marsh H. W. (1984a). Self-concept: The application of a frame of reference model to explain paradoxical results. *Australian Journal of Education, 28*, 165-181.

Marsh H. W. (1984b). Self-concept, social comparison, and ability grouping: A reply to Kulik and Kulik. *American Educational Research Journal, 21*, 799-806.

Marsh H. W. (1987). The big-fish-little-pond effect on academic self-concept. *Journal of Educational Psychology, 79*, 280-295.

Marsh, H. W. (1993). Academic self-concept: Theory measurement and research. In J. Suls (Ed.), *Psychological perspectives on the self, 4*, 59–98. Hillsdale, NJ: Erlbaum.

Marsh, H. W., and Shavelson, R. J. (1985). Self-concept: Its multifaceted, hierarchical structure. *Educational Psychologist, 20*, 107–123.

Marsh, H. W., Kong, C. K., and Hau, K. T. (2000). Longitudinal multilevel models of the big-fish-little-pond effect on academic self-concept: Counterbalancing contrast and reflected-glory effects in Hong Kong high schools. *Journal of Personality and Social Psychology, 78*, 337–349.

Marsh, H. W., Walker, R., and Debus, R. (1991). Subject specific components of academic self concept and self efficacy. *Contemporary Educational Psychology, 16*, 331-345.

Marshall, H. H., and Weinstein, R. S. (1984). Classroom factors affecting students' self-evaluations. *Review of Educational Research, 54*, 301–326.

Mc Dowell I., Newell C. (1987). *Measuring Health: a Guide to Rating Scales and Questionnaires.* Oxford University Press, New York.

Pajares F. (2000) Schooling in America: myths, mixed messages, and good intentions. Lecture delivered at Emory University, Cannon Chapter, January 27, 2000. (On-line) Available at: http//www.cc.emory.edu/EDUCATION/mpf/greatteacherlecture.html.

Pajares, F., and Miller, M.D. (1994). The role of self-efficacy and self-concept beliefs in mathematical problem-solving: A path analysis. *Journal of Educational Psychology, 86*, 193-203.

Pavot W., Diener E. (1993). Review of the Satisfaction with Life Scale. *Psychological Assessment, 5*, 164-72.

Perry C. and Marsh H.W. (2003). Relations Between Elite Athlete Self-Concept And International Swimming Performance. Paper presented at NZARE AARE, Auckland, New Zealand, November 2003 (PER03785).

Rogers, C. R. (1959). A theory of therapy, personality, and interpersonal relationships as developed in the client-centered framework. In S. Koch (Ed.), *Psychology: A study of a science, 3*, 184–256. New York: McGraw-Hill.

Ryff C. D. (1989a). Happiness Is Everything, or Is It? Explorations on the Meaning of Psychological Well-Being. *Journal of Personality and Social Psychology, 57, 6*, 1069-81.

Scheirer, M. A., and Kraut, R. E. (1979). Increasing educational achievement via self-concept change. *Review of Educational Research, 49*, 131-150.

Shavelson, R. J., Hubner, J. J., and Stanton, G. C. (1976). Self-concept: Validation of construct interpretations. *Review of Educational Research, 46*, 407–441.

Singelis T. M. (1994). The measurement of independent and interdependent self-construals. *Personality and Social Psychology Bulletin, 20*, 580-591

Skaalvik, E. M., and Skaalvik, S. (2002). Internal and external frames of reference for academic self-concept. *Educational Psychologist, 37*, 233-244.

Snygg, D., and Combs, A. (1949). *Individual behavior.* New York: Harper.

Strein, W. (1993). Advances in research on academic self-concept: Implications for school psychology. *School Psychology Review, 22*, 273-284.

Wells, L. E., and Marwell, G. (1976). *Self-esteem: Its conceptualization and measurement.* Beverly Hills, CA: Sage.

Wylie, R. (1974). *The self-concept: Vol. 1. A review of methological considerations and measuring instruments* (rev. ed.). Lincoln: University of Nebraska Press.

Wylie, R. (1979). *The self-concept: Vol. 2. Theory and research on selected topics* (rev. ed.). Lincoln: University of Nebraska Press.

In: The Concept of Self in Education, Family and Sports   ISBN 1-59454-988-5
Editor: Anne P. Prescott, pp. 191-206   © 2006 Nova Science Publishers, Inc.

Chapter 8

"THE CONCEPT OF THE INDEPENDENT AND INTERDEPENDENT SELF AND SOCIOLOGICAL THEORY: INTER-DISCIPLINARY CROSS-FERTILIZATION"

Bernadette E. Dietz

Associate Professor of Sociology, University of Cincinnati Clermont College

ABSTRACT

The concepts of self and identity have increasingly received attention in the social psychology literature, with theory development and empirical research springing from both psychological and sociological social psychology. The cross-cultural work of anthropologists and psychologists led to the distinction between the independent self and the interdependent self. It is hypothesized that people reared in cultures with highly individualistic values tend to develop a view of self as an independent agent, while those reared in cultures with highly collectivist values develop a view of self as interdependent with others. Recent work has refined these concepts and their measurement, and has developed the theoretical ideas further. Research has found variation in these aspects of self within single cultures. There are great potential benefits of cross-fertilization between the disciplines of psychology and sociology. This chapter examines the conceptions of the independent and interdependent self within the framework of sociological theory, particularly Practice Theory and Identity Theory. This is approached through discussions of the development of the self and of how the self influences behavior. This effort raises new theoretical questions to be addressed in both disciplines, particularly questions related to the relationship of power to the independent and interdependent self, and self-meanings.

INTRODUCTION

Social scientists from various disciplines have shared an interest in gaining a greater understanding of the self. The self is often seen as a link between the larger society and the individual. It represents a mechanism through which the society and culture influence and shape the behavior of individuals. The self is also typically conceptualized as a vehicle of individual and group agency, providing for the opposite direction of influence from the individual to the larger community and society [Callero 2003]. The following pages bring together particular theories of the self and identity that have sprung from anthropology, psychological social psychology, and sociological social psychology in an attempt to further our understanding of the self and the link between the self and society and to raise new research questions.

Over the years there has been little cross-fertilization between sociological and psychological theory. There are potentially great benefits from a bringing together of some of these theories and findings. One recent example of this kind of attempt compared and contrasted sociological and psychological identity theories. It was pointed out in this work that it is not always wise to attempt to integrate divergent theories [Hogg et al. 1995]. However, our understanding of social phenomena can be enhanced greatly by an awareness of the theory and findings of both sociology and psychology, the questions addressed by each, and the concepts found useful.

This chapter will address some ways in which sociological theory and psychological theory can inform each other. First, an overview of theory and some findings related to the concepts of the independent and the interdependent self will be presented. These concepts were introduced by psychologists who were informed by anthropological findings. Then useful sociological theory will be examined in relation to issues of the development of self and the influence of the self on behavior. Finally, research questions and promising areas for future research are discussed. It is concluded that to move forward in our understanding of the self, particularly the independent and interdependent self, greater attention is needed to two major issues. One is the relationship of power relations and stratification systems to the independent and interdependent self. It is argued here that power can exert itself most fully through its influence on the self-conceptions of groups, and particularly on the independent and interdependent self. The second is the elaboration of the complexity of self-meanings. This chapter presents an argument that the independent self and interdependent self, as one of the most basic and abstract elements of self, act as lenses through which actors interpret others, situations, and the self.

THEORY

The *self* has often been viewed by social scientists as "…all of the individual's cognitions and emotions relating to the self" [Rosenberg 1992, p.596]. This approach to the definition of the self has been shared by the fields of sociology and psychology. There are, however, differences of emphasis in how these two social sciences define the self. Psychologists tend to view the self in terms of cognitions and personality tendencies that are influenced by social factors and in turn influence behavior [Wylie 1961]. Psychologists have referred to the self as a schema, a cognitive framework of knowledge, and as a theory about self. In this view, the self contains facts and constructs and hypotheses related to the self, as well as values and aspirations that may represent possible or potential selves [Schlenker 1985].

Sociological social psychologists emphasize the self as a regulatory reflexive process that occurs in social interaction. The self is also seen as an object of reflection [James 1890, Mead 1934]. It has been stated, therefore, that the self is both a social

force (the acting, reflecting subject) and a social product (a concept of self as an object created through the social interaction and reflection process) [Rosenberg 1981]. The reflexive process produces a *personal self* and also a *public self* as it is visible and known to others.

The idea of the public self was referred to in the early work of the psychologist William James [1890] in which he stated, "...a man has as many social selves as there are individuals who recognize him and carry an image of him in their head" [James 1890, p.294]. Here he indicates that the self is a public and social phenomenon, arising in the interaction process. James' early work also suggests the idea that there is some sense of unity and continuity to the self. What is often referred to as the "I", or the acting subject, is the source of self-observation and sense of continuity, while the "me", or empirical self, is that which can be observed [James 1890].

A further distinction among dimensions of self focuses on the *biographical self* built up over time and experienced as enduring versus the *situated self* experienced in a particular situation. This includes the distinction made between personal identity, social identity, and situated identity. *Personal identity* that includes aspects of the self seen as unique to the individual (e.g. one's name, personality characteristics), while *social identity* includes aspects of self that are tied in to social life (e.g. social statuses, group memberships). Both these types of identity develop over time and have been characterized as biographical identity elements because they relate to a continuity of experience and are experienced as an enduring self. *Situated identity*, on the other hand, refers to aspects of self as they are invoked in particular immediate situations and roles [Hewitt 1991].

Both psychological and sociological conceptualizations of the self have been heavily influenced by a "western view" of the individual in which the person is viewed as a unique and independent entity whose behavior is influenced by a set of internal characteristics, such as personality traits, abilities, and motives [Markus AND Kitayama 1991, p.224]. Currently there is a growing recognition of an alternative to this western view of self and of the fact that the self may differ greatly among various cultures of the world.

The Interdependent Self and the Independent Self

Markus and Kitayama [1991] introduced the concepts of the independent and interdependent self-construal which refer to thoughts, feelings, and actions related to the self in relation to the group. They state,

> ...the Western notion of the self as an entity containing significant dispositional attributes, and as detached from context, is simply not an adequate description of selfhood. Rather, in many construals, the self is viewed an *inter*dependent with the surrounding context, and it is the "other" or the "self-in-relation-to-other" that is focal in individual experience [Markus AND Kitayama 1991, p.225].

The *independent self-construal* is associated with Western individualistic cultures while the interdependent self is associated with Asian collectivist cultures. The person with an independent self sees herself as a unique person, separate from others, with internal traits, thoughts, and abilities that are separate from the characteristics of the social situation. This type of self involves an emphasis on expressing the self, seeking one's own goals, and communicating in a direct fashion. Others are viewed in a similar fashion, as independent actors whose internal thoughts, feelings, and traits must be understood in order to understand their behavior. To the person with a highly independent self-construal, the self is experienced as a private inner self.

The person with an *interdependent self-construal* sees himself as a part of a group, intertwined with others, and as influenced greatly by the social situation and context. This type of self involves an emphasis on relationships, fitting in to the group, coordinating one's behavior to the needs of the group, and communicating in an indirect fashion. To a person with this type of self, others are viewed similarly as intertwined in relationships and as having their actions molded by the specifics of the situation. Hence, reading the context allows one to communicate more indirectly and this often helps to maintain harmonious relationships. To this type of person, the public self takes center stage with the most significant aspects of self found in relationships and contexts rather than inside the individual. In fact, "…for the interdependent self, others are included *within* the boundaries of the self because relations with others in specific contexts are the defining features of the self" [Markus AND Kitayama 1991, p.245].

Even the person with a highly interdependent self is expected to experience a private or inner sense of self to some degree. Social functioning requires a notion of self as distinct from the physical environment and from other people. Also, it is the case that people are aware of internal experience involving some continuity of thought and feeling that is not directly visible to the others. These factors would tend to create some sense of a private, independent self in individuals [Markus AND Kitayama 1991]. Similarly, it appears that even a person with a highly independent view of self experiences the interdependent nature of their social activity to some level.

Culture is posited to influence the relative development of these differing types of selves, with an independent self more commonly found in cultures with an individualistic value orientation and an interdependent self more likely found in cultures with collectivist values [Markus AND Kitayama 1991, Triandis 1989]. These important dimensions of culture were distinguished in the Anthropological work of Hofstede (1980). The concepts of *individualism* and *collectivism* refer to the differing ways the individual relates to the group in various cultures. *Individualistic cultures* give priority to individual needs and goals, defining and treating people as separate and unique entities with personal longstanding traits. Individualism has been pronounced generally in Northern and Western Europe, North America, and Australia. The empirical work of Hofstede (1980) suggests the United States is the most individualistic of the countries studied. *Collectivist cultures* give priority to the group needs and goals, tending to define and treat people as members of groups, intertwined with others and social situations. Generally, collectivism is found when cultures of Asia, Africa, South America and the Pacific Islands are studied.

The concern with this distinction between individualist and collectivist cultures mirrors a long-standing concern of Sociologists with the overlapping distinction between "folk societies" and "urban societies". It is argued that processes of industrialization and urbanization encourage the development of the urban lifestyle, involving increased complexity, heterogeneity, impersonality, and progress and change. In the urban society, individuals are viewed as independent actors and there is little group solidarity [Thio 1998]. There is much overlap between this distinction and that of the individualist and collectivist culture. However, high levels of collectivism are found in societies that are highly industrialized and urban, in Japan for example. Questions remain concerning how values of individualism and collectivism relate to distinctions such as socialism and capitalism, and homogeneity and heterogeneity. There is room for further development of these concepts and for theory and research related to the macro-forces that create these differences among societies, but this is not the focus of this chapter.

Research has tended to support the hypothesis that the independent self is more common in individualistic cultures and the interdependent self more common in collectivist cultures [e.g. Bochner 1994, Singelis 1994, Trafimow et al. 1992, Triandis 1989]. Refinements of measurement and theory have taken place over time. Recent work has indicated that cultures are more complex than the basic individualism-collectivism distinction suggests. When individualism and collectivism are measured within each of the different social domains of family, close friends, colleagues, and strangers, great variety is found within samples of Japanese and American university students. For example, the Japanese sample showed lower collectivism scores related to family than did the American sample. Findings were related to cultural change occurring in both countries, but also illustrate the complexity of culture [Matsumoto et al. 1996].

Recent empirical work on self-construals suggests that the independent self and the interdependent self are not polar opposites, but can co-exist within a person in varying levels [Cross AND Markus 1991]. In one empirical study, overall differences found between Asian-American groups in comparison with Caucasian-American groups were consistent with the hypothesis (Asian groups showing more interdependence of self), but evidence indicated that the two sub-scales were very weakly correlated [Singelis 1994], indicating that to be measured as having a highly independent self does not preclude the possibility of also having a highly interdependent self. This finding suggests this dimension of self is more complex than previous work indicated. It may be productive to measure the independence/interdependence of self within various domains, as the Matsumoto et al. [1996] research attempted in their research on cultural values and behaviors.

Work on the independent and interdependent self has primarily focused on attempts to measure these self-construals, cultural and group differences in the self, and theory on behavioral and attitudinal outcomes of these types of selves. Little discussion has occurred representing attempts to understand the process involved in the development of these different types of selves. Markus AND Kitayama [1991] address this issue briefly stating that the cultural context is influential through normative imperatives imparted to members to be, for example, independent and expressive of one's unique self. They also mention the influence of the varying institutions in various societies and how these structure different types of relationships amongst members. It is instructive to also draw upon available theories and findings from the perspective of sociological social psychology to address this issue. This is discussed further below.

Sociological Theory of Self Development

Sociological theory concerning social influences on the self can provide insights into the development of the independent and the interdependent self. Further empirical examination of the independent and the interdependent self offers an opportunity to sociological and psychological social psychologists to gain a fuller understanding of contextual influences on the self. Sociological work on self-development has sometimes focused on the broad context of this development and has sometimes emphasized the micro-interaction processes involved in the construction of and change in the self and self concept. Others have attempted to incorporate linkages between macro-level features of societies and micro-level social relations. An understanding of this linkage is key to an explanation of the reciprocal influence between the individual and society. Therefore, theoretical ideas that include this link will be discussed below.

A body of sociological work, known as the social structure and personality approach, examines shifts in culture and social structure and links these to changes in self. This work has sometimes been criticized for making generalizations that ignore the complexity of the social world and the rich diversity of groups. In response to this potential problem, Callero [2003] states, "...the most enduring and informative analyses are often those that link together historical shifts in the political economy, change in particular social settings, and critical alterations in self-experience" [Callero 2003, p.122]. This is consistent with the suggestion of Markus AND Kitayama [1991] stated above that to understand influences on the self we need to examine not only the features of social institutions but also how these structure relationships with others in particular situations. Some sociological work attempts these linkages (e.g. Kusserow 2004, Sennett 1998, Hochschild 1997, Giddens 1991, Bourdieu 1977).

The French sociologists Pierre Bourdieu [1977] presented a Theory of Practice that fulfills the requirement of linking the macro structure and culture to people's experiences and relationships in social situations, and is particularly promising as a useful approach to the study of the independent and interdependent self. The theory focuses on how social structures become internalized by individuals sharing a position in the structure, particularly a social class position. Bourdieu introduced the concept of *habitus* which is defined as "systems of durable, transposable dispositions...principles of the generation and structuring of practices and representations which can be objectively 'regulated' and 'regular' without in any way being the product of obedience to rules" [Bourdieu 1977, p.72]. So, Bourdieu proposes an alternative to the influence of stated cultural rules and obedience to these. Habitus reflects culture and consists of internalized structures, ways of perceiving, interpreting, and acting that are shared among a group or class, including tastes, dispositions, beliefs, expectations, and aspirations. These may be subjective and appear as unique internal traits of individuals, but in reality they are not just properties of the individual. Rather they are shared among members of a group who share a common position in the social structure. Habitus includes the taken for granted and what is often thought of as common sense. It is internalized by individuals beginning with early socialization experiences. The independent and interdependent self can be considered habitus knowledge since they are conceptions that are socially defined and shared amongst members of groups.

Sociologists tend to argue that power issues should remain at the forefront of social theory. Postmodern theorists argue that the self is a direct result of the exercise of power and can only be understood in relation to specific historical systems of discourse. This approach emphasizes that the self is a social construction [Callero 2003]. Bourdieu [1977] emphasizes in his work the way power relationships are reproduced into future generations by habitus, such as relations of social class. For example, dispositions like intelligence are often seen as reflecting individual hierarchies of ability, but in reality reflect social hierarchies (involving types of cultural capital that reflect economic capital and influence chances for mobility). Social institutions, like education, promote dominant group interests and conceptions of the world.

The independent and interdependent self are among the most abstract, fundamental aspects of self, since they reflect one's most basic view of self in relation to others. As such, I posit this is an aspect of self through which the exercise of power can exert itself most fully. If this sense of self is molded through social forces reflecting dominant group interests, it has great potential to shape behavior across contexts. The presence of a habitus of the independent self rather than the interdependent self may contribute to the reproduction and even heightening of power relationships and economic inequalities. Research suggests that those with an interdependent self are more likely to not only view themselves as intertwined with others in social situations, but also view others and their behaviors from that same vantage point. Singelis [1994] found that those with the interdependent self were more likely than those with the independent self, when presented with a hypothetical conversation between two people, to attribute the cause of the peoples' behavior to the situation rather than internal traits. Therefore, those with an independent self may be less likely to assign importance to social forces as explanations of social class positions in society and more likely to assign importance to internal traits of individuals, thereby blaming the victims of systems of social inequality.

In addition to the above, the Practice theory does acknowledge the dynamic nature of society and leaves room for human agency to create social change. To Bourdieu, habitus knowledge is flexible and fluid. It may vary amongst groups and individuals, and sometimes challenges social structures rather than simply reflecting culture and social structure. This suggests that due to individual variation and the interaction between individual characteristics and features of local social contexts, there may be times when an individual's or a group's habitus may not fit with the current social environment and may create challenge. Role conflict and psychological dissonance may occur, as well as overt forms of challenge to the existing order. There also may be times when a habitus itself contains elements that either encourage or discourage challenge. As in the example given above, it is argued here that those with an interdependent self are more likely to challenge an economic order that sustains inequality and poverty. This is argued because those with an interdependent self are more likely to recognize that individual behaviors and outcomes are products of social situations.

According to the ideas of Bourdieu [1977] the linkage of social structures to individual internalization occurs through a variety of processes. Direct teaching is one of these processes and includes statements of rules, beliefs, and values. Perhaps more importantly, a multitude of unconscious modes of informal socialization impart habitus knowledge without participants' conscious awareness. These modes include daily practices and patterns of interaction, rituals, discourses, and proverbs that model the principles of the habitus. For example, as children learn alongside parents in the home they internalize a taken for granted relationship between parents and children and a division of labor between the sexes. These unconscious processes should be particularly important in the development of the independent and interdependent self, since these involve fundamental conceptions and assumptions of self in relation to others.

One recent empirical study used an ethnographic method and is a particularly good example of the application of this approach to the study of individualism. The author used Bourdieu's theory as a framework and examined child rearing and individualistic values and conceptions within three communities in the U.S. The author finds evidence that a distinction can be drawn between hard and soft individualism, that community and social class structures influence child rearing activities of parents and pre-school teachers, and that child rearing is associated with an internalization of a particular type of individualistic values and conception of people. The author does not attempt to measure the self of participants, but does examine the conception of children expressed and reinforced by parents and teachers, and sometimes by the children themselves. This conception has implications for the future economic and social positions of youth. *Hard individualism* in contrast to *soft individualism* refers to a view of the individual as a "...singular unit 'against' the world, as contrasted to...a singular unit 'opening up' or out into the world" [Kusserow 2004, p.26]. A distinction is also drawn between two types of hard individualism, one "projective" (valuing toughness to allow one to break through to a higher class level) and one "protective" (valuing toughness to deflect dangers) [Kusserow 2004].

The author concludes that individualism shows itself in varying forms for families in different classes and types of communities. Individualism has "uniquely tailored meanings and uses for...parents..." and "...it becomes a form of explanation or solution to the central issues and meanings in the lives of these parents" [Kusserow 2004, p. 24]. The work of Kusserow illuminates how the broader context of the social class system in the U.S. and the local community context shape groups' daily social relations, concerns, beliefs, and values that then become deeply internalized in the habitus. The habitus is viewed by members as including natural, internal tendencies of individuals, rather than being recognized as socially created. Each style of individualism reflected in the habitus prepares youth to fit into the social world and class status of parents. The higher class community in the study valued soft individualism. One working class community valued hard, projective individualism, while the other valued hard, protective individualism. This latter difference was associated with a difference in characteristics of the working class communities. The working class community that was more diverse and had much higher crime rates valued the protective form of hard individualism, while the other, having more sense of community togetherness and pride, valued the projective form.

This work details the different social relations and processes of internalization of the habitus in the three communities. Kusserow notes differences in interactional behaviors, body styles, language used, and even pamphlets given from pre-schools to parents as important in the internalization processes. For example, parents and teachers in the higher income community encouraged the development of the soft individualism habitus through using soft tones of voice, warm and open facial expressions, and closer body proximity, all creating a soft environment where the child is encouraged to open up to a receptive world. Metaphors used illustrated their conceptions of people, specifically their children. In this higher class community the children were often referred to as "flowers" and "delicate" and life described as a "canvas upon which the child can spread her wings" [Kusserow 2004, p.176]. Children were seen as needing gentle care and an open environment to encourage their development to their full potential. A safe place was created in pre-school for show and tell activities, encouraging self expression. The author interprets the soft individualism found in this community as a particularly psychologized view, where the child is viewed as having a true self that must be developed and expressed.

In contrast, working class community members encourage the internalization of hard forms of individualism. For example, parents and teachers used harsher language and louder tones of voice with children, expressing negative emotions more often, and maintaining greater physical distance from children. Metaphors used to describe children included "superman", "hardy", and "resilient" and life was often described as "a tough mountain to climb" [Kusserow 2004, p.176]. Children were seen as needing to be toughened to face the world. Show and tell activities in pre-school were often attended by teasing requiring the child to defend their stories. These and other processes encouraged the development of a habitus of hard individualism in these youth.

Bourdieu's Theory of Practice [1977] provides a useful framework for the study of the development of the self. On the other hand, theory and empirical findings related to the independent and the interdependent self could provide an avenue of research that may lead to insights that will aid in the further development of theory on the internalization of habitus and the relationship of power to the self. A promising research agenda could focus on further outlining the contextual features of societies and communities that are associated with the types of selves, how these features shape social relations and behaviors for groups in different positions in the social structure, and the implications of these differences for the self. Importantly, the relationship of power and systems of inequality to the self should be forefront in this agenda.

There is a growing body of cross-cultural empirical work examining individualism and collectivism and the two types of selves. Much of it has contrasted China and/or Japan with the U.S. and some has delved into the processes that produce different types of selves in the two societies, but generally this work lacks the guidance of a theoretical framework. For example, Hamaguchi [cited in Markus AND Kitayama 1991] points out the word for self used in Japan is *jibun*, which means "one's share of the shared life space" [p. 228], suggesting one way language may be involved in reflecting social life and shaping views of self in relation to other. Similarly, differences in metaphors and proverbs used in societies have been noted, for example the popular Japanese proverb stating that the nail that sticks up must be hammered down has been frequently cited as an example of the imparting of collectivist values. Studies of the varying school environments and social relations in Japan compared to the U.S. have been enlightening. Various studies have suggested that, in contrast to U.S. classrooms, Japanese classrooms create a setting and frame interactions so as to encourage students to value the group, find a place for themselves in groups, and satisfaction in group involvements. Peak [1989] and Lewis [1989] both found that Japanese teachers set a minimum standard for student behavior, leaving some authority to place limits on behavior in the group itself, thus encouraging the development of skills of self-restraint and tolerance and an understanding of the group's needs. Schneider AND Silverman [2003] point out how Japanese students are interacted with as members of cooperative classroom work groups and how students often remain in these work groups for years.

The cross-cultural research cited above has been extremely informative about linkages between general cultural value systems and aspects of self, and about various socialization processes. Some work has begun to examine cultural change in Japan [e.g. Matsumoto et al. 1996]. More of this type of analysis in the future may help us further understand the reciprocal influence of society and the self. This cross-cultural research has focused less heavily on defining important features of the broader context that shape the local social environment, and on differences within the societies among groups located at different places in the social structure. It has also tended to ignore how power relations that are reflected and reinforced by the self. Addressing these areas should lead to a further understanding of the development of the self.

Identity Theory, the Self and Behavior

Research has suggested associations between type of self (independent versus interdependent) and behavior and between type of cultural values (individualistic versus collectivist) and behavior. Some of these findings will be discussed later. Sociological Identity theory [Stryker 1980] is a useful framework to apply to further understand the independent and interdependent self and how these influence behavior. On the other hand, Identity theory may be developed further through attempts to address these types of selves and the research findings related to these in its framework. Identity theory is a structural theory that stems from the Symbolic Interactionist tradition and emphasizes that the self mediates the relationship between society and the individual. The theory seeks to explain role performance behavior, which reflects the influence of both the self and the society. While not all behaviors reflect social positions with associated expectations (roles), role performances do account for a great deal of social behavior.

Identity theory defines *identities* (or role-identities) as, "internalized positional designations" that exist when a person, "is a participant in structured role relationships" [Stryker 1980, p.60]. So, when a person occupies a social status (or social position) they will have an associated identity. An individual may have identities as a sociologist, teacher, mother, wife, friend, Democrat, and motorcyclist and these taken together make up the self. These identities carry *meaning* for individuals and therefore, provide self-meanings and a sense of self-worth.

Other kinds of social attributes, such as gender, race, and social class are treated in Identity theory as more generalized statuses because they do not carry specific behavioral roles. They exert great influence on the self indirectly through their effect on the social positions a person can occupy (e.g. one born into poverty has less chance of becoming a physician than one born into wealth.), through the relative importance of the identities (e.g. occupational identities may be more important to males than females), and through an influence on the nature of individual interactions with others (e.g. people tend to come into contact with other people of similar social class position) [Hogg et al. 1995]. So the self reflects society. However the theory also specifies a reciprocal relationship between self and society. The individual, to varying degrees in different positions and situations, has some ability to role-make rather than simply role-play [Stryker 1980].

The self is seen as organized, according to Identity theory. One important way that identities are organized is in a hierarchy of *salience*. The higher an identity is in the salience hierarchy, the greater the likelihood that it will be called upon in situations and that it will be important in defining the self. The salience of an identity is influenced by *commitment*. "To the degree that one's relationships to specified sets of other persons depend on being a particular kind of person, one is committed to being that kind of person" [Stryker 1980, p.61].

Affective commitment will be greater to the degree that ties to particular sets of others are important to a person. *Interactional commitment* will be greater the larger the number of roles (and hence, role partners) associated with the identity. The greater the commitment to an identity, the higher it will be in the salience hierarchy, and therefore, the more likely it will be called upon to guide behavior in situations. Other factors that are posited to increase salience are the degree the identity is evaluated positively, the degree that the role expectations from others to whom one is committed are congruent, the greater the number of persons in this set of others for whom the identity is also highly salient [Stryker 1980].

The salience hierarchy of identities, according to the Identity theory, exerts an influence on behavior in several ways. The higher an identity is in the salience hierarchy the greater the likelihood that behavior will be congruent with the associated role expectations, the more likely situations will be seen as a chance to perform the associated role, and the more likely a person will seek out situations in which to perform the role [Stryker 1980]. A body of research has tested hypotheses from the Identity theory. Much of it has focused on commitments, salience, and time spent engaging in particular role performances and generally finds support for the theory [e.g. Stryker AND Serpe 1982]. Some research has examined the influence of particular generalized statuses, such as gender, and suggests that these statuses are related to identity salience and commitment (e.g. Bielby 1992, Thoits 1986].

While Identity theory does not specifically incorporate the independent and the interdependent self, it does address the role of generalized statuses, such as gender. The independent self and interdependent self can be considered examples of this type of generalized status. However, the independent/interdependent self should be treated as even more abstract and basic qualities of the self than such statuses as gender. Markus AND Kitayama [1991] argue this same point saying, "These construals recruit and organize the more specific self-regulatory schemata" [p. 230]. Identity theory provides a framework for understanding how they may organize the self in this way. According to this theory, generalized statuses influence the structure of the self and behavior through their influence on identities and the salience hierarchy of identities. They exert an influence on identities through the three mechanisms mentioned above.

Identity theory then would suggest that the independent/interdependent self influences identities through, first, an effect on the positions one can or will occupy. Research indicates that the self is a motivating force, with individuals displaying self-enhancement [Kaplan 1980] and self-consistency motives [Schwartz AND Stryker 1970]. Individuals with an independent self should be motivated to take on roles that will allow them to express what they see as their inner qualities related to the more independent aspects of self. The individual with an interdependent self should be motivated to take on roles that allow them to express their interconnected-ness with others. This individual may be more likely than one with an independent self to take up softball than tennis, and more likely to take a job in which they work closely and cooperatively with others because of the particularly interdependent nature of these roles. Taking on roles that are consistent with the individual's view of self, and values, will be more likely to enhance self-esteem and contribute to a consistent view of self.

The second way the general type of self influences identities is through its effect on the relative importance of identities. Identity theory states that higher levels of affective commitment to identities contributes to their salience, and commitment varies by status. Research has found, for example, that gender as a generalized type of status is associated with identity commitment and salience so that women show higher salience of, and commitment to, family identities than do men [Bielby 1992]. The individual with an interdependent self should place greater importance on maintaining relationships and would as a result have a higher commitment level to identities than the individual with the independent self. They may also have greater commitment and salience levels to identities that particularly involve interdependent activity with others. Research using the Twenty Statements Test to measure self-construals has tended to find that those from collectivist cultures complete the "I am" sentences with more social statuses and group memberships than do those from more individualistic cultures, who complete the sentence with more statements of psychological attributes [Bochner 1994, Triandis et al. 1990, Cousins 1989, Bond AND Cheung 1983]. This is often interpreted to mean that group oriented elements are more central and salient to those from collectivist cultures.

The independent/interdependent self should also influence identities through the third process stated in the Identity theory, its effect on the nature of social relations and patterns of interaction. Other generalized statuses like race, ethnicity, and social class are associated with varying interaction patterns in such a way that individuals tend to interact with in-group members more heavily than out-group members. This patterning may also occur in relation to the independent/interdependent self, especially since this self was in all probability developed within a cultural or sub-cultural group and social network that placed more value on either independence or interdependence. The type of self should influence social interactions in a second way. Markus AND Kitayama [1991] suggest that the basis of self-esteem and self-satisfaction differ for the independent and the interdependent self. For those with an independent self, self-esteem is enhanced by a person's ability to express the self and validate their internal attributes. For those with an interdependent self, self-satisfaction is enhanced by the ability to fit the self into a group and to maintain harmony. If this is the case, self-esteem/satisfaction motives would differ between the two types of selves and would certainly influence the individual's goals for social interactions and their behavior. Identity theory then would suggest that, through this mechanism, the independent/interdependent self influences who a person comes into contact with (which may influence role opportunities), but also how a person interacts with others and how they perform their roles.

The independent and interdependent self should exert an influence on identities and their salience and therefore on behavior, as the above discussion indicates. There may be a fourth way these selves influence behavior. This is through their influence on the *meaning* of identities for the individual. Identity theory indicates that behavior is influenced by identities and their salience, but also by the particular meaning of these identities for the actor [Stryker 1980]. It is likely that whether a person has a predominantly independent self or an interdependent self will color the meaning of other generalized statuses and of particular identities. Because of the abstract, fundamental nature of these aspects of self, it is posited here that they act as a lens through which the actor interprets particular situations, others, events, and the self. Independent and interdependent self-meanings may be channeled through specific identities to influence behavior. For example, it is likely that an occupational identity would differ in meaning such that for those with an independent self, internal traits, skills, and abilities would be central, while for those with an interdependent self, occupational relationships would be more central. These differences in meaning then should shape occupational behavior.

Identity theory is a useful framework to guide our understanding of how the independent and interdependent self influence role performance behaviors and can help social scientists make sense of relationships found in empirical research. For example, research has found that those from collectivist cultures are more likely to avoid dissent and open confrontation and to behave in ways that preserve harmony amongst members of a group than are those from individualistic cultures [Schneider AND Silverman 2003]. Identity theory suggests that this can be explained by a greater level of salience of and affective commitment to various identities, and especially those that allow for the expression of interdependence, amongst those with an interdependent self. Also, the greater level of interdependence built into the meaning of identities can explain this relationship. For those with interdependent selves, identities that preserve harmony are more likely to be invoked and the meaning of identities is more likely to reflect interrelationships.

Research has also found that individuals from cultures with strongly collectivist values (e.g. East Asian cultures) are less likely to exhibit social loafing during cooperative group work than those from cultures with individualistic values (e.g. U.S.) and are more likely to display social facilitation where their performance is heightened in the group [Earley 1993]. Identity theory posits that when identities are highly salient, behavior will be more congruent with role expectations. This suggests an explanation for the greater social facilitation found in collectivist cultures. Those with an interdependent self are likely to rank identities that express interdependence highly in their salience hierarchy. Therefore, when confronted with a cooperative work situation these individuals should be likely to readily invoke a salient identity with a strong cooperative component. The high level of salience of the identity invoked is expected to be associated with a greater congruence of behavior with role expectations. The interdependent person is more likely in this type of situation to attempt to fulfill the expectations of work partners and therefore, put a great effort into the work. In contrast, those with independent selves are less likely to have identities that are both highly cooperative and highly salient and thus less likely to invoke such an identity in cooperative situations.

Identity theory provides a useful framework within which to understand the independent and interdependent self and role performance behavior. In addition, further work on these generalized aspects of self and how they shape self-meanings may prove valuable in efforts to refine the Identity theory. Sociological Identity theorists have pursued much more work on particular role-identities than they have on the influences of the more generalized statuses. Social psychologists from the field of psychology have focused more heavily on generalized statuses, such as theorists and researchers using the Social Identity theory framework [Tajfel AND Turner 1979]. A reasonably broad theory of self and behavior should incorporate the various levels of identity

CONCLUSION

Social Psychologists in the fields of Psychology and Sociology have shown an interest in developing a deeper understanding of the self and how it operates as a link between the individual and the larger society. There has been a growing recognition of the diversity in conceptions of self in both fields. A body of work is developing by Psychologists and Anthropologists on some of these differences. This chapter has focused on their work on the distinction between the independent and the interdependent self and has brought these ideas together with theoretical ideas from Sociological Social Psychologists in an attempt to raise new research questions.

After initial discussion of the self and the independent and interdependent self, this chapter focused on development of the self, and then on the influence of the self on behavior. The Practice theory of Bourdieu was used as a framework to discuss the development of self and the internalization of a habitus of independence and interdependence that represents a self-schema. This theory emphasizes how the broader cultural and structural context become internalized as habitus knowledge through several processes, some overt and some very subtle [Bourdieu 1977]. Although a body of research has begun to build that examines the independent and interdependent self, several questions about the development of these kinds of selves need further attention. What features of the local social worlds of groups (both within one society and cross-culturally) have an influence on the development of an independent or an interdependent self? How are these local social worlds shaped by the broader culture and social structure? How is the exercise of power involved in the development of an independent or interdependent self? What processes are involved in the internalization of the habitus related to self in relation to others?

The Sociological Identity theory was used as a framework to discuss the self and its influence on behavior. The independent and interdependent self are treated here as generalized statuses, like gender, within the Identity theory framework. As such, it is concluded that these types of selves should influence behavior through their influence on the identity salience hierarchy and through their influence on the meaning of identities. Several questions would be particularly beneficial to address in future research in this area. How do generalized social statuses, like the independent and the interdependent self, color the meanings of more particular identities? How do differences in self-meanings related to independence and interdependence influence behavior in situations?

It is concluded here that the independent and interdependent self are among the most abstract and fundamental aspects of self. Research and theoretical development now can benefit most from a particular emphasis on first, the relationship of power to the independent and interdependent self, and second, the self-meanings associated with each of these types of selves. In general, power in relation to the self has not received a great deal of attention by Sociologists or Psychologists and it may be that the most profound effect of the exercise of power can be observed in its influence on the self conceptions of groups. Self-meaning has been studied more in the field of Psychology than in Sociology. Power relations and self-meanings are at the heart of an understanding of the reciprocal relationship between the individual and the society.

From a Sociological perspective, the individual is to a great degree a product of society. On the other hand, individuals, behaving collectively, create and sustain society. Similarly, the self can be said to be a social product, but also is influential in the continual negotiation of meaning and social space that creates and sustains social patterns. The self may be implicated in the reproduction of inequalities, or may be instrumental in creating social change. Bourdieu's theory [1977] emphasizes that the process of internalization of a habitus is shaped by contextual power relations. The theory, however, argues that a habitus sometimes challenges the existing structure. For example, it is posited here that a habitus of independence of self detracts from the possibilities of challenge to the economic order because of its psychologized view of self and others, while the interdependent self may lend itself to challenge of an economic order that results in inequalities and poverty. Symbolic

Interactionist theory asserts that people create meaning and that they act on the basis of meaning. An understanding of the construction of meaning is central to an understanding of the self, and the link between the self and society.

Investigation of the type of research questions posed here, with an emphasis on relations of power and meaning, should lead to a further understanding of the independent and interdependent self and to further refinements of theory of the self and society.

ACKNOWLEDGEMENTS

The author wishes to thank Lora Hasse and Dan Goodman for comments on earlier drafts of this manuscript.

REFERENCES

Bielby, D. D. (1992) Commitment to work and family. Annual Review of Sociology, 18:281-302.

Bochner, S. (1994) Cross-cultural differences in the self concept. Journal of Cross- Cultural Psychology, 25 (2), 273-283.

Bond, M. H., AND Cheung, T. S. (1983) The spontaneous self-concept of college students in Hong Kong, Japan, and the United States. Journal of Cross-Cultural Psychology, 14: 153-171.

Bourdieu, P. (1977) Outline of a theory of practice. Cambridge: Cambridge University Press.

Callero, P. (2003) The sociology of the self. Annual Review of Sociology, 29, 115-133.

Cousins, S. D. (1989) Culture and self-perception in Japan and the United States. Journal of Personality and Social Psychology, 56(1): 124-131.

Cross, S. E., Markus, H. R. (1991) Cultural adaptation and the self: Self-construal, coping, and stress. Paper presented at the annual meeting of the American Psychological Association, San Francisco.

Earley, P. C. (1993) East meets west meet mideast: Further explorations of collectivistic versus individualistic work groups. Academy of Management Journal, 36: 319-348.

Giddens, A. (1991) Modernity and self-identity. Stanford: Stanford University Press.

Hewitt, J. P. (1991) Self and society. Boston: Allyn AND Bacon.

Hochschild, A. R. (1997) The time bind. New York: Henry Holt and Company.

Hofstede, G. (1980) Culture's consequences: International differences in work-related values. Beverly Hills: Sage.

Hogg, M. A., Terry, D. J., AND White, K. M. (1995) A tale of two theories: A critical comparison of identity theory with social identity theory. Social Psychology Quarterly, 58, 255-269.

James, W. (1890) The principles of psychology. New York: Holt.

Kaplan, H. B. (1980) Deviant behavior in defense of self. New York: Academic Press.

Kusserow, A. (2004) American individualism: Child rearing and social class in three neighborhoods. New York: Palgrave Macmillan.

Lewis, C. C. (1989) From indulgence to internalization: Social control in the early school years. Journal of Japanese Studies, 15 (1): 139-157.

Markus, H. R., Kitayama, S. (1991) Culture and the self: Implications for cognition, emotion, and motivation. Psychological Review, 98, 224-253.

Matsumoto, D., Kudoh, T, AND Tekeuchi S. (1996) Changing patterns of individualism and collectivism in the United States and Japan. Culture and Psychology, 2, 77-107.

Mead, G. H. (1934) Mind, self, AND society. Chicago: University of Chicago Press.

Peak, L. (1989) Learning to become a part of the group: The Japanese child's transition to preschool life. Journal of Japanese Studies, 15 (1): 93-123.

Rosenberg, M. (1992) The self-concept: social product and social force. In M. Rosenberg AND R. Turner (Eds.), Social psychology: Sociological perspectives (pp. 593-624). New York: Basic Books.

Rosenberg, M. AND Kaplan, H. B. (1982) Principles of self-concept formation: Introduction. In M. Rosenberg AND H. B. Kaplan (Eds.), Social psychology of the self- concept (pp. 174-178). Arlington Heights, IL: Harlan Davidson, Inc.

Thio, A. (1998) Sociology. New York: Longman.

Schlenker, B. R. (1985) Introduction: Foundations of the self in social life. In B. R. Schlenker (Ed.), The self in social life (pp.1-32). New York: McGraw-Hill Book Company.

Schneider, L. AND Silverman, A. (2003) Global sociology: Introducing five contemporary societies. Boston: McGraw-Hill.

Schwartz, M. AND Stryker, S. (1970) Deviance, selves, and others. Washington, D.C.: American Sociological Association.

Sennett, R. (1998) The corrosion of character. New York: Norton.

Singelis, T. M. (1994) The measurement of independent and interdependent self- construals. Personality and Social Psychology Bulletin. 20 (5), 580-591.

Stryker, S AND R. T. Serpe (1982) Commitment, identity salience, and role behavior: Theory and research example. In W. Ickes AND E. S. Knowles (Eds.), Personality, roles, and social behavior (pp.199-218). New York: Springer-Verlag.

Stryker, S. (1980) Symbolic interactionism: A social structural version. Menlo Park: Benjamin/Cummings Publishing Company.

Tajfel, H. AND Turner, J. (1979) An integrative theory of intergroup conflict. In W. G. Austin AND S. Worchel (Eds.), The social psychology of intergroup relations (pp. 33-47). Monterey: Brooks-Cole.

Thoits, P. A. (1986) Multiple identities: Examining gender and marital status differences in distress. American Sociological Review, 51: 259-272.

Trafimow, D., Triandis, H. C., AND Goto, S. G. (1991) Some tests of the distinction between the private self and the collective self. Journal of Personality and Social Psychology, 60, 649-655.

Triandis, H. C., McCusker, C., and Hui, C. H. (1990) Multimethod probes of individualism and collectivism. Journal of Personality and Social Psychology, 59: 1006-1020.

Triandis, H. C. (1989) The self and social behavior in differing cultural contexts. Psychological Review, 96, 506-520.

Wylie, R. C. (1961) The self-concept. Lincoln: University of Nebraska Press.

In: The Concept of Self in Education, Family and Sports
Editor: Anne P. Prescott, pp. 207-217

ISBN 1-59454-988-5
© 2006 Nova Science Publishers, Inc.

Chapter 9

THE RELATIONSHIP BETWEEN SELF-CONCEPT SCALES AND SOCIAL DESIRABILITY

John Hattie[*]
University of Auckland, New Zealand
Richard Fletcher
Massey University, Albany
David Watkins
University of Hong Kong, Hong Kong

ABSTRACT

This study investigates the relationship between Social Desirability and a number of different self-concept measures. At least two of the major Social Desirability dimensions (Denial and Overconfidence) are common to some of the dimensions of self-concept. In this paper we argue it is important to ensure that the self-concept tests are not influenced by a third dimension, Impression Management.

INTRODUCTION

When individuals are presented with self-report surveys, it is often claimed that they may respond in a socially desirable way, rather than in terms of how they truly conceive themselves on the construct of interest. Any confounding influence of Social Desirability therefore brings into question the validity of such self-report measures. This paper addresses the relationship between Social Desirability and self-concept scales, and demonstrates that only some dimensions of Social Desirability need to be avoided as other dimensions of Social Desirability can be considered integral parts of a person's self-concept.

[*] Please address all correspondence to: John Hattie. School of Education, 10th Floor Fisher Building, University of Auckland, Private Bag 92019; Email: j.hattie@auckland.ac.nz

Social Desirability was defined by Edwards (1957; 1990) as the tendency people have to respond to test items in a way that is socially acceptable in order to gain the approval of others. More recently King and Bruner (2000) similarly defined Social Desirability as "the pervasive tendency of individuals to present themselves in the most favourable manner relative to prevailing social norms and mores." (p.80). Groves (1989) claimed Social Desirability was a judgement about the value of a particular attribute, in a particular culture, and that socially desirable responses are those where there is a tendency to give overly positive descriptions – although we would add that it may also involve minimising overly negative descriptions. Most personality or affective scales aim to measure an individual's propensities on the dimension of interest, and not have the meaning of scores influenced by other sources of variability such as trying to appear to be socially desirable. It is perhaps not surprising, therefore, that Social Desirability has been considered a biased and unwanted source of variance and many attempts have been made to find ways to remove this unwanted variance. Groves (1989), for example, reviewed studies that showed how respondents over-reported or under-reported on their behaviour probably because of Social Desirability, and suggested methods to reduce this bias (see also Bradburn, Sudman, Blair, and Stocking, 1979; Schwarz, 1999).

Although most researchers agree that Social Desirability is a problem when interpreting test results, there is less agreement as to the reasons for the desirability responses. For example, it could be that some respondents are 'more' sensitive and responsive to the situational and cultural demands (Crowne and Marlowe, 1964); some respondents may be forestalling rejection or providing an avoidance response; some respondents may be involved in Impression Management; or it may be that some psychological attributes include aspects of Social Desirability. It is this latter claim that is more fully explored in this study.

THE SUB-DIMENSIONS OF SOCIAL DESIRABILITY

In a major review of the many instruments to assess Social Desirability, Paulhus (1991) noted the low correlations between many of these instruments and argued that this was because these measures differentially assessed two different dimensions of Social Desirability. The first, he termed 'Self-Deception Enhancement' or an honest but overly positive self-presentation; and the second he termed 'Impression Management' or self-presentation tailored to an audience. Paulhus developed a new measure to more directly measure these two major components – the Balanced Inventory of Desirable Responding (BIDR). The BIDR is a 40-item scale based on a series of situations ("I am not a safe driver when I exceed the speed limit", "When I hear people talking privately, I avoid listening"), and respondents rate their agreement on a seven-point scale (Not True to Very True). After allowing for reverse items, a high score for each of the two sub-scales "are attained only by subjects who give exaggeratedly desirable responses" (Paulhus, 1991, p. 37).

The Impression Management items were based on the assumption that respondents over-report their performance of a wide variety of desirable behaviours and under-report undesirable behaviours. Because the claims "involve overt behaviours (e.g., I always pick up litter) any distortion is presumably a conscious lie" (Paulhus, 1991, p. 37). Individuals high on Impression Management are more responsive to social influences and they prefer low profile situations to avoid evaluations by others (Paulhus, 1991). In another version of BIDR, Paulhus, Reid and Murphy (1987) divided Impression Management into two factors: Enhancement (promoting positive qualities) and Denial (disavowing negative qualities). For the final scale, however, only one factor (Impression Self-Deception) was preferred. The final set of Self-Deception items were based on the assumption that participants tend to deny having psychologically threatening thoughts or feelings (e.g., hating one's parents) or making exaggerated claims of positive cognitive attributes (overconfidence in one's judgement).

RELATIONSHIP BETWEEN SOCIAL DESIRABILITY AND SELF-CONCEPT

One of the arguments of this paper is that, from a conceptual perspective, it should not be surprising that there are strong relationships between many aspects of self-concept and aspects of Social Desirability – and no attempt to reduce this covariance is meaningful. For example, it is known that the Self-Deception aspects of Social Desirability correlate with self-concept (Winters and Neale, 1985). This is not because of any measurement artefact, but because various aspects of Self-Deception, for some individuals, are an integral part of their conceptions of self (see also Kroner and Weekes, 1996).

Fiske and Taylor (1984), for example, noted that "Instead of a naïve scientist entering the environment in search of the truth, we find the rather unflattering picture of a charlatan trying to make the data come out in [a] manner most advantageous to his or her already-held theories" (p. 88). Individuals tend to judge positive traits to be overwhelmingly more characteristic of their self than negative attributes, positive personality information is efficiently processed and easily recalled whereas negative personality information is poorly processed and difficult to recall. People show poorer recall for information related to failure than to success, recall task performance as more positive than it actually was, perceive that poor abilities are common but favoured abilities are rare and distinctive, consider the things people are not proficient at are less important than the things that we are proficient. People have a pervasive tendency to see themselves as better than others, and self-ratings are generally significantly more positive than observers' ratings. People do overinflate, and have high confidence and low denial when referencing attributes of themselves.

Impression Management, however, is more concerned with impressing others ("purposefully tailoring their answers to create the most positive social image", Paulhus, 1991, p21) and it therefore may interfere with defensible estimates of self-concept. It would seem desirable to attempt to minimise the involvement of Impression Management in the assessment of self-concept as Impression Management involves a conscious shift that is related to the situation (in the present instance, the test situation), and it relates to conscious attempts to dissemble and to self-present in a way that is tailored to a particular audience. This dissimilitude is less the case with Self-Deception as it can be a meaningful and important component of a person's self-concept. Self-reports of self-concept should represent these aspects of Self-Deception, but self-reports could be masked by Impression Management when students try to impress the test administrator/interpreter with beliefs about themselves not necessarily related to actual self-concept. Reducing the Impression Management dimensions of Social Desirability may increase the predictive validity of self-concept measures.

Hence, it would be expected that Self-Deception could be related to various aspects of self-concept, whereas Impression Management could confound the self-concept estimates, and/or could form a separate dimension. If, to the contrary, Impression Management is related to many dimensions of self, then these self scales are not assessing self-concept. In such a case, Social Desirability (at least a factor relating to Impression Management) is confounding the self-reports of self-concept. Reducing the Impression Management part of Social Desirability may, therefore, increase the predictive validity of self-concept measures.

The current research involves two studies. The first study explores the dimensionality of the BIDR and demonstrates that it can be used to meaningfully identify the three major dimensions of Social Desirability: Impression Management-Enhancement, Impression Management-Denial, and Self-Deception. The second study relates the items from these three dimensions to a variety of self-concept measures. It uses a structural equation model to ascertain which of the dimensions of Social Desirability relate to the various self-concept measures.

STUDY 1: THE FACTOR STRUCTURE OF THE BIDR

Method

Sixteen of the BIDR items were chosen for this study. These items were deemed most appropriate for high school students and were chosen from across the various dimensions noted above. Items excluded primarily related to situations unlikely to have been experienced by the majority of these students (e.g., "I am a lover", "The reason I vote is because my vote can make a difference") or because of the language may not have been universally understood by the sample (e.g., "I am a completely rational person"). The items were administered, as part of a larger study, to a sample of 767 14-19 year old adolescents across four high schools in New Zealand. Each item was scored on a seven-point Likert scale from "Not True" to "Very True." As prescribed by Paulhus (1991), the final score for each item was a 1 (when the student responded with the two extreme points, 6 and 7, or 0 if they responded with 1 through 6). There were 517 males and 230 females (and 20 students for whom sex was not recorded), and the distribution across ethnic groups where E1qaz78%, Maori 4%, Pacific Island 10%, Asian 3%, and Others 3%.

Results

A maximum-likelihood factor analysis using oblimin rotation was used on all items, specifying two, then three factors. For the two-factor solution there was evidence of the expected Impression Management and Self-Confidence factors, but there were too many items loading on unexpected factors for this to be considered a clear finding. The three-factor solution was more readily interpretable. Table 1 presents the factor loadings and correlations between the factors for the three-factor solution for the New Zealand sample in the middle three columns of the table.

Table 1. Maximum-likelihood Factor Pattern for the Social Desirability Items Across the Two Samples

No.		NZ Sample			USA Sample		
		IM	CO	DN	IM	CO	DN
Factor 1: Impression Management (IM)							
14	I always obey laws, even if I'm unlikely to get caught	.42	.02	.05	.64	.04	.05
16	I never take things that don't belong to me	.60	.05	-.04	.55	.00	.04
15	I have never dropped litter on the street	.35	.06	-.03	.48	-.05	-.12
18	I don't gossip about other people's business	.30	.03	.02	.46	-.02	-.06
17	I have never damaged a library book or store merchandise without reporting it	.59	-.06	-.05	.43	.06	.08
12	I never swear	.33	.05	.00	.39	.02	.00
Factor 2: Self-Deception-Overconfidence (OC)							
2	I always know why I like things	.05	.50	.06	.00	.69	-.17
9	I am very confident of my judgements	.01	.63	-.01	.00	.51	.00
3	Once I've made up my mind, other people can seldom change my opinions	.05	.25	-.03	-.01	.32	.00
6	I never regret my decisions	.03	.41	.10	.16	.30	.00
Factor 3: Self-Deception-Denial (DN)							
11	I don't always know the reasons why I do the things I do	-.02	.08	.36	-.21	.01	.50
10	I sometimes tell lies if I have to	.15	-.09	.33	-.34	.00	.51
1	It would be hard for me to break any of my bad habits	-.02	.09	.32	-.06	-.01	.52
5	It's hard for me to shut off a disturbing thought	-.06	.09	.48	.00	-.11	.47
13	I sometimes try to get even rather than forgive and forget	.18	-.06	.26	.16	.00	.34
8	I rarely appreciate criticism	-.05	-.05	.38	.14	.01	.30
Correlations between the factors							
		1	2	3	1	2	3
	Impression Management	1.00			1.00		
	Self-Deception-Overconfidence	.32	1.00		.31	1.00	
	Self-Deception-Denial	.26	.21	1.00	.13	.22	1.00

The Impression Management factor is as expected given the development of the scale as outlined by Paulhus. It includes items where the participants are purposively tailoring their answers to create the most positive social image. The students claim that they never damage library books, always obey, never take unaccounted leave, never drop litter, or never swear.

The Self-Deception factor, however, splits into two separate factors with a low correlation between these factors ($r = .21$). All the items that needed reversing (from negative to positive) are on one of these factors (Denial), and all the positive items are on the other (Confidence). This division of positive and negative items has been often noted in the measurement literature although it is far from clear whether the reasons for the split is because of linguistic issues (Chapman and Tunmer, 1997), artefactual problems (Hansford and Hattie, 1982); or conceptual or psychological reasons.

In the present case, it could be claimed that Self-Deception about negative events relates more to a lack of confidence (or a tentativeness or denial), and Self-Deception about positive events more relates to overconfidence (or a surety of opinions and beliefs). If these two factors were opposite ends of a continuum of confidence it would be expected that the correlation between the two factors would be negative, but it is small and positive. Hence, we recommend that the two aspects of Self-Deception be considered separately. Rather than call them under- and overconfidence (which implies they are two ends of a continuum), we prefer to label them Denial and Overconfidence, and both these factors are part of Self-Deception. That is, a person considered high in Self-Deception could find it hard to shut off a disturbing thought (Denial) and/or be very confident of his or her judgements (Confidence).

STUDY 2: THE RELATION BETWEEN BIDR AND SELF-CONCEPT

Method

As part of a larger study, the same 16 items from the BIDR, along with a number of self-concept scales, were administered to a sample of 230 15-19 year old adolescents in a large high school in North Carolina. The scales were administered to the group over a morning period, with frequent rest intervals. The school principal and teachers were in attendance throughout the testing and this markedly improved the on-task behaviour of the students. There were 123 males and 107 females who completed the tests, and the majority where European 78%, with the remainder being Asian-Pacific Island 2%, Hispanic 4%, African American 10%, or American-Indian/Alaskan 3%).

As the aim was to assess the relationships between Social Desirability and self-concept scales, a number of different self-scales were used. These included self-concept scales relating to Academic, Peers, Family, Physical, and Self-confidence. Items from five self-concept scales were used, and total scores for each dimension within each scale were used in the structural model. It is therefore one of the strengths of this study that a variant of the multitrait-multimethod design is used by incorporating a number of self-concept measures.

The first scale, the "About Myself" scale by Song and Hattie (see Hattie, 1992) is a 35-item scale based on a hierarchical conception of self-concept, with seven facets grouped under three dimensions (see Hattie and Marsh, 1995; Shavelson, Hubner, and Stanton, 1976). The scales used included Academic self-concept (which is divided into Achievement, Ability, and Classroom sub-scales), Social self-concept (which is divided into Peers and Family), Physical self-concept, and Confidence in self. The items for the seven facets represent a wide variety of statements related to how students describe themselves.

The second scale is the Harter (1988) Self-Perception Profile for Adolescents. This profile includes eight self scales, of which three were chosen for the present study: Scholastic Competence (Academic), Peer Likeability (Friends), Physical Appearance (Physical). A two-step answer process was used, whereby participants were first asked to consider the type of adolescents they are most like (e.g., "Some kids feel like they are just as smart as other kids their age" or "Other kids aren't so sure and wonder if they are as smart"), and then indicate whether that descriptive is "Really true for me" or "Sort of true for me". We used three items from the Academic scale (e.g., "I think doing well in school is important"), five from the Friends (e.g., "I think that having a lot of friends is important"), and three from the Physical scale (e.g., "I think that my physical appearance is important"). There is no Harter scale related to Family self-concept.

The third scale is the Self Attributes Questionnaire (SAQ) devised by Pelham and Swann (1989). This is a 10-item scale that asks the students to rate various aspects of their self-concept. A rating from 1 (Not At All Important) to 10 (Extremely Important) is provided, indexed with an adjective ranging from bottom 5%, lower 10%, through to upper 10%, and top 5%. Under each of these is still another cue as to the percentage in the population, viz. 0-5%, 6-10% for the bottom two categories, to 90-95% and 96-100% for the top two categories. This scale was completed in relation to Academic, Peers, Family, And Physical self-concept.

The fourth scale was also devised by Pelham and Swann (1989) and is called the Personal Importance scale (PI). It is a 10-item scale that asks the adolescents to rate "How personally important each self dimension is to you compared to other people your age and sex". The same rating scale as the SAQ was used.

The final scale is the Rosenberg (1965) self-esteem scale, which is among the most popular global scales of self-worth and includes ten items constructed to form a Guttman scale. The scale assesses "confidence in self" as the items relate to expressions of confidence, self-efficacy and control.

Results

A maximum-likelihood factor analysis with oblimin rotation indicated that there were three meaningful factors: Impression Management, Overconfidence and Denial (three rightmost columns in Table 1). The same pattern of loadings was found as in Study 1. The factor pattern is most clear, in that the items load substantially on only one factor (and closer to zero loadings elsewhere), and the correlations between the factors are sufficiently low to be confident that there are three separate and meaningful factors.

Total scores were obtained for each of the three factors and as there were differing numbers of items for each factor, these were converted as if there were six items per scale (thus the range was 0 to 36). The mean for Impression Management is 18.94 (SD=5.87), for Overconfidence is 22.28 (SD=5.13), and Denial, 23.00 (SD=5.13). Thus, the students were higher on Denial and Overconfidence , and lower on Impression Management.

The estimates of reliability for the various self-concept scales were all sufficiently high to provide confidence in using these scores: Song and Hattie Achievement .67, Ability .87, Peers .76, Family .81, Physical .57, Confidence .63; Harter Academic .50, Peers .52, Physical .57, SAQ .71 (recall there is only one item per scale so the total alpha is reported here); PI Academic .66, Peers .64, Family .71, Physical .78; and Rosenberg .77. The scores from similar domains correlated more highly with each other than they did with scales from different dimensions (e.g., for the three Family scales the average correlation was .53 with each other, and .30 with the other dimensions). On average, the loadings on like-factors were 1.5 greater than the loadings on unlike-factors.

Structural equation modelling was used to relate the various dimensions of self-concept to the three Social Desirability scales. For the self-concept part of the model, each of the same name self-concept scales was constrained to load onto an appropriately named latent dimension. Thus, the academic scales from Song and Hattie (Academic, Achievement, Classroom), Harter Academic, SAQ Academic, And PI Academic were all constrained to load onto a factor termed "Academic Self-concept". The final model specified that the five self-concept dimensions (Academic, Peers, Family, Friends, and Confidence) related to the three Social Desirability dimensions (Impression Management, Self-Deception–Denial, and Self-Deception–Overconfidence).

The fit of the model was acceptable (chi-square = 1208.99, df = 558, Tucker-Lewis index = .97, and RMSEA of .072). A close inspection of the modification indices showed there were no further structural paths that, if freed to be estimated, would statistically significantly reduce the degree of fit. This is particularly important for the Social Desirability factors as, for example, none of the paths from Impression Management to any of the self-concept factors were statistically significant.

The items from the Harter scale had the lowest loadings on each self-concept dimension suggesting that this scale may be assessing dimensions somewhat different from the others, but it is retained in this analysis, as removing these scales did not markedly improve the overall fit of the model, or change the structural weights. Further research as to why the Harter scale is assessing different aspects of self-concept to the other scales is warranted. The factor loading for the Song and Hattie classroom scale on Academic is lower than desired. This is somewhat less surprising when prior research has indicated it also has strong loadings on Friendship, reflecting how the concepts that many students have of themselves in classrooms are as much related to friends as to academic beliefs (Hattie, 1992).

An inspection of the factor loadings for the Impression Management and Denial Social Desirability latent dimensions indicate that each item is making a contribution. The Overconfidence scale, however, is dominated by two items, "I always know why I like things" and "I am very confident of my judgements", whereas the other two items, "Once I've made up my mind, other people can seldom change my opinions", and "I never regret my decisions", make a negligible contribution (which is a pattern not surprisingly similar to the factor pattern from the exploratory analysis above). The first two, and dominant, items are most related to Overconfidence, hence the retention of the title.

The correlations between the three Social Desirability factors indicate a high negative relationship between Impression Management and Denial (-.42), otherwise the three Social Desirability factors are close to being independent dimensions (see Figure 1). 1qaz Most important, there are no structural relations between Impression Management and any of the self-concept dimensions. This indicates that the self-concept scales are assessing attributes not related to Impression Management, and if the latter dimension is desired in a study or profile of an individual, then a separate scale of Impression Management needs to be included in the battery. More important, these self-concept dimensions are not affected by a person's desire to systematically over-report on desirable and under-report on undesirable behaviours.

There are two negative structural paths from Denial to Academic and to Overconfidence. Thus students who had high scores on Denial tended to lower their self-esteem estimates on Academic and Overconfidence, but not on Physical, Family, or Friends. The Overconfidence attribute of Social Desirability was positively related to all self-concept dimensions. As predicted, therefore, the Confidence aspect of Self-Deception is an intricate part of self-concept.

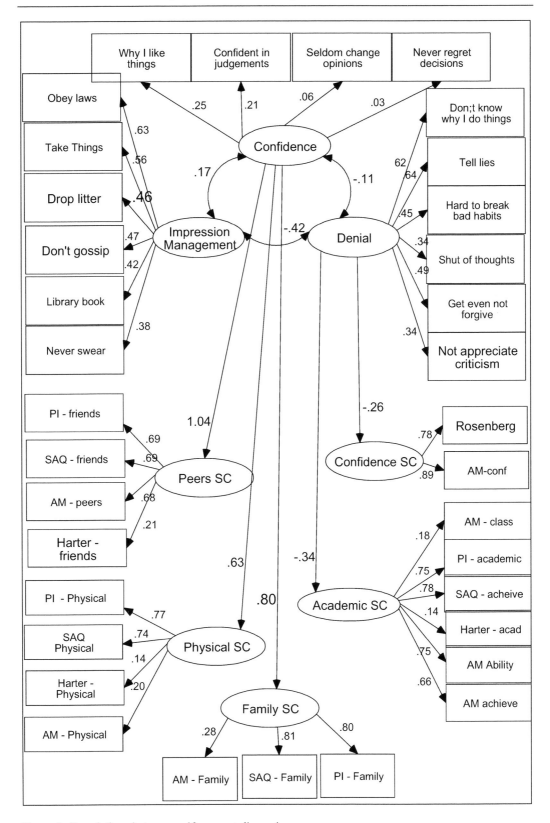

Figure 1. Correlations between self-concept dimensions

DISCUSSION

Self-deception, which we have divided into Overconfidence and Denial, can reflect an honest appraisal of a person's self-concept. Impression Management, however, is more associated with the desire to present oneself in a socially conventional way, and hence can mask self-reports of a person's self-concept. In the various scales used in this study there were no effects between self-concept dimensions and Impression Management.

Overconfidence is related to those attributes of self-concept where we are more interested in receiving a view from others. Peers, Physical and Family self-concept all involve an appraisal of how others see us. It appears that we may be overconfidently biasing our beliefs about how others see us, and thus engaging in self-serving biases when we interpret the viewpoints of others. But when we are making appraisals about how we project ourselves to others (Confidence and in the Academic domain) we are more likely to engage in Denial. There seems to be a relationship between receiving information about the self and Overconfidence, and between projecting information to others and Denial.

As to the question of whether researchers should remove the Social Desirability components from self-report measures of self-concept, the answer is No and Yes. The two aspects relating to Self-Deception, Denial and Overconfidence, can be important parts of self-concept and removing these components may reduce the predictive validity of self measures(see also Fisher and Katz, 2000). On the other hand, it is desirable to reduce the Impression Management aspects that can be evident in self-report measures. Such an appearance to "look good" or present oneself in the most favourable manner relative to prevailing social mores reduces the validity of the self-concept measure. Certainly, the current measures of self-concept are not influenced by Impression Management. As noted by Zerbe and Paulhus (1987), Impression Management can be a potential confounding variable as such a "conscious presentation of a false front, such as deliberately falsifying test responses to create favourable impressions" is unwanted (p.253).

REFERENCES

Bradburn, N. M., Sudman, S., Blair, E., and Stocking, C. (1979). *Improving interview method and questionnaire design*. San Francisco: Jossey-Bass.

Chapman, J. W., and Tunmer, W. E. (1997). A longitudinal study of beginning reading achievement and reading self-concept. *The British Journal of Educational Psychology, 67*(3), 279.

Crowne, D. P., and Marlowe, D. (1964). *The approval motive*. New York: Wiley.

Edwards, A. L. (1957). The Social Desirability variable in personality assessment and research. New York: Dryden.

Edwards, A. L. (1990). Construct validity and Social Desirability. *American Psychologist, 45*, 287-298.

Fisher, R. J., and Katz, J. E. (2000). Social desirability bias and the validity of self-reported values. *Psychology and Marketing, 17*(2), 105-120.

Fiske, S. T., and Taylor, S. E. (1984). *Social cognition*. New York: Random House.

Groves, R. M. (1989). *Survey errors and survey costs*. New York: John Wiley and Sons.

Hansford, B., and Hattie, J. A. (1982). Communication apprehension: An assessment of Australian and US data. *Applied Psychological Measurement, 6*, 225-233.

Harter, S. (Ed.). (1988). *Self-Perception Profile for Adolescents USA*. Denver, Colorado: University of Denver.

Hattie, J. (1992). *Self-concept*. New Jersey: Erlbaum.

Hattie, J., and Marsh, H. W. (1995). Future research in self-concept. In B. Bracken (Ed.), *Handbook on self-concept* (pp. 421-463). New Jersey: Erlbaum.

King, M. F., and Bruner, G. C. (2000). Social desirability bias: A neglected aspect of validity testing. *Psychology and Marketing, 17*(2), 79-103.

Kroner, D. G., and Weekes, J. R. (1996). Socially desirable responding and offence characteristics among rapists. *Violence Vict, 11*(3), 263-270.

Paulhus, D. L. (1991). Measurement and control of response bias. In J. P. Robinson, P. R. Shaver and L. S. Wrightsman (Eds.), *Measures of personality and social psychological attitudes* (pp. 17-59). New York: Academic Press.

Paulhus, D. L., Reid, D. B., and Murphy, G. (1987). The omnibus study of desirable responding. Unpublished manuscript: University of British Columbia.

Pelham, B. W., and Swann, W. B. (1989). Self-Attributes Questionnaire. *Journal of Personality and Social Psychology, 57*, 672-680.

Rosenberg, M. (1965). *Society and the adolescent self-image*. Princeton, New Jersey: Princeton University Press.

Schwarz, N. (1999). Self-reports: How the questions shape the answers. *American Psychologist, 54*, 93-105.

Shavelson, R. J., Hubner, J. J., and Stanton, G. C. (1976). Self-concept: Validation of construct interpretations. *Review of Educational Research, 46*(3), 407-441.

Winters, K. C., and Neale, J. M. (1985). Mania and low self-esteem. *Journal of Abnormal Psychology, 94*, 282-290.

Zerbe, W. J., and Paulhus, D. L. (1987). Socially desirable responding in organisational behaviour: A reconception. *Journal of Management Review, 12*, 250-264.

INDEX

D

F

G

intuition, 7
issues, 35, 41, 43, 45, 79, 84, 88, 147, 149, 155, 192, 196, 198, 212

J

Japanese, 195, 199, 206
judgment, 124, 180, 181, 186
justification, 71

K

knowledge, viii, 2, 3, 4, 5, 6, 8, 9, 10, 19, 20, 43, 47, 48, 49, 115, 116, 118, 122, 130, 150, 154, 181, 193, 196, 197, 204

L

labor, 160, 197
lack of confidence, 212
language, 12, 45, 174, 198, 199, 210
language skills, 12
laws, 211
leadership, 11, 187
learned helplessness, 105
learners, 2, 9, 10, 18
learning, vii, 1, 2, 3, 4, 5, 6, 7, 8, 9, 10, 11, 12, 13, 15, 16, 17, 18, 19, 20, 21, 26, 28, 29, 35, 36, 37, 38, 39, 40, 41, 42, 43, 44, 45, 46, 47, 48, 57, 58, 67, 68, 72, 84, 123, 124, 130, 145, 151
learning behavior, 58
learning environment, 20
learning outcomes, 8, 41, 47
learning process, 8, 57
learning task, 8
legislation, 12
lending, 62
level of depression, 95
liability, v, 111, 147
life experiences, 78, 84, 143
life satisfaction, ix, 179, 180, 181, 186, 187
life span, 69, 85, 89, 172, 175
lifestyle, 195
limitation, 68, 108, 170
linear function, 145
LISREL model, 170
listening, 208
literacy, 1, 12, 18, 43, 47
literature, ix, 7, 35, 53, 54, 58, 68, 76, 84, 85, 119, 137, 155, 180, 181, 186, 191, 211
living conditions, 159
local community, 198

location, 8
locus of control, 81
loneliness, 74
longitudinal study, 55, 70, 216
love, 137

M

major depression, 95, 112
maladaptive, 58
male(s), 61, 79, 80, 81, 85, 88, 89, 96, 98, 100, 113, 158, 185, 186, 187, 200, 210, 212
management, x, 10, 12, 86, 89, 110, 111, 205, 207, 208, 209, 210, 211, 213, 214, 216, 217
marital conflict, 155, 156, 167, 173, 175, 176
marital status, 206
marriage, 172
mastery, 52, 53, 54, 57, 58, 76, 77, 78, 79, 81, 82, 89, 99, 110
mathematical achievement, 70
mathematics, vii, 2, 7, 11, 12, 42, 44, 47, 48, 51, 52, 53, 55, 56, 57, 58, 59, 60, 61, 64, 65, 66, 67, 68, 70, 72, 73
mathematics tests, 12
matrix, 43, 162
meanings, ix, 191, 192, 198, 200, 202, 203, 204
measurement, ix, 1, 5, 6, 7, 15, 16, 17, 43, 46, 47, 48, 71, 72, 88, 97, 113, 116, 119, 122, 123, 125, 130, 132, 133, 134, 135, 136, 149, 150, 151, 177, 188, 189, 191, 195, 206, 209, 211
measures, x, 5, 14, 16, 17, 22, 35, 52, 53, 56, 58, 59, 62, 63, 68, 70, 95, 97, 98, 100, 102, 108, 117, 120, 121, 122, 123, 124, 125, 126, 142, 143, 150, 151, 154, 161, 162, 165, 168, 170, 207, 208, 209, 210, 212, 216
media, 94
medication, 94, 105, 108, 109
memory, 9, 118, 121, 123, 124
memory biases, 124
mental ability, 72
mental disorders, 96
mental health, 59, 107, 110, 113, 145
mental illness, 93, 95, 109, 110, 111
mental retardation, 93
mentor, 43
meta-analysis(es), 47, 94, 105, 107, 111, 120
metacognition, ix, 153, 167, 169, 171
methodology, 5, 45
Ministry of Education, 12, 13, 22, 46, 48
minority, 76
misunderstanding, 124
modeling, vii, 14, 43, 45, 51, 55, 62, 69, 139, 174, 213

Q

R